H Clay

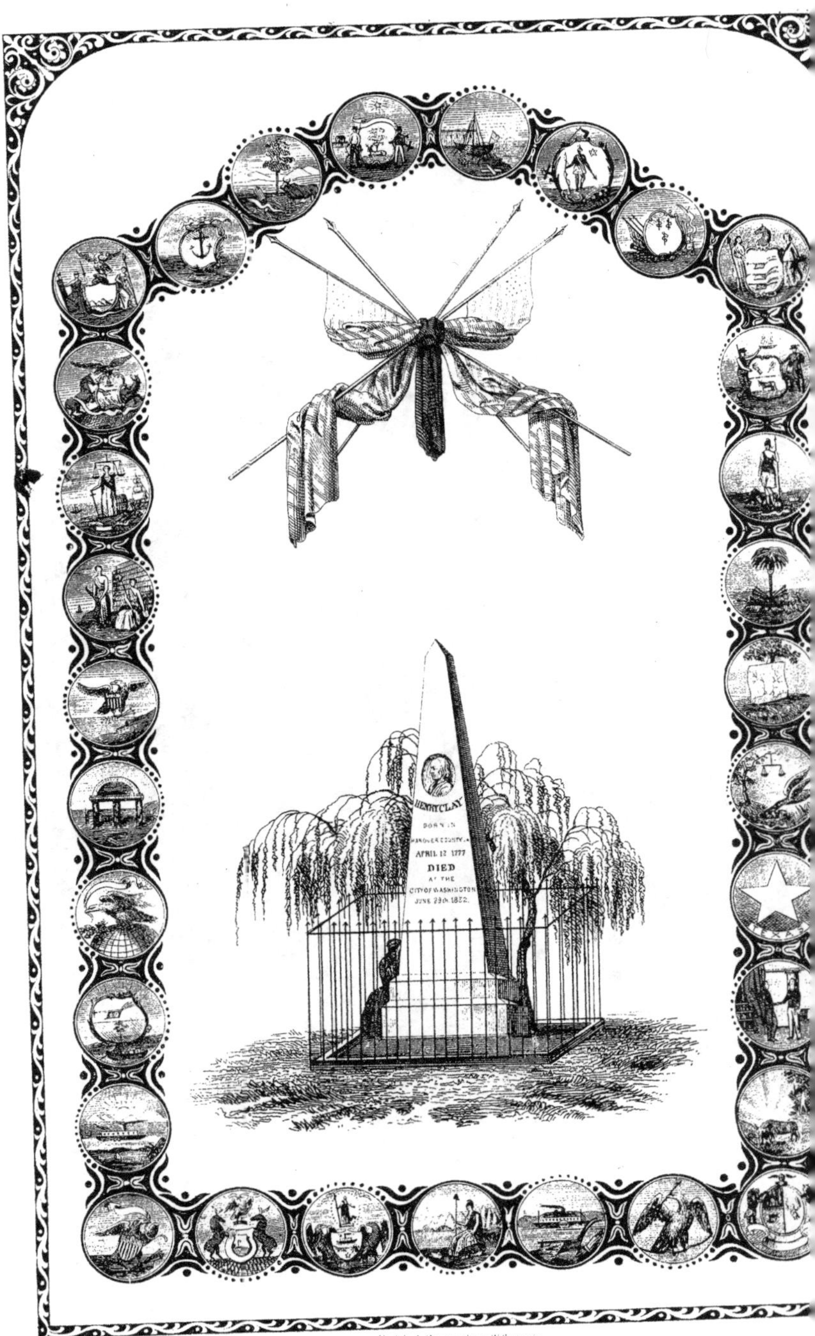

Engd. by J. Meyer & Co. [illegible] William St.

IN COMMON COUNCIL OF THE

City of New York

The following message was received from his Honor the Mayor announcing

THE DEATH OF THE

HON. HENRY CLAY

MAYOR'S OFFICE

New York, June 30th 1852.

To the Honorable the Common Council:

Gentlemen: The nation is called on to mourn the loss of one of her wisest and best sons Henry Clay the devoted patriot, the enlightened statesman the eloquent orator, is no more. After a lingering and painful illness he closed a long and eventful life, leaving behind him a name which will be cherished and admired, wherever the English tongue is spoken as the champion of freedom the defender of the oppressed.

His death is not merely a national loss, but throughout the world the friends of freedom will mourn it. Long years of devotion to his country's welfare, and unceasing efforts for her advancement have secured to him the gratitude and affection of his countrymen and friends, as warm and true as man could ever claim.

But I need not speak of Mr Clay's character or services they are inscribed, in letters of imperishable glory, on the pages of our country's history.

I make the official announcement of his death, assured that the representatives of the first commercial city of the Western world, will testify their regard for the memory of the departed patriot and sage, by such measures as are adapted to the mournful occasion.

A C Kingsland Mayor.

Engr. by F. Mayer & Co. [illegible] William St.

In connection with the foregoing

ALDERMAN

William H. Cornell

Presented the following Preamble and Resolutions

Whereas, *The melancholy and afflicting intelligence has been officially communicated to this Board, that death has closed the mortal career of the illustrious* **Henry Clay** *United States Senator, the renowned statesman, the accomplished diplomatist, and the eloquent orator, and*

Whereas, *It is befitting us, as a great and free nation, possessing a warm and ardent appreciation of the virtuous and patriotic services of the illustrious men of the republic, while living, and that, when an all wise* **Providence** *in his infinite wisdom, deems it necessary to call from this earthly pilgrimage, one of its most eminent personages, we deeply feel the oppressing sadness that surrounds us and that, in the demise of* **Henry Clay** *we fully realize a nation's bereavement. Not only have his virtues and talents endeared him to the people of the* **UNITED STATES** *but to the whole world, who will, with melancholy cheerfulness, render to his memory their unanimous tribute of respect. The justly renowned, but lamented Henry Clay has from his indomitable energy, his accomplished statesmanship, and his diplomatic ability,*

Eng'd by F. Mayer & Co. 93 William St

occupied, in the **Councils** of the nation, the highest positions of honor for more than half a century. His heroic conduct, through a long and useful life, entirely devoted to the service of his country, will forever serve as a bright example for the present and future generations. His noble and disinterested love of country has stamped him emphatically one of the greatest men of his time. His glowing sentiments of patriotism knew no **South**, no **North**, no **East**, no **West**. He was generous without ostentation, thoroughly republican in his sentiments, and simple in his manners, winning respect and golden opinions everywhere among the virtuous and good, by the calm dignity and urbanity of his deportment. Dearly beloved in his family circle and by all who had daily or occasional intercourse with him; he has left behind him a name that future generations will revere and bless. When the sombre clouds of fanaticism, with their dark, foreboding aspect, threatened our country's peace, the great champion of human freedom, notwithstanding he had, like the venerable **Cincinnatus**, retired from the turmoils of public life, came forth again at his country's call, once more buckling on the mighty armor of conciliation, sacrificing all factions of party, dispelling the aspirations of sectional dissensions, for the preservation and perpetuity of our glorious constitution and the Union, and thus we find him expiring at the **Capital** of the nation, among the representatives of this wide extended republic. His powerful and comprehensive mind, ardently enlisted in the cause of his country, was ever ready to assist in promoting its glory, usefulness, and indissolubility. He was enraptured with profound respect and love for the principles of our **Republican** and moral institutions, many of which acknowledge, with paternal gratitude, numberless favors from his fostering care. But the sun of his personal usefulness has forever set, and the nation will long deplore his loss. His deeds, like the everlasting hills, will stand as noble examples to guide posterity in promoting the best interest of our happy **Union**: therefore be it

Eng'd by F. Mayer & Co. [illegible] William St

Resolved That the chambers of the respective Boards of the **Common Council** be draped in mourning, and remain so for ninety days; that the members wear the usual badge of mourning for the same period; that it be earnestly recommended to the citizens to close their places of business on the day of the funeral obsequies; that the proprietors of public places, and owners of ships and other vessels be requested to hoist their flags at half mast during the day.

Resolved That a Committee of seven members from each **Board** together with the President thereof, be appointed to carry out the foregoing preamble and resolution, and to make all such arrangements as they may think advisable and proper

Resolved That the **Clerk** of the **Common Council** be directed to transmit a certified copy of the foregoing preamble and resolutions to the family of the deceased patriot

Adopted By the Board of Aldermen June 30.th 1852 and Aldermen William H. Cornell, Wesley Smith, William J. Brisley, William M. Tweed James M. Bard, Sylvester L. H. Ward and John Boyce appointed such committee on the part of said Board.

Adopted By the Board of Assistants June 30.th 1852 and Assistant Aldermen Isaac O. Barker, Thomas Woodward, John J. Tait, William Anderson, William H. Wright, J. Benson McGown, and Jacob H. Valentine appointed such committee on the part of said board.

Approved By the **Mayor** July 1st 1852.

D. T. Valentine **Clerk of Common Council.**

Engd. by F. Mayer & Co. 9 William St

REPORT
OF THE
COMMITTEE OF ARRANGEMENTS
OF THE
COMMON COUNCIL OF NEW YORK,
OF THE OBSEQUIES
FINIS
IN MEMORY OF THE
HON. HENRY CLAY.
Maclees Sc

PRESENTED BY ALDERMAN WM. H. CORNELL.

McSPEDON & BAKER,
PRINTERS.

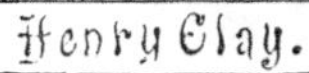

Board of Aldermen.

Resolved, That the Clerk of the Common Council cause to be published, in an appropriate manner, the report of the Committee of Arrangements on the obsequies of the Hon. Henry Clay, late United States Senator.

D. T. VALENTINE, *Clerk*.

THE JOINT SPECIAL COMMITTEE of the Common Council, appointed to make arrangements for rendering a suitable testimony of respect to the memory of the Hon. HENRY CLAY, late United States Senator from the State of Kentucky, respectfully

REPORT:

That they entered upon the performance of the melancholy duty assigned them, appreciating its high consideration, its sacred trust and arduous responsibilities, with a sincere conviction of its importance; conscious that, however assiduously their duties might be performed, no additional lustre would be attached to the memory of the great man whose death the united voice of the American people deplores.

Your Committee deem it highly proper that something more than a superficial notice of the events of the day should be recorded in connection with their report of the obsequies of the man whose name stands first among the giant intellects of our great statesmen. Long as we had expected the event of his demise, and prepared as the whole country should have been for its announcement, we find ourselves wholly unfitted to record the sad intelligence. A great and good man has fallen. A nation mourns at his bier, and laments the loss of one who, in its greatest perils, has been its savior. One so far above and beyond ordinary men; so pure in public life; so unselfish and disinterested in his private life; so excellent a husband; so good a father; so faithful a friend, and so bold and inflexible a patriot, that we feel entirely unable to speak of him according to his worth.

Henry Clay was a man to mark the age in which he lived. His mind was a fitting counterpart of the whole casket in which it was enshrined. His manners were graceful and impressive. Those who came in contact with him felt the charm of his influence; and this attachment of his friends grew upon them, till no political misfortune could remove it. They were his friends in prosperity and in the prospect of power, but more his friends in adversity. Nature had formed him in her finest mould, and had stamped him with the seal of her own nobility. The heart of the nation throbs with melancholy emotions at the departure, from the field of his glories, of the man whom the whole world revered as a patriot, from his innate love of country—as a statesman, from intuition and from practice—as a philanthropist, from pure benevolence and a love of liberty. The dignified graces of Mr. CLAY's character can best be appreciated by those who knew him in the private walks of life. His impulses were generous and disinterested. He had an utter scorn of all that was sordid, selfish or deceitful. He who could say, "I would rather be right than be President," was not likely to hold in high esteem those whose ambition was unregulated by principle, or whose moral sense was facile to the moulding touch of self-interest. His eminent services in the councils of the nation, rendered during a series of more than fifty years, (a circumstance with few parallels in the annals of the world,) will ever adorn the brightest pages of American history. The purity of his motives, his stern and unrelenting intrepidity for his country's rights and her glory, will forever exist with fervency and freshness in the memory of a grateful people. When foreign outrage left his country no alternative but disgrace, or a resort to arms, he was found among the foremost to maintain the dignity and honor of his country. Born and cradled amid the excitement of the Revolution, the first songs which the ears of his childhood heard, were those which the struggle for freedom inspired. The important period through which he has lived in such prominence before the world, will ever render his memory inseparable from the history of his country. As in future years the results of civil and religious liberty in South America shall glow with increasing brightness, their fires shall add new lustre to the name of him who was the early and ardent advocate of their rights. As long as the heroism of Greece shall be admired, and the garlands of her poets endure, so long shall the name of HENRY CLAY be cherished by every heart that beats in unison with the pantings of liberty.

His intellect was expansive and comprehensive; his eloquence vigorous, and, to an extraordinary degree, fascinating and persuasive; his heart brave and honest; his affections warm and pure, and his patriotism ardent, devoted and disinterested. When the factions and calumnies of the present day are past by, succeeding generations will pronounce a grateful eulogy upon his public services, and rank him among the most distinguished public benefactors. Posterity will then pronounce, with equal truth and justice, "during the course of a long and arduous public life, he made his country's interests the end and aim of his exertions. He never sacrificed a principle to secure the favor of a party, or yielded an opinion from the fear of its unpopularity. He sought first and principally the extension of republican freedom, and as the best means of securing it, labored with all the energy of his eloquence, to maintain unimpaired the union of the states. He incorporated himself with no party that regarded the general government in the light of an unwieldy and inert mass, powerless of good; but supported the true theory which regards the union as an active and vivifying principle, pervading all sections, cementing them together by the ties of mutual interest and convenience, and availing itself of its great resources to produce the most certain and expeditious communication between them."

Your Committee, in view of the foregoing suggestions have compiled, from authentic and reliable sources, a summary of the proceedings at Washington, from the hour of his death; along the route; in this city, and until the arrival of the body at Lexington, Kentucky, its final resting place; estimating a full record of all the transactions as valuable reminiscences for future reference, and adopted as a slight testimony of the appreciation entertained of his many virtues, his eminent services, and patriotic devotion to his country.

Announcement of the Death of Henry Clay.

HENRY CLAY died in Washington City, D. C., on Tuesday, June 29th, 1852, at seventeen minutes past eleven o'clock, in the seventy-sixth year of his age. His death was announced in this city, by telegraph, about half past eleven o'clock, A. M. The sad news was soon spread to all parts of the city. All the public buildings, places of amusement, the shipping in the harbor, and every flag-staff immediately displayed the American flag at half mast, and a melancholy gloom was thrown over the whole city. The courts, immediately on receipt of the sad intelligence, delivered eloquent eulogies, and adopted resolutions expressive of the deep sympathy entertained for the deceased, and all public meetings, as an evidence of respect for his memory, adjourned. Measures were also immediately taken for convening the Common Council, for the purpose of adopting suitable arrangements expressive of the high esteem in which the memory of the distinguished dead is held, and of rendering such public demonstrations as are usually called for, by the citizens generally, upon similar occasions.

On the day of Mr. CLAY's death at Washington, the President of the United States issued the annexed circular to the several Heads of Departments:

EXECUTIVE MANSION,
TUESDAY, HALF PAST 12 O'CLOCK, P. M.

SIR:—The tolling bells announce the death of the Hon. HENRY CLAY. Though this event has been long anticipated, yet the painful bereavement could never be fully realized. I am sure all hearts are at this moment too sad to attend to business; and I therefore respectfully suggest that your department be closed for the remainder of the day.

MILLARD FILLMORE.

Both branches of the Common Council were convened on the next day, when the following proceedings were had:

Proceedings of the Common Council.

BOARD OF ALDERMEN.

JUNE 30, 1852.

PRESENT—Richard T. Compton, Esq., President; Abraham Moore, Dudley Haley, John Boyce, William M. Tweed, William J. Brisley, Charles Francis, Wesley Smith, Daniel F. Tiemann, James M. Bard, S. L. H. Ward, Asahel A. Denman, William H. Cornell.

The President announced that the Board was convened by the Mayor, pursuant to a request made by a majority of the members elected.

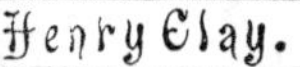

The following message was received from his Honor the Mayor, announcing the death of the Hon. HENRY CLAY:

MAYOR'S OFFICE,
NEW YORK, JUNE 30th, 1852.

To the Honorable the Common Council:

GENTLEMEN :—The nation is called on to mourn the loss of one of her wisest and best sons. HENRY CLAY, the devoted patriot, the enlightened statesman, the eloquent orator, is no more. After a lingering and painful illness, he closed a long and eventful life, leaving behind him a name which will be cherished and admired, wherever the English tongue is spoken, as the champion of freedom—the defender of the oppressed. His death is not merely a national loss, but throughout the world the friends of freedom will mourn it. Long years of devotion to his country's welfare, and unceasing efforts for her advancement, have secured to him the gratitude and affection of his countrymen and friends, as warm and true as man could ever claim. But I need not speak of Mr. CLAY's character or services—they are inscribed, in letters of imperishable glory, on the pages of our country's history.

I make the official announcement of his death, assured that the representatives of the first commercial city of the Western world, will testify their regard for the memory of the departed patriot and sage, by such measures as are adapted to the mournful occasion.

A. C. KINGSLAND, *Mayor.*

Which was accepted, and ordered on file.

In connection with the above, Alderman CORNELL presented the following preamble and resolutions :

Whereas, The melancholy and afflicting intelligence has been officially communicated to this Board, that death has closed the mortal career of the illustrious HENRY CLAY, United States Senator, the renowned statesman, the accomplished diplomatist, and the eloquent orator; and

Whereas, It is befitting us, as a great and free nation, possessing a warm and ardent appreciation of the virtuous and patriotic services of the illustrious men of the republic, while living, and that, when an all-wise Providence, in his infinite wisdom, deems it necessary to call from this earthly pilgrimage, one of its most eminent personages, we deeply feel the oppressing sadness that surrounds us—and that, in the demise of HENRY CLAY, we fully realize a nation's bereavement. Not only have his virtues and talents endeared him to the people of the United States, but to the whole world, who will, with melancholy cheerfulness, render to his memory their unanimous tribute of respect. The justly renowned, but lamented HENRY CLAY, has, from his indomitable energy, his accomplished statesmanship, and his diplomatic ability, occupied, in the councils of the nation, the highest positions of honor for more than half a century. His heroic conduct, through a long and useful life, entirely devoted to the service of his country, will forever serve as a bright example for the present and future generations. His noble and disinterested love of country has stamped him emphatically one of the greatest men of his time. His glowing sentiments of patriotism knew no South, no North, no East, no West. He was generous without ostentation, thoroughly republican in his sentiments, and simple in his manners, winning respect and golden opinions everywhere, among the virtuous and good, by the calm dignity and urbanity of his deportment.

Dearly beloved in his family circle, and by all who had daily or occasional intercourse with him, he has left behind him a name that future generations will revere and bless.

When the sombre clouds of fanaticism, with their dark, foreboding aspect, threatened our country's peace, the great champion of human freedom, notwithstanding he had, like the venerable CINCINNATUS, retired from the turmoils of public life, came forth again at his country's call, once more buckling on the mighty armor of conciliation, sacrificing all factions of party, dispelling the aspirations of sectional dissensions for the preservation and perpetuity of our glorious constitution and the Union; and thus we find him expiring at the capital of the nation, among the representatives of this wide extended republic. His powerful and comprehensive mind, ardently enlisted in the cause of his country, was ever ready to assist in promoting its glory, usefulness, and indissolubility. He was enraptured with profound respect and love for the principles of our republican and moral institutions, many of which acknowledge, with paternal gratitude, numberless favors from his fostering care. But the sun of his personal usefulness has forever set, and the nation will long deplore his loss. His deeds, like the everlasting hills, will stand as noble examples to guide posterity in promoting the best interests of our happy Union ; therefore be it

Resolved, That the chambers of the respective Boards of the Common Council be draped in mourning, and remain so for ninety days; that the members wear the usual badge of mourning for the same period; that it be earnestly recommended to the citizens to close their places of business on the day of the funeral obsequies; that the proprietors of public places, and owners of ships and other vessels, be requested to hoist their flags at half mast during the day.

Resolved, That a Committee of seven members from each Board, together with the President thereof, be appointed to carry out the foregoing preamble and resolution, and to make all such arrangements as they may think advisable and proper.

Resolved, That the Clerk of the Common Council be directed to transmit a certified copy of the foregoing preamble and resolutions to the family of the deceased patriot.

Which were unanimously adopted, and Aldermen CORNELL, SMITH, BRISLEY, TWEED, BARD, WARD and BOYCE, together with the President, appointed such Committee on the part of this Board.

Alderman WILLIAM M. TWEED, of the Seventh Ward, seconded the motion of Alderman CORNELL, and said,—

Mr. PRESIDENT:—Our whole country is again in tears! Scarcely were the remains of the lamented CALHOUN cold in the tomb, ere another brilliant and magnanimous statesman has gone to his silent and eternal repose! "When sorrows come, they come not in single spies, but in battalions," said one of old, whose wisdom I fully realize on this mournful occasion.

Sir, I trust that I love the glorious principles of democracy as life itself; but I thank God that I am American enough never to forget those who never forgot their country. Those great Americans, who have literally worn themselves out in the public service, I will ever hold in grateful remembrance, regardless of their political or religious creed.

The great fathers of the Revolution were chiefly superseded by JACKSON, CALHOUN, CLAY and WEBSTER, to whom our mighty destinies have been mainly intrusted during the present century. The lot of these illustrious men was wisely cast in States, whose domestic institutions and local interests, were, in many respects, widely dissimilar. But they all realized that they breathed the same national air,—all amicably met in the same national council,—and all watched, with sleepless eyes, the common welfare of their beloved country. WEBSTER alone remains, like the last leaf of a withered foliage. JACKSON, "whose eye, in battle, flashed like a rifle, and whose voice drowned the cannon," was first gathered to his fathers. CALHOUN, whose eagle eye, compressed lip, and prophetic voice commanded the admiration of his countrymen, followed the wise and courageous JACKSON. And now we are summoned to the mausoleum of HENRY CLAY!

On this solemn occasion, it affords me a melancholy pleasure to briefly scan the past. Being probably the youngest member of this body, I cannot be supposed to have long mingled in public affairs, but, with all deference, I trust that I am tolerably familiar with our national history, and that I am especially familiar with the lives of JEFFERSON and HAMILTON, those great intellectual giants of the Revolution, who laid the eternal foundation of the two leading political parties of our country. And it has been my happy fortune to be a living witness of a moiety of the public career of JACKSON and CALHOUN, (the warm admirers of JEFFERSON,) and of CLAY, a devoted disciple of HAMILTON. Now, although they all widely differed on those great national questions that have divided and distracted the country during most of the present century, yet they all profoundly loved their country, and strove to surpass each other in their enthusiastic efforts to perpetuate our glorious institutions to the remotest period.

Sir, with what national pride should we all contemplate the youthful JACKSON, when, at the peril of instant death, he hurled defiance at the British officer who commanded him to black his boots, while in captivity. Again, behold him, with his knapsack, in his solitary march from Carolina to Tennessee, in search of a forest home,—as Judge and Representative,—a Senator with JEFFERSON, in '96, listening to the wise counsels of that illustrious statesman; contending hand to hand, and foot to foot, with the South Western Indians,—at the battle of New Orleans,—the twice-elected president of the freest, happiest, and mightiest nation in the whole journey of the sun,—utterly destroying a gigantic national moneyed institution, because he conceived it to be a deadly foe to democratic liberty; a man who loved and served his country with all the zeal and fidelity of the immortal WASHINGTON.

Now behold the timid and thoughtful CALHOUN, while a New England student, as he enters the legislature of South Carolina, a mere youth,—in the halls of Congress, and in the front rank as an orator and statesman,—his energy and patriotism during our country's second struggle with Great Britain,—resisting the adoption, by Congress, of the tariff, abolition, and overshadowing monetary schemes of northern and western statesmen,—in his memorable collision with JACKSON, on nullification,—in the Senate, breasting the wide-spread bankruptcy of '37, and restoring order out of chaos,—his great ability as Chief of the War and State Departments,—his masterly diplomacy in the acquisition of Texas,—his dying efforts on the

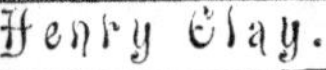

floor of the Senate; and in all we behold the deep and thrilling eloquence of DEMOSTHENES, the wisdom of JEFFERSON, and the patriotism of JACKSON.

And now behold HENRY CLAY, in the mill of Hanover, a poor boy,—as he scales the Alleghanies in pursuit of a new abode in the wilds of Kentucky,—in the legislature of his adopted state,—in the lower House of Congress, on the leading Committee, and Speaker at several consecutive sessions,—as the advocate of peace abroad, and of peace at home, both in the private and public arena; whose burning eloquence in the Senate assembly, paralyzed the conspirators against the liberties of his country. Now, although I opposed, and ever shall, the leading features of his national policy, yet I always admired his sterling patriotism, his powerful eloquence, and his earnest advocation of what he conceived to be essential to his country's welfare.

Mr. President, and members of the Common Council of New York: Where are the men to fill the vacant seats of these exalted statesmen? Alas! they do not exist. But men of kindred genius will again arise among us, if we are true to the God of liberty and of nations,—if we are true to that beneficent Being, who bore us in triumph through the bloody scenes of the Revolution, and who has so faithfully guarded our liberties to this remote day. JACKSON, CALHOUN, CLAY! let the verdure of their graves forever bloom, and emit undying fragrance. Forever let their sacred memory be green in our hearts. Forever let us gratefully remember their noble deeds, and impart them to our children, as worthy of their highest emulation. Let those now on the stage of human action, closely imitate their spotless example and their incredible sacrifices from youth to age. Let us profoundly cherish the precious relics of political wisdom they have bequeathed us, and adopt them as genial sunlight in our pilgrimage through the dark and untrodden future. Let us do all this, and God will bless us (as worthy of his continued protection) with another brilliant galaxy of mighty spirits, to guard us against those, within and without our borders, who would effect our country's ruin.

Three noble oaks are fell'd at last,
That stood erect so many years,
'Neath summer skies, and winter's blast,
Falling amid their country's tears!

JACKSON! CALHOUN! CLAY! touching sounds—
That thrill the soul like muffled drum!
Names wont to cheer, 'mid fortune's frowns,
Like the full moon or mid-day sun.

Who fought and spoke in thrilling strain,
For liberty and all her train;
Who all were true, from youth to age,
As any of historic page.

Farewell, fathers! cold in the ground!
Who loved and served thy race so well;
Thy sons still live, to guard thy mound,
And thy great deeds their children tell.

On motion, the Board then adjourned.

D. T. VALENTINE, *Clerk.*

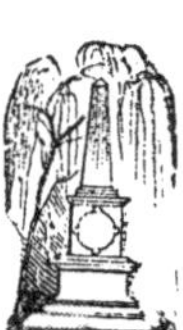

BOARD OF ASSISTANT ALDERMEN.

JUNE 30, 1852.

PRESENT—Jonathan Trotter, Esq., President, in the chair; Messrs. Brown, Tait, Mabbatt, O'Brien, Rodman, Woodward, Wells, Anderson, Bouton, McGown, Wright, Wheelan, Barker, Rogers and Valentine.

The President announced that the Board had been called together by his Honor the Mayor, pursuant to the third section of the amended charter, for the purpose of taking such measures as the members may deem proper in relation to the death of the Hon. HENRY CLAY.

Mr. Barker presented the following resolutions, viz :

Resolved, That this Board has received, with feelings of deep regret, the intelligence of the death of Hon. HENRY CLAY, late a Senator in Congress, from the State of Kentucky.

Resolved, That in common with our constituents and the whole nation, we mourn the loss of the great man who has filled and adorned so many public stations, and in whom, by a happy combination, were united the highest characteristics of the orator, the patriot, the statesman and the sage.

Resolved, That our admiration of his character, and our sorrow at his loss, are increased by the reflection that he crowned his splendid labors by devoting, with all the ardor of his earlier years, the evening of his life, and the last efforts of his genial spirit and his matchless eloquence, to reconciling sectional animosities, and to vindicating and preserving that glorious Union, in whose service he had so long and so faithfully labored.

Resolved, That it is our solace, on this melancholy occasion, to reflect that the close of his life was serene and tranquil, supported by the consolations of affection and religion ; that the sun of his glory descended unclouded ; that he now reposes, all feelings of party forgotten, and by universal consent, and with a fame forever identified in the annals of the world, with the history of the country and of liberty.

Resolved, That penetrated by these feelings, and desirous of testifying, however faintly, our appreciation of a character so lofty and services so distinguished, a Committee of five from the Board of Assistant Aldermen be appointed, to confer with a like Committee from the Board of Aldermen, to devise suitable measures, on behalf of the city of New York, in honor of the memory of the deceased.

The resolutions having been read, Mr. BARKER rose, and addressed the Board as follows:

Mr. PRESIDENT :—I feel embarrassed in attempting to add any remarks to the resolutions which have been presented upon this mournful occasion, for I feel my incompetency to the task.

We have been convened this evening, on the occasion of the death of the Hon. HENRY CLAY, who has long been the pride and the glory of the American republic.

HENRY CLAY, the man of the nation, who for half a century has stood first in the front ranks, as an orator, a statesman and a patriot, is now numbered with the dead. That great and heroic soul, which knew no impulses but those of patriotism and philanthropy, has passed away from these mortal scenes. The millions of this wide extended country, with the millions of the friends of liberty in other lands, will receive the news of this event with emotions too deep for utterance.

At the mention of his name, we are now hushed in silence and grief. There is now no hurrah for him who so often carried with him the people with an enthusiasm so unbounded. He has made his last appeal to his countrymen, and that was for the union of this glorious confederacy. We all know how that appeal has been answered. He is now silent, and sleeps the sleep of death, but he has left with us the triumph of his glorious deeds to brighten our path for the future.

It is needless, in this place, to recount the various acts of a life devoted to the service of his country. They are the theme of youth and the admiration of age.

His countrymen had been for some time warned that a mortal disease had attacked his majestic and stately form, yet the melancholy tidings of his death, though softened by their expected coming, have sank deeply and permanently into every heart.

The great man of this nation has been taken away, but time, endless time, will recall the glories of his past life, and many a page of his country's history will be adorned and illuminated with the actions, the wisdom, and the eloquence of HENRY CLAY.

The resolutions were unanimously adopted, and Messrs. BARKER, WOODWARD, TAIT, ANDERSON and WRIGHT, appointed the Committee.

Mr. BARKER then moved that the resolutions be sent to the Board of Aldermen for concurrence.

Which was carried.

The above resolutions were subsequently received from the Board of Aldermen, so amended as to increase the Committee to seven.

Whereupon, the amendment was concurred in, and the President added Messrs. McGowN and VALENTINE to said Committee.

FROM THE BOARD OF ALDERMEN.

Preamble and resolutions in favor of adopting suitable measures in relation to the death of HENRY CLAY.

Unanimously concurred in.

On motion, the Board then adjourned.

EDWARD SANFORD, *Clerk.*

Pending the proceedings in this city, ceremonies of the most interesting, but melancholy character, commensurate with the love the deceased was held by the nation, and which your Committee deem worthy of being recorded, took place at the Capital.

Funeral Solemnities in Washington.

Pursuant to the arrangements prescribed by the Committee of the Senate, the members of the Senate and of the House of Representatives, together with public bodies and associations, military companies, and civic authorities, assembled at the National Hotel, where the body had lain since life departed; and from thence the melancholy funeral procession passed to the Senate chamber, so long the theatre of his glories.

As the body was borne to the centre of the chamber, the Rev. Dr. BUTLER, Chaplain to the Senate, in full canonicals, read part of the Episcopal ritual—

"I am the resurrection and the life, saith the Lord."

In consonance with the solemn service over the dead was the scene there presented—sombre and sad.

The President of the United States, and the Speaker of the House of Representatives, were seated with the President of the Senate. The body of the Senate, the representatives of state sovereignties, were grouped, on the two innermost semicircular rows of chairs, around the lifeless form of their late colleague. The Committee of Arrangements, and the Committee to convey the body to Kentucky, and the pall-bearers, with the Kentucky delegation in the House of Representatives, as chief mourners, and a number of personal devoted friends, were also in close proximity to the inanimate form of the deceased.

The members of the House of Representatives filled the outer circles, except such parts as were devoted to the large diplomatic corps, the Cabinet of the President of the United States, the officers of the Army and Navy, among whom were Major-General SCOTT, Commander-in-chief, and Commodore MORRIS. With the Municipal Councils of the city of Washington, were the officers of neighboring cities, and others, official and unofficial.

A shield of fragrant and sweetly-culled flowers was placed upon the sarcophagus, as a memorial of affection for the deceased statesman within. The pure white and brightly variegated flowers contrasted sadly with the rich folding drapery of black cloth, additionally relieved by its silver ornaments. The sarcophagus, in which the remains were inurned, resembles the outlines of the human body. The handles, the face-plate, the plate for inscribing the name, and other plates, are of massive silver, beautifully wrought and chased, having appropriate emblems, among which appear wreaths of laurel and oak, with a full-blown rose, and sprig of oak with its acorns detached from their parent stem, showing the work of the fell destroyer. The plate, near the centre of the sarcophagus, bore the simple inscription,

The utmost silence prevailed ; all present, including the crowded auditory in the galleries and lobbies, were deeply impressed with the solemnity of the occasion. Amidst the contemplations to which this scene gave being, the chaplain's voice broke on the listening ear—

"But some man will say, How are the dead raised up? and with what body do they come?"

The answer is furnished by the residue of the fifteenth chapter of 1st Corinthians, which the chaplain impressively read for the consolation of the bereaved living.

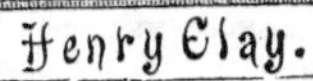

A SERMON

DELIVERED IN THE SENATE CHAMBER OF THE UNITED STATES,

ON THE OCCASION OF THE

FUNERAL OF THE HON. HENRY CLAY,

BY THE

REV. C. M. BUTLER, D.D.,

CHAPLAIN OF THE SENATE.

"How is the strong staff broken, and the beautiful rod!"—JER. xlviii. 17.

"BEFORE all hearts and minds in this august assemblage, the vivid image of ONE MAN stands. To some aged eye, he may come forth, from the dim past, as he appeared in the neighboring city of his native state, a lithe and ardent youth, full of promise, of ambition, and of hope. To another, he may appear as, in a distant state, in the courts of justice, erect, high strung, bold, wearing the fresh forensic laurel on his young and open brow. Some may see him in the earlier, and some in the later, stages of his career, on this conspicuous theatre of his renown; and to the former he will start out, on the background of the past, as he appeared in the neighboring chamber, tall, elate, impassioned—with flashing eye and suasive gesture, and clarion voice, an already acknowledged 'Agamemnon, King of Men;' and to others, he will again stand in this chamber 'the strong staff' of the bewildered and staggering state, and 'the beautiful rod,' rich with the blossoms of genius, and of patriotic love and hope, the life of youth still remaining to give animation, grace, and exhaustless vigor, to the wisdom, the experience, and the gravity of age. To others he may be present as he sat in the chamber of sickness, cheerful, majestic, gentle—his mind clear, his heart warm, his hope fixed on heaven, peacefully preparing for his last great change. To the memory of the minister of God, he appears as the penitent, humble, and peaceful Christian, who received him with the affection of a father, and joined with him, in solemn sacrament and prayer, with the gentleness of a woman and the humility of a child. 'Out of the strong came forth sweetness.' 'How is the strong staff broken, and the beautiful rod!' But not before this assembly only, does the venerated image of the departed statesman, this day, distinctly stand. For more than a thousand miles—East, West, North and South—it is known and remembered, that at this place and hour, a nation's representatives assemble to do honor to him whose fame is now a nation's heritage. A nation's mighty heart throbs against this capitol, and beats through you. In many cities banners droop, bells toll, cannons boom, funereal draperies wave. In crowded streets, and on sounding wharfs, upon steamboats and upon cars, in fields and in work-shops, in homes, in schools, millions of men, women and children, have their thoughts fixed upon this scene, and say mournfully to each other, 'This is the hour in which, at the capitol, the nation's representatives are burying HENRY CLAY.' *Burying* HENRY CLAY! Bury the records of your country's history—bury the hearts of living millions—bury the mountains, the rivers, the lakes, and the spreading lands from sea to sea, with which his name is inseparably associated, and even then you would not bury HENRY CLAY—for he lives in other lands, and speaks in other tongues, and to other times than ours.

"A great mind, a great heart, a great orator, a great career, have been consigned to history. She will record his rare gifts of deep insight, keen discrimination, clear statement, rapid combination, plain, direct and convincing logic. She will love to dwell on that large, generous, magnanimous, open, forgiving heart. She will linger, with fond delight, on the recorded and traditional stories of an eloquence that was so masterful and stirring, because it was but *himself*, struggling to come forth on the living words—because, though the words were brave and strong, and beautiful and melodious, it was felt that, behind them there was a *soul*, braver, stronger, more beautiful, and more melodious, than language could express. She will point to a career of statesmanship which has, to a remarkable degree, stamped itself on the public policy of the country, and reached, in beneficent practical results, the fields, the looms, the commercial marts, and the quiet homes of all the land, where his name was, with the departed fathers, and is with the living children, and will be, with successive generations, an honored household word.

"I feel, as a man, the grandeur of this career. But as an immortal, with this broken wreck of mortality before me, with this scene as the 'end-all' of human glory, I feel that no career is truly great but that of him who, whether he be illustrious or obscure, lives to the future in the present, and, linking himself to the spiritual world, draws from GOD the life, the rule, the motive, and the reward of all his labor. So would that great spirit which has departed say to us, could he address us now. So did he realize in the calm and meditative close of life. I feel that I but utter the lessons which, living, were his last and best convictions, and which, dead, would be, could he speak to us, his solemn admonitions, when I say that statesmanship is then only glorious when it is *Christian:* and that man is then only safe, and true to his duty and his soul, when the life which he lives in the flesh is the life of faith in the SON of GOD.

" Great, indeed, is the privilege, and most honorable and useful is the career, of a Christian American statesman. He perceives that civil liberty came from the freedom wherewith CHRIST made its early martyrs and defenders free. He recognizes it as one of the twelve manner of fruits on the Tree of Life which, while its lower branches furnish the best nutriment of earth, hangs on its topmost boughs, which wave in Heaven, fruits that exhilarate the immortals. Recognizing the State as GOD's institution, he will perceive that his own ministry is divine. Living consciously under the eye, and in the love and fear of GOD; redeemed by the blood of JESUS; sanctified by His spirit, loving His law, he will give himself, in private and in public, to the service of his SAVIOR. He will not admit that he may act on less lofty principles in public than in private life, and that he must be careful of his moral influence in the small sphere of home and neighborhood, but need take no heed of it when it stretches over continents and crosses seas. He will know that his moral responsibility can not be divided and distributed among others. When he is told that adherence to the strictest moral and religious principle is incompatible with a successful and eminent career, he will denounce the assertion as a libel on the venerated Fathers of the Republic—a libel on the honored living and the illustrious dead—libel against a great and Christian nation—a libel against GOD himself, who has declared and made 'godliness profitable for the life that now is.' He will strive to make laws the transcripts of the character, and institutions illustrations of the providence of GOD. He will scan with admiration and awe the purposes of GOD in the future history of the world, in throwing open this wide continent, from sea to sea, as the abode of freedom, intelligence, plenty, prosperity and peace; and feel that, in giving his energies with a patriot's love to the welfare of his country, he is consecrating himself, with a Christian's zeal, to the extension and establishment of the Redeemer's kingdom. Compared with a career like this, which is equally open to those whose public sphere is large or small, how paltry are the trade of patriotism, the tricks of statesmanship, the rewards of successful baseness! This hour, this scene, the venerated dead, the country, the world, the present, the future, GOD, duty, heaven, hell, speak trumpet-tongued to all in the service of their country, to *beware* how they lay polluted or unhallowed hands

'Upon the ark
Of her magnificent and awful cause.'

"Such is the character of that statesmanship which alone would have met the full approval of the venerated dead. For the religion which always had a place in the convictions of his mind, had also, within a recent period, entered into his experience and seated itself in his heart. Twenty years since, he wrote—'I am a member of no religious sect, and I am not a professor of religion. I regret that I am not. I wish that I was, and trust that I shall be. I have, and always have had, a profound regard for Christianity, the religion of my fathers, and for its rites, its usages and observances.' That feeling proved that the seed sown by pious parents, was not dead, though stifled. A few years since, its dormant life was re-awakened. He was baptized in the communion of the Protestant Episcopal Church; and during his sojourn in this city, he was in full communion with Trinity Parish.

"It is since his withdrawal from the sittings of the Senate, that I have been made particularly acquainted with his religious opinions, character, and feelings. From the commencement of his illness he always expressed to me his persuasion that its termination would be fatal. From that period until his death, it was my privilege to hold frequent religious services and conversations with him in his room. He avowed to me his full faith in the great leading doctrines of the Gospel—the fall and sinfulness of man, the divinity of CHRIST, the reality and necessity of the Atonement, the need of being born again by the Spirit, and salvation through faith in a crucified Redeemer. His own personal hopes of salvation he ever and distinctly based on the promises and the grace of CHRIST. Strikingly perceptible on his naturally impetuous and impatient character, was the influence of grace in producing submission and a 'patient waiting for CHRIST,' and for death. On one occasion, he spoke to me of the pious example of one very near and dear to him, as that which led him deeply to feel and earnestly to seek for himself the reality and the blessedness of religion. On another occasion, he told me that he had been striving to form a conception of heaven; and he enlarged upon the mercy of that provision by which our SAVIOR became a partaker of our humanity, that our hearts and hopes might fix themselves on him.

On another occasion, when he was supposed to be very near his end, I expressed to him the hope that his mind and heart were at peace, and that he was able to rest with cheerful confidence on the promises and in the merits of the Redeemer. He said, with much feeling, that he endeavored to, and trusted that he did repose his salvation upon CHRIST; that it was too late for him to look at Christianity in the light of speculation; that he had never doubted of its truth; and that he now wished to throw himself upon it as a practical and blessed remedy. Very soon after this, I administered to him the sacrament of the LORD's Supper. Being extremely feeble, and desirous of having his mind undiverted, no persons were present but his son and his servant. It was a scene long to be remembered. There, in that still chamber, at a week-day noon, the tides of life flowing all around us, three disciples of the SAVIOR—the minister of GOD, the dying statesman, and his servant, a partaker of the like precious faith—commemorated their SAVIOR's dying love. He joined in the blessed sacrament with great feeling and solemnity—now pressing his hands together, and now spreading them forth, as the words of the service expressed the feelings, desires, supplications, confessions, and thanksgivings of his heart. His eyes were dim with grateful tears, his heart was full of peace and love! After this he rallied, and again I was permitted frequently to join with him in religious services, conversation and prayer. He grew in grace and in the knowledge of our LORD and SAVIOR JESUS CHRIST. Among the books which, in connection with the Word of GOD, he read most, were 'Jay's Morning and Evening Exercises;' the 'Life of Dr. Chalmers,' and 'The Christian Philosopher Triumphant in Death.' His hope continued to the end, to be, though true and real, tremulous with humility rather than rapturous with assurance. When he felt most the weariness of his protracted sufferings, it sufficed to suggest to him that his Heavenly Father doubtless knew that, after a life so long and stirring, and tempted, such a discipline of chastening and suffering was needful to make him more meet for the inheritance of the saints; and at once words of meek and patient acquiescence escaped his lips.

"Exhausted nature at length gave way. On the last occasion when I was permitted to offer a brief prayer at his bedside, his last words to me were that he had hope only in CHRIST, and that the prayer which I had offered for his pardoning love and his sanctifying grace, included every thing which the dying need. On the evening previous to his departure, sitting for an hour in silence by his side, I could not but realize, when I heard him, in the slight wanderings of his mind to other days, and other scenes, murmuring the words, '*My mother! Mother! Mother!*' and saying, '*My dear wife!*' as if she were present; and frequently uttering aloud, as if in response to some silent Litany of the soul, the simple prayer, 'LORD have mercy upon me.' I could not but realize then, and rejoice to think how near was the blessed reunion of his weary heart with the loved dead and with her—Our dear LORD gently smooth her passage to the tomb!—who must soon follow him to his rest, whose spirits even then seemed to visit and to cheer his memory and his hope. Gently he breathed his soul away into the spirit world.

'How blest the righteous when they die!
 When holy souls retire to rest,
How mildly beams the closing eye!
 How gently heaves the expiring breast!

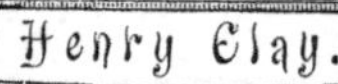

'So fades the summer cloud away;
So sinks the gale when storms are o'er;
So gently shuts the eye of day;
So dies the wave upon the shore!'

"Be it ours to follow him in the same humble and submissive faith to Heaven. Could he speak to us the counsels of his latest human and his present heavenly experience, sure I am, that he would not only admonish us to cling to the SAVIOR in sickness and in death; but adjure us not to delay to act upon our first convictions, that we might give our best powers and fullest influence to GOD, and go to the grave with a hope, unshadowed by the long worldliness of the past, or by the films of fear and doubt resting over the future.

"The strong staff is broken, and the beautiful rod is despoiled of its grace and bloom; but, in the light of the eternal promises, and by the power of CHRIST's resurrection, we joyfully anticipate the prospect of seeing that broken staff erect, and that beautiful rod, clothed with celestial grace, and blossoming with undying life and blessedness, in the Paradise of GOD."

The ritual of the Episcopal Church, at the burial of the dead, closed the solemn service, and the body was removed to the rotunda, when the silver plate, covering the glass over the face of the corpse, was removed, the President and the Cabinet, Senators, Representatives, Diplomatic Corps, officers of the Army and Navy, Clergymen and Physicians, and all present, drew near, and, amid the most impressive silence, took a last view of the features of the great and illustrious deceased.

At the conclusion of the ceremonies, the procession proceeded to the railroad depot, in the following order:

The Chaplains of both Houses of Congress.
Physicians who attended the deceased.

Committee of Arrangements.

Mr. HUNTER,	Mr. COOPER,
Mr. DAWSON,	Mr. BRIGHT,
Mr. JONES, of Iowa,	Mr. SMITH.

Pall Bearers.

Mr. CASS.	CORPSE.	Mr. PRATT,
Mr. MANGUM,		Mr. ATCHISON,
Mr. DODGE, of Wis.		Mr. BELL.

Committee to attend the remains to Kentucky.

Mr. UNDERWOOD,	Mr. FISH,
Mr. JONES, of Tenn.	Mr. HOUSTON,
Mr. CASS,	Mr. STOCKTON.

The Family and Friends of the deceased.
The Senators and Representatives from the State of Kentucky, as mourners.
The Sergeant-at-Arms of the Senate.
The Senate of the United States, preceded by their President *pro tempore*, and Secretary.
The other Officers of the Senate.
The Sergeant-at-Arms of the House of Representatives.
The House of Representatives, preceded by their Speaker and Clerk.
The other Officers of the House of Representatives.
Judges of the United States.
Officers of the Executive Departments.
Officers of the Army and Navy.

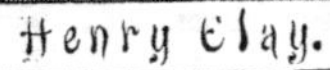

The Mayor and Corporation of Washington, and of other Cities.
Civic Associations.
Military Companies.
Citizens and Strangers.

On the arrival of the corpse at the depot, it was placed in a car appropriately decorated, and confided to the Committee appointed to accompany it to Kentucky. The funeral cortege soon after arrived, and halted for the night at

Baltimore,

where the whole people came out to attest, by fit observances, their affection and sorrow. The coffin was placed for the night in the Exchange, upon a magnificent cenotaph, erected in the centre of the rotunda, in charge of the Independent Greys, as a guard of honor.

On the following morning the corpse was removed from the Exchange to the cars, attended by the Mayor, City Council, officers of the Army and Navy, the Independent Greys, (guard of honor,) civic associations and the citizens of Baltimore, generally. The whole city wore a melancholy aspect; business was generally suspended; the buildings on the streets through which the procession passed, and in other parts of the city, were decorated with the mournful habiliments of death. The bells tolled and minute guns were fired during the passage of the procession.

The body was placed in a car appropriately draped with black crape, and the cars, provided for the funeral cortege, were similarly decorated.

At Elkton, Md., the cortege was met by a Committee from the State of Delaware, to whom the Baltimore Committee delivered their venerated charge, accompanied with a beautiful and appropriate address; which was very feelingly responded to by the Committee from Delaware. When the cars reached

Wilmington,

a large civic and military escort was in attendance, and the remains and escort, consisting of the Baltimore and Washington Committees, were received by the Committee of Arrangements appointed by the City Council, and escorted to the City Hall, where a guard of honor was stationed, and the plate being removed from the sarcophagus, an immense concourse of people, male and female, passed through the lines and took a last look at the features of the deceased.

At every station where the cars stopped, they were met by thousands, who were anxious to obtain a view of the body. Houses were decked with mourning, bells tolled, and minute guns fired, as the train passed along.

Philadelphia.

The cortege arrived at Philadelphia at night, and was received at the depot by the corporate authorities, firemen, military and citizens. The Washington Greys acting as the guard of honor to the corpse. The firemen carried lighted torches, and rockets were fired, during the passage of the procession, from the depot to the Hall of Independence. The procession as it moved through the entire route to the Hall of Independence, was grand, solemn and

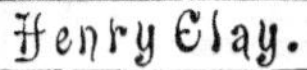

imposing beyond any thing of the kind that has ever taken place in that city. The whole population appeared to be gathered on the line of march, and a deep, reverent, eloquent silence, like the silence of death itself, pervaded the mighty multitude; above it all, rendered more audible and impressive by the contrast, was heard the slow, measured tread of the long funeral train, the tolling bells, the booming minute gun, and the mournful roll of the muffled drum.

The city authorities had made every preparation for the reception of the remains. The hall was heavily hung with black cloth, and the square was brilliantly illuminated.

The scene in the venerable hall was one which pen could not describe. The hour was midnight. The body was surrendered, in a feeling speech, by the Chief Marshal, Major Fritz, into the keeping of the city authorities. The chairman of the Committee of Arrangements, Mr. Wetherill, was so overcome by his feelings, that he could not reply.

As the spectators passed around the bier, and took a last look at the coffin, then encircled in a wreath of green and rare flowers, the silence of death pervaded the room. Tears were freely shed, and the deepest sorrow was depicted on every countenance.

At an early hour on Saturday morning, the doors of the hall were thrown open, and the people, to the number of thousands, of both sexes, and of all ages, were admitted to take a last look of the magnificent coffin. The face of the corpse was not exposed, as the effect of the light on it, in Baltimore, produced such a marked change, as to show the necessity of the utmost caution, in order to preserve the lineaments of the great man perfect, for the gratification of his family and nearest friends, when the body shall reach its final resting-place in Kentucky.

The corpse was placed in the hearse and conveyed to the steamer Trenton, followed by the several committees, and the marshals of the obsequies. The band played a farewell dirge, and the Washington Greys gave the parting salute. The steamer was heavily draped in black, and her bell tolled in mournful harmony with the dirge-like toll of the bells of the city. At nine o'clock the boat moved off. A large throng of spectators stood gazing sadly after her until she was lost to view on the river.

At Tacony,

The Committee of Councils delivered the corpse into the custody of the officers and Committee of Congress, charged with the duty of conveying it to Ashland. A large number of citizens accompanied the remains to Tacony; a number also came on to

Trenton.

The remains reached Trenton shortly after 10 o'clock. Their arrival was announced by the firing of minute guns by a company of artillery, and an immense concourse, which had collected, uncovered as the train approached. The church bells were also tolled, and all the buildings in the vicinity of the depot were appropriately draped.

At Princeton,

There was a very general suspension of business, and over the railroad an immense arch was erected, and draped in mourning, with mottoes expressive of the general grief at the nation's loss. The places of business and dwellings in the vicinity were also in mourning.

Similar demonstrations of sympathy and respect were exhibited at New Brunswick, Elizabethtown, Rahway, and, indeed, at all places along the route.

At Newark,

The remains were met by the Committee of Jersey City, and a large body of military, while the firing of minute guns and the tolling of bells betokened the general sorrow. The stores and places of business were mostly closed, and all the principal buildings were decked in mourning.

Order of Proceedings in New York.

THURSDAY, JULY 1.

The Joint Committee held its first official meeting this day, and immediately entered upon the performance of the duties assigned them. It being then understood that the mortal remains of the revered Henry Clay would be brought to this city, *en route* for Kentucky. Ample measures were promptly adopted to complete all the arrangements designed for the reception of the body, characteristically appropriate of the occasion, and in a manner adequate to his merits and exalted station. A delegation from the Clay Festival Association, waited upon the Committee, and presented the following communication:

"The undersigned, duly constituted a committee, with power to act in behalf of the 'Clay Festival Association,

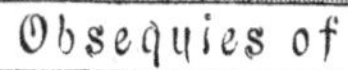

respectfully represent that they have been organized as an association, the past seven years, having for its object the celebration of the birthday of HENRY CLAY, by an annual festival. That many of them were closely allied to him by ties of personal friendship and unity; and that all this has been done free from any political considerations.

"That we now, in common with our fellow-citizens, mourn his loss, but, that from the very nature of our organization, it is manifest that the ties which connect us with the illustrious dead, is of a strong and affectionate character.

"We therefore respectfully request of your honorable committee, that we may be permitted to occupy such position and take such action, that would seem to be not only appropriate, but our proper right.

"*First.* We respectfully ask of you to be permitted to do service in attendance upon the body of the deceased during its stay in New York.

"*Second.* We ask that we may be permitted to act as mourners upon the occasion of the procession.

M. R. BREWER,
President Clay Festival Association.

KENNETH G. WHITE, }
JOSIAH P. KNAPP, } *Vice Presidents.*

BENJ. DRAKE,
Chairman Executive Committee.

JAS. L. BERRIEN, *Sec'y.*

JOS. M. PRICE,
WM. S. DUKE,
HORATIO REED,
GEORGE F. WOODWARD,
H. N. LOUDON,
DAVID WEBB,
JOHN T. BARNARD,
A. W. ROGERS."

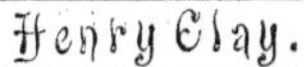

FRIDAY, JULY 2.

A telegraphic despatch was received from the Hon. JOSEPH R. UNDERWOOD, (from Baltimore,) stating that the body of Mr. CLAY would arrive in this city on Saturday afternoon.

Whereupon, Aldermen BRISLEY, BARD, and Assistant Aldermen BARKER, WRIGHT and McGOWN, were appointed a Committee to proceed to Philadelphia, to confer with the delegation having charge of the body. Delegations from the Clay Festival Association and Whig General Committees were invited to accompany the Committee.

Company D, Washington Greys, Capt. JAMES LITTLE, was selected as a guard of honor, on the reception of the body; also, during its stay in the city, and at its departure.

Letters of invitation were issued to the Mayor, Governor, Lieut. Governor and the Heads of Departments of the State, Common Council, Heads of Departments, Judges of Courts, officers of the Army and Navy, members of Congress, State Senate and Assembly, Foreign Ministers and Consuls, Society of Cincinnati, Collector, Naval Officer and Surveyor of the Port, and other civil officers of the United States, &c., &c.

The following notice was issued, and ordered to be published in the newspapers of the day:

"The Special Committee of the Common Council of the city of New York, appointed to make suitable arrangements to pay respect to the Hon. HENRY CLAY, deceased, respectfully announce to their fellow-citizens, that intelligence has been received that the remains may be expected to arrive in this city this day, Saturday, 3d inst., at one o'clock, P. M., at the Battery, from whence they will be taken to the City Hall, and there remain until the Congressional delegation determines to proceed onward.

"It is requested by the Committee that the persons having charge of the various church bells, will cause them to be tolled during the hours of one and two o'clock, P. M.

"It is also recommended that the shipping in our harbor display their flags at half mast, and that proprietors of hotels and other public buildings, do likewise.

"The Committee earnestly request, that from the hour above named, until the close of the day, business of every kind be suspended in respect to the memory of the deceased.

"Delegates who will participate in the reception of the remains, will take their position in the line on the Battery, in the order arranged upon with the Committee of the Common Council, as the shortness of time will preclude further notice.

It is designed that the obsequies in honor of the deceased will take place at some future time, of which due notice will be given.

WILLIAM H. CORNELL, WESLEY SMITH, WILLIAM J. BRISLEY, WILLIAM M. TWEED, JAMES M. BARD, S. L. H. WARD, JOHN BOYCE, RICHARD T. COMPTON, Pres't.	*Committee of the Board of Aldermen.*
ISAAC O. BARKER, THOMAS WOODWARD, JOHN J. TAIT, WILLIAM ANDERSON, WILLIAM H. WRIGHT, S. BENSON McGOWN, J. H. VALENTINE, JONATHAN TROTTER, Pres't.	*Committee of the Board of Assistant Aldermen.*

On the same day his Honor the Mayor issued the following

Proclamation.

MAYOR'S OFFICE, JULY 2, 1852.

In respect to the memory of the departed sage and patriot, HENRY CLAY, whose remains will reach this city on Saturday, the 3d inst., on their route to the West, the public offices of the city will be closed, on that day, after 12 o'clock, M.

A. C. KINGSLAND, *Mayor*.

On Saturday morning, the Committee assembled, preparatory to proceeding to Jersey City, where they were to receive the body. The Committee, accompanied by the Mayor, members of the Common Council, City officers, Clay Festival Association, United States Government officers, Company D, Washington Greys, (guard of honor) and a large number of invited guests, proceeded to the Battery, and embarked on board the steamer Philadelphia for Jersey City.

Upon the arrival of the train bearing the funeral cortege, the Hon. JOSEPH R. UNDERWOOD, was introduced to Mr. MANNERS, Mayor of Jersey City, who spoke in behalf of the Committee, as follows:

"Mr. CHAIRMAN:—We come, in behalf the people of Jersey City, to express the deep sympathy which we all feel in the loss of the distinguished statesman, whose remains you have in charge. He has fallen in the autumn of life, laden with its richest honors. But, 'We come to *bury*, not to praise him.' We desire to unite with you in this solemn, mournful procession, and render every service in our power, befitting this melancholy occasion, and to invite you to remain in our city a sufficient length of time to allow its citizens an opportunity of paying their last sad tribute of respect to the illustrious dead, whom in life they never failed to honor."

Senator UNDERWOOD responded in a brief but chaste and feeling address, in which he adverted to the public and private worth of the deceased statesman—to which a tribute has been paid by the people along the entire route from Washington. He also expressed his desire that the request for the resting of the remains at Jersey City be granted.

At the arrival of the cars, minute-guns were fired, and the bells were tolled. The procession was formed at the depot, and marched to the boat. The Jersey City Continentals, as a guard of honor, and the officers of the Hudson Brigade, accompanied by a band of music, escorted the procession of the various committees to the boat. As they moved through the streets, the heads of the entire mass of spectators were uncovered, and not a voice disturbed the effect of the measured tramp of the feet, the deep, sad music of the funeral march, or the more distant tolling bells and booming cannon. Tears fell from many eyes. As soon as all were on board the boat Philadelphia, she moved off into the stream, and on her way to the Battery, Mayor MANNERS returned the remains to the Senatorial Committee, with some appropriate remarks, and introduced AMBROSE C. KINGSLAND, Mayor of New York, to the Committee, who, in behalf of the City of New York Committee, received the charge. During the passage of the steamer, a very beautifully arranged wreath, composed of oak leaves, was presented by Dr. BENJAMIN DRAKE to the Senatorial Committee, with the following address, viz :

" GENTLEMEN SENATORS:—In behalf of the Clay Festival Association, I respectfully ask your permission to place near the body of our illustrious friend a last but humble, though fitting testimonial of our regard and affection. It is a CIVIC WREATH, composed not of the laurel, the triumphant gatherings of the battle field, but of the leaves of the oak. Such a decoration the Romans of old were wont to bestow upon their most meritorious citizens. We loved Mr. CLAY in life, and his memory is near to us in death. We have further to ask that a delegation from our body, may be permitted to attend his honored remains to their final resting place, in Kentucky."

Senator UNDERWOOD, in behalf of the Committee of the Senate, briefly assented, and stated in reference to the emblem of the oak leaves, that it was in keeping with all that had transpired on the route from the Capitol to this city.

On the arrival of the boat at the wharf, the coffin was placed in a splendidly decorated open hearse, drawn by eight gray horses, appropriately caparisoned. The procession was formed in the following order:

Sergeants-at-Arms of both Boards.
The Mayor.
Presidents of the Boards of Aldermen and Assistants.
Sergeant-at-Arms of the Senate.
The Senate Committee.
The Common Council of New York.

The Common Council of Jersey City.
The Jersey City Continentals.
Citizens of New Jersey, Philadelphia, Baltimore and Washington.

WASHINGTON GREYS, AS A GUARD OF HONOR.	HEARSE.	WASHINGTON GREYS, AS A GUARD OF HONOR.

Clay Festival Association, as mourners.
The Whig General Committee,
Democratic Whig Young Men's Committee.
Citizens.

The procession moved up Broadway to Chatham street, up Chatham street to the east gate of the Park, when they entered and rested in front of the City Hall. The body was then taken from the hearse and conveyed to the Governor's room, (which had been appropriately trimmed for the occasion,) followed by the military and the committees. It was then placed upon a beautiful cenotaph; and as soon as the sentinels were stationed to guard the coffin, the anxious multitude were allowed to walk around the bier, and take a last look of that which contained but the dust of HENRY CLAY.

As the procession passed along to the City Hall, the bells were tolled, minute guns were fired from the Battery, the forts and shipping in the harbor. The buildings along the line of the procession, and in other parts of the city, were dressed in mourning. There was an almost entire cessation from business, and a general feeling of grief seemed to pervade our whole population.

The body remained in the Governor's room during the night and throughout the next day (Sunday, July 4th, the seventy-sixth anniversary of American Independence.) The inhabitants of this city, Brooklyn, Williamsburgh, Hoboken, Staten Island and other places adjacent to New York, availed themselves of this opportunity of rendering their mite to the general sorrow of the nation, and testifying their love, admiration and respect of the illustrious dead, and to take a final look at the coffin wherein is confined all that remains of the once great man of the nation! There he lay, on the very spot where, a few years ago, he stood proudly erect, affable, and self-possessed—the pleased and pleasing recipient of a people's homage—admiring women crowding the levee, happy to grasp his hand, and little girls pressing onward to snatch a kiss from his venerable lips. On that very spot—lifeless and wasting—encased in iron cerements—there reposed all that remained of the great, illustrious, and almost worshipped, HENRY CLAY. What an impressive contrast! The glorious anniversary of our country's independence was full of the manifestations of public grief. The stars and stripes of our national banners were darkened with the emblems of mourning. The flags at half mast, the tolling bells, the minute-gun, the muffled drum, the solemn countenance and the mournful tread of the passing spectator, told of a nation's sorrow for the loss of one of the most illustrious and loved in its councils.

The facilities for admitting visitors were admirably arranged. Upwards of one hundred thousand persons visited the remains during the evening of Saturday and on Sunday. There was a constant procession passing throughout the day, and all conducted without the slighest confusion. The coffin and floor around the cenotaph, was covered with flowers, which the affection of visitors, prompted with feelings of gratitude, to place near the body as they passed by.

Departure of the Remains from New York.

LEAVING THE CITY HALL.

AT two o'clock, on Monday morning, the remains of HENRY CLAY were removed from the Governor's room, accompanied by the Committee of Arrangements of the Common Council, escorted by Company D, Washington Greys, as guard of honor, with the Clay Festival Association, as pall bearers, to the steamboat Santa Claus, (which had been chartered to convey the remains to Albany,) lying at the foot of Murray street.

The scene was solemn and impressive, as the full moon lent its rays to lighten the pathway of the funeral procession; the slow march, the tolling bell, and the mournful roll of the muffled drum added to the general solemnity. At the moment when the association and guard of honor were drawn up in line, to permit the remains to pass to the boat, the band suddenly struck up the air, "Should old acquaintance be forgot." The effect cannot be described—there was scarcely a dry eye in the whole assemblage. The steamboat was decorated in a neat and appropriate manner—the outside being festooned with black and white linen, while the flags, which run half mast, were trimmed with crape. The ladies' cabin was hung with crape, and in the centre was arranged a cenotaph, upon which the coffin was placed, and then covered with a heavy black velvet pall. A committee of six of the military and six of the Clay Festival Association, waited as guard until the hour arrived for the boat to start.

The coffin, which rested in the saloon, was covered with a magnificent canopy of crape, and on the top were strewn flowers of the choicest kind. Near the head was a beautiful wreath, made from the "IMMORTILLE" (or life everlasting flower) brought from France, and presented by Mrs. ANN S. STEPHENS, the poetess, with a request that it might be placed on the tomb of HENRY CLAY, in Kentucky. It is a bright yellow, while a cross of a dark brown of the same flower is worked in it. It was admired by all as a fit emblem to the memory of HENRY CLAY, who will live forever in the hearts of his countrymen. The civic wreath, presented by the Clay Festival Association, and with the same request, also adorned the top, while the laurel wreath from Philadelphia, and the boquets from Baltimore and Washington were placed around it, and had all maintained their fragrance and beauty.

DEPARTURE FROM NEW YORK.

At 11 o'clock, a gun was fired, which was the signal for starting—the bell commenced tolling, and the boat was soon underway. The following is a list of the funeral cortege:

Mourners.—THOMAS H. CLAY, son of Mr. CLAY; HENRY CLAY, Jr., grandson, Lexington; Hon. Mr. WHITE, Kentucky; Hon. Mr. WILLIAMS, Kentucky; Mrs. CARTER.

Senate Committee.—Hon. J. R. UNDERWOOD, Hon. J. C. JONES, Hon. R. F. STOCKTON, Hon. H. FISH, Hon. S. HOUSTON, Hon. L. CASS.

ROBERT BEALS, Sergeant-at-Arms, U. S. Senate; R. P. ANDERSON, Assistant do.

Committee in charge of the coffin.

Committee of the Clay Festival Association, to escort the remains to Lexington.

Common Council of New York.

Company D, Washington Greys.

Clay Festival Association.

Delegations from the General Committees.

Invited Guests.

PASSAGE UP THE RIVER.

The bell of the steamer was kept constantly tolling, and as we passed the steamboats upon the river, bound for New York, they stopped for a few moments, lowered their flags at half mast, minute-guns were exchanged, and they commenced tolling their bells. At all the landings we passed, similar demonstrations were shown. As we neared West Point, the booming cannon reverberated from hill to hill. Cozzens' Hotel immediately lowered the American flag, and as we passed West Point a body of the cadets were drawn up in line, and stood on the embankment, with heads uncovered. A national salute was fired from the boat, while the band on the boat played a beautiful funeral dirge.

At NEWBURGH, where the boat arrived soon after three o'clock, and where there was a grand celebration, the cortege was honored with a national salute of thirteen guns, fired one each minute. The boat was detained here some twenty minutes, during which time the citizens were allowed to pass on board and view the coffin. The greatest feeling was manifested, and the flags that had been raised to celebrate our country's national day, were lowered to half mast, as a token of respect for the memory of the deceased. The church bells were tolled as the boat left the wharf, and minute-guns were fired.

POUGHKEEPSIE.—As we passed the village of Poughkeepsie, crowds had assembled on the adjoining hills and docks. The flags were at half mast, and the people stood with heads uncovered. A small boat came out from the shore, and threw on board a beautiful boquet, to which was attached a note, which read as follows:

"The Ladies of Poughkeepsie in memory of HENRY CLAY."

HYDE PARK.—Here the people assembled on the wharf in large numbers, and stood with heads uncovered as the boat passed; a salute was fired from the shore, and the American flag, trimmed with crape, floated at half mast.

KINGSTON AND RHINEBECK.—The bells were tolling as we passed by these two places, minute-guns were fired, and every token of the deepest sympathy manifested.

As we passed the residence of General DE PEYSTER, at Tivoli, we noticed a portion of his regiment drawn up in line, and when the boat was directly opposite, they fired a volley, as if firing over the grave of a comrade.

The grounds were tastefully trimmed in mourning, and from the boat presented a beautiful appearance.

The "LIVINGSTON" places were also decorated in mourning, and had guns stationed on prominent points, firing salutes.

UPPER AND LOWER RED HOOK—BRISTOL AND CATSKILL, presented the same tokens of the general grief.

HUDSON.—The docks and Round House Hill were completely crowded with people. We noticed thirty-one young ladies, dressed in white, with black scarfs thrown across their shoulders, and in their right hands the American flag, trimmed with black crape. The boat stopped her engine as we went by—minute-guns were fired and bells tolled.

From Hudson up to Albany, there was a constant firing of cannon from the shore, and every demonstration was shown to tell the grief the whole country felt.

During the day we passed the steamboats North America, Columbia, Armenia and Utica, each one of which stopped as we went by, lowered their colors and tolled their bells.

The steamboat Baltic, of Albany, having on board the Committee of Arrangements, the Whig General Committee, a delegation of the Democratic Committee, and one hundred of the Burgess Corps and citizens, came down the river to meet the Santa Claus. The Baltic remained at Castleton; and at half past nine o'clock the approach of the Santa Claus was announced by the tolling of bells and the firing of minute-guns. The Baltic's bell commenced tolling, and minute-guns were fired in response to the Santa Claus.

The Albany Committee of Arrangements having been received on board the latter boat by the Committee of the New York Common Council, and introduced to the Senatorial Committee, the Baltic led the way to Albany. The night was perfectly still, and not a sound was heard upon the water but the tolling of the bells on the boats, and the booming of the minute-guns, now answered at Albany.

Upon the arrival of the boats at Albany, the body of Mr. CLAY was placed in the possession of the Corporate authorities by the Chairman of the Committee of Arrangements, with the following remarks:

GENTLEMEN OF THE CORPORATION OF THE CITY OF ALBANY :—As the representatives of the city of New York, we have a mournful duty to perform. Within a few days we were honored with the custody of a relic of inestimable value,—we were intrusted with the mortal remains of HENRY CLAY, the venerated sage—the pure patriot, and the distinguished statesman.

It now becomes our sad office, having, we believe, faithfully performed our trust, to impose upon your honored city the same pleasing but melancholy duty that was assigned us. Pleasing—because you have within your keeping the "last of earth" of one of the most brilliant sons of this great and prosperous nation;—melancholy, because, by this afflicting dispensation of Divine Providence, our country has sustained an irreparable loss. We have been permitted to drop a sympathetic tear over the body of this great and good man, who, though now dead, yet speaketh through his glorious works. His memory is embalmed in the recollections of a grateful and devoted people, and his precepts are indelibly stamped upon their hearts.

We mourn his loss, not as those who mourn without hope ; for although the mortal part of him, whose eloquence, virtue and wisdom is the admiration of the world, be dead, still, we sincerely believe his spirit has fled to happy regions of eternal bliss, and, like a guardian angel, watches over and points us to his precepts and examples.

Sirs, this valuable relic of the immortal HENRY CLAY, we confide to your care, with the assurance that while it remains in your keeping, it will be treasured and appreciated with as high consideration as his life was virtuous and patriotic.

It is now upon its way to its final resting-place, where we hope it may peacefully rest until it is awakened by the thrilling call from the great trump on the resurrection morn.

The remains were received by Alderman JAMES D. WASSON, in behalf of the Corporate authorities of Albany, in a very touching and eloquent response.

The body was taken on shore and placed in a splendid funeral car, when a procession of military, firemen, and citizens generally, speedily formed, notwithstanding the lateness of the hour,—eleven o'clock. The public buildings and many of the stores and houses on the line of the procession were draped in mourning, and brilliantly illuminated.

As the procession passed up State street, (the firemen bearing torches) the scene was one of the most impressive and remarkable that had occurred since the remains left

Washington. Arriving at the gates of the capitol, the military opened to the left, and the remains were removed from the car and carried into the hall of the capitol. The closing ceremonies occupied until near two o'clock, when the doors of the capitol were closed, and the Burgess Corps were left in charge, as a guard of honor.

Departure of the Remains from Albany.

A special train of cars were in readiness to receive the corps at half-past eight o'clock. As they passed the Mansion House, Company D, Washington Greys, Capt. James Little, of New York city, to whom all honor be given, in their devotion to the remains of Mr. Clay, were drawn up in line, and paid the usual military honors. The Burgess Corps accompanied the remains to Buffalo. A large crowd of spectators had gathered at the depot, anxious to catch a last look of the coffin that contained the remains of the illustrious dead. At nine o'clock, precisely, the train, consisting of three passenger cars and a locomotive, appropriately trimmed, left the depot. The crowd taking off their hats as the cars moved out—the utmost silence was preserved, the deepest feeling was manifested.

Your Committee, after taking leave of the mourners, Senate Committee, and others, accompanying the body to Kentucky, the authorities and people of Albany, and having, in their humble judgment, performed their duty to the honored dead, returned to the boat, which soon after departed for New York, where they arrived early on the following morning.

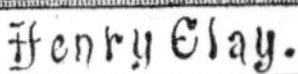

Simultaneous with the proceedings of the Common Council, and the action of your Committee, several of the Civic Societies of this city, Members of the Bar, and others, held meetings and adopted the following proceedings :

THE SOCIETY OF CINCINNATI.

NEW YORK, JULY 2, 1852.

The Corporation of this city have decided to render appropriate honors to the memory of the Hon. HENRY CLAY, deceased, who has been so highly distinguished for his pre-eminent talents, the purity and disinterestedness of his patriotism, and his uniform devotion to the great interests of his country, during his long and useful life ; and the members of our society, being descendants of those patriots who fought the battles of the revolution, which secured to our beloved country its independence, and the power to establish our glorious Union ; and as this distinguished patriot has, on all occasions, by his great talents, his energy and perseverance, eminently contributed to sustain and preserve that Union ; it is, therefore, proper that we should unite with our fellow-citizens in rendering the highest honors to his memory. The members of this society will assemble at the City Hall to-day, at the hour designated by the Committee of the Corporation, in their advertisement in the papers, for the ceremonies to take place, for the purpose of joining in the solemnities to be observed on the melancholy occasion.

By order.

GEN. ANTHONY LAMB, *Pres't.*

E. P. MARCELLIN, *Secretary.*

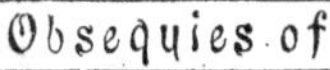

CLAY FESTIVAL ASSOCIATION.*

Immediately upon the melancholy tidings of the death of HENRY CLAY reaching this city, the following notice was issued to the members of the Association:

"CLAY FESTIVAL ASSOCIATION.—*The Great Commoner is no more! HENRY CLAY sleeps with the departed Patriots of the Republic!*—The members of this Association are notified that a meeting will be held at City Hotel, corner of Broadway and Howard streets, on this (Wednesday) evening, June 30th, 1852, at 8 o'clock, to take such action as may be proper in paying a just tribute to the memory of HENRY CLAY.

M. R. BREWER, *President.*

KENNETH G. WHITE, } *Vice Presidents.*
JOSIAH P. KNAPP, }

JAS. L. BERRIEN, *Secretary.*

A large number responded to the call, when M. R. BREWER, Esq., the President, addressed the Association, alluding, in a very pathetic and eloquent manner, to the great and irreparable loss the whole nation had sustained, and announced that the object of the present meeting was mainly to adopt measures suitable to the occasion, and to render a fitting tribute of respect to the memory of the great Commoner, HENRY CLAY.

Upon motion, it was unanimously resolved, that a committee be appointed to prepare resolutions, expressive of the sentiments and feelings of the Association.

It was further resolved that a committee be appointed to confer with the public authorities; that a deputation proceed to Washington, to meet the remains of Mr. CLAY; that the room be hung in mourning for the space of six months, and that the members wear the usual badge for thirty days.

* This Association was organized in 1845, for the sole purpose of commemorating the birthday of HENRY CLAY; and its annual festivals have always been marked with the highest enthusiasm, indicative of the love and admiration of the members for the sage and patriot.

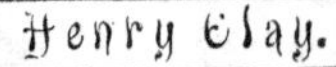

FRIDAY, JULY 2.

The meeting of the Association, numerously attended, met pursuant to adjournment. M. R. BREWER, Esq., in the chair, assisted by two Vice Presidents.

KENNETH G. WHITE, Esq., from the committee appointed to draft resolutions, reported the following :

Resolved, That in the death of HENRY CLAY, whose public life was a continued benefit and blessing to the people of the United States, this Association has sustained a calamity awakening the most poignant feelings of regret, and the deepest emotions of sorrow.

Resolved, That assembling once more in the place where we have so often met to rejoice in some fresh triumph of his commanding genius, or to do homage to some new display of his exalted patriotism ; though it is with subdued and saddened feelings we stand here, like bereaved children around the grave of a beloved father; we still experience a feeling of noble exultation in the recollection that his whole life bore testimony to his lofty sentiment, that he "WOULD RATHER BE RIGHT THAN BE PRESIDENT."

Resolved, That while the nation mourns the loss of her purest patriot, her most gifted statesman, her wisest sage, and her first citizen, it is ours to sorrow over a departed father, guide and protector. That while theirs is the grief of friendship, ours is the keener sorrow of kindred.

Resolved, That our affection for the illustrious deceased was not the blind attachment of political partizanship, but the higher, purer and nobler devotion, inspired by the spotless integrity of his character, his lofty and disinterested patriotism, his enlightened statesmanship, and his imperishable devotion to the interests and the honor of the country, of which he was the most distinguished ornament.

Resolved, That while with sorrowing hearts and trembling hands we record the loss sustained by ourselves, by the country, and by mankind, still it is not without holy joy and consolation that we look back to the sublime example of his virtues, and the unclouded purity of his fame. In these, a priceless inheritance descends to future ages from his life; and his death bequeaths a still richer legacy, as illustrating, in one of the greatest of our race, the divine truth, that "this corruptible shall put on incorruption, and this mortal put on immortality." Down from the heights of heaven, the eloquent voice of the sainted patriot and sage comes thrilling to our hearts in the touching language of paternal affection—"MAY YOU TOO DIE THE DEATH OF THE RIGHTEOUS," and readily, heartily and solemnly do we respond—"MAY OUR END BE LIKE HIS!"

Resolved, That we tender to the relations and family of the deceased our heart-felt sympathies in this heavy affliction, and that we mourn and sorrow with them in a common bereavement.

Resolved, That the rooms of our Association be hung in mourning for six months, and that the individual members wear the usual badge for thirty days.

Resolved, That a copy of these resolutions be furnished to his family, signed by the members of the Association.

The resolutions were seconded by ERASTUS BROOKS, Esq., as follows:

"MR. CHAIRMAN:—I cannot suffer the question to be put upon the resolutions which have been read, without the utterance of one word from some member of this Association in their behalf. I know how idle for the dead are our words of praise and our tears of sorrow; but among the survivors of the dead the heart finds relief in contemplating the greatness and in reciting the virtues of those whose presence on earth we are not permitted to recall. Our great political father, the friend of our youth and of our mature years, is DEAD! The wise counselor of the government, through more than forty years of public service, is NO MORE! The constant and consistent advocate of constitutional liberty, the peace-maker of the country, abroad and at home—the defender of the freedom of the oppressed in the old world and the new, now sleeps the sleep of death. He rests from his labors; and, at peace with GOD and man, his spirit reposes in the blissful quiet of that celestial paradise toward which all his entire heart, and all his hopes finally aspired.

"The funeral procession of HENRY CLAY is now marching from the city of Washington, where the great statesman died, and where he rendered so many eventful services to his country, to the destined repose of the grave in his own Kentucky. His body, surrounded by the President of the United States, and cabinet ministers, by statesmen of all parties, by the representatives of the army and navy, by senators and representatives in congress, by foreign ambassadors, and by the most distinguished men of the earth, has been mantled and coffined in the Senate chamber, which he adorned by his presence and immortalized by his genius. The light of heaven has for the last time looked down through the dome of the capitol, the corner-stone of which was laid by GEORGE WASHINGTON, upon the remains of him, who sought, by word and deed, through all his life, to illustrate and defend the principles of the Father of his

Country. His seat is vacant, and no more shall we there behold his majestic form, or hear the music of that voice which charmed all our ears, and made captive all our hearts.

> "The applause of listening senates to command;
> The threats of pain and ruin to despise:
> To scatter plenty o'er a smiling land,
> And read his history in a nation's eyes."

was the ambition of HENRY CLAY.

"But, Mr. Chairman, I will not now add to the recital of his virtues. I read with satisfaction, sanctified by the calamity which we could not control, of the thousands and tens of thousands who with full hearts and streaming eyes are this evening doing homage to the memory of the dead. To night his body rests on its pilgrimage to the tomb, surrounded by guards of honor, composed of citizens, senators and soldiers, in the city of Philadelphia, within the Hall of Independence—a fitting resting place for the remains of the greatest American of the nineteenth century, as WASHINGTON was of that age which gave freedom to the people and a constitution to the government.

"Mr. Chairman:—The funeral train, with all its sad attendants, will be here to-morrow. We shall not see HENRY CLAY as when last he was among us, surrounded by the beauty and gayety of the ball-room, the genial attractions of the festive board, and with eyes beaming with joy as they gazed upon one alike loved, honored and admired. We behold, in contrast now the curtain of death, rising before us. The long living idol of our hearts is before us, voiceless as death, and inanimate as the grave. The sweet sounds of a past welcome which thrilled all hearts, and the glad strains of past merriment which stirred the blood within our veins to quicker motion, and a new life, has changed to the solemn dirge, the deep tolling bell, and the minute gun. All that we see and hear reminds us of a void never on earth to be filled. But let us thank GOD that though men die, our love, our affections, and our remembrances of their virtues, live. The summer shall pass, and the fresh green leaves around us fade away with the decay of nature, as the autumn and winter of the year shall, like kindred drops, mingle their days together; but in all seasons, may the life and death, the principles and the example of HENRY CLAY bloom, as in perpetual youth, in the hearts of all true patriots and good men."

The meeting was also impressively and feelingly addressed by Hon. WILLIS HALL and others.

The resolutions were unanimously adopted, ordered to be engrossed on parchment, and enclosed in a suitable case, to be transmitted to the family of the deceased.

These resolutions were engrossed, and have been enclosed in a case, of which the following is an illustration:

The case is a column, designed and executed by Mr. JOHN MOST, emblematic of the position of HENRY CLAY, in the history of his country—a "PILLAR OF THE STATE." The shaft is of beautiful ebony, in token of mourning; the base and capital are of ivory, elaborately carved with the leaves of the oak and acorns. The ornaments are silver bands, embossed also with the leaves of the oak. The capital is removable, and in the hollow of the column is deposited the scroll containing the resolutions, signed by the individual members of the Association.

Dr. DRAKE, the chairman of the Executive Committee, reported that the Joint Committee of Arrangements of the Honorable Common Council, had kindly allotted to the Association, the position as chief mourners of the illustrious dead, upon the reception of his remains in this city, and that suitable badges would be provided for the occasion, with a recommendation to the members to appear in black clothing.

The chairman further reported that a civic wreath had been prepared, to be placed upon the coffin of our illustrious and venerated friend.

It was further recommended that a deputation, consisting of seven of the associates, be selected to accompany the remains to the final resting place, at Lexington.

All of which, report and recommendation, were unanimously approved, and the following named gentlemen were selected as the deputation to accompany the remains.

JOSEPH M. PRICE,
JOSIAH P. KNAPP,
ALFRED G. PECKHAM,
JAMES R. WOOD,
DAVID WEBB,
DANIEL L. PETTEE, and
NICHOLAS CARROLL.

In accordance with the previous arrangements, the Association assembled at the Apollo rooms, on the morning of July 3d, 1852;—the members dressed in black, with crape upon the left arm—the officers wearing black mourning scarfs, and, preceded by their Sergeant-at-Arms, marched in procession to Castle Garden, where they had been invited by the Honorable Common Council to accompany them in a steamboat, to receive the remains at Jersey City.

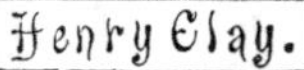

After a short detention at Jersey City the corpse arrived, and was received on board of the boat, the Association having formed on each side of the entrance. The bier was carried through, escorted by the military of Jersey City, and finally committed to the charge of the authorities of New York, in an eloquent address of Senator UNDERWOOD, which was appropriately responded to by his Honor A. C. KINGSLAND, Mayor of the city of New York.

Upon the arrival of the remains at Castle Garden, the Association formed, accompanied by the near relatives and neighbors of Mr. CLAY, immediately behind the hearse, and followed the remains to the Governor's room, City Hall.

After having divided themselves into committees of six, they remained constantly in attendance, night and day, at the room in which was deposited all that was mortal of the great commoner.

In accordance with the previous arrangement, that the remains should be removed on the morning of the 5th—the celebration of the national anniversary occurring on that day—the whole Association remained in attendance at the City Hall, for the purpose of accompanying the corpse to the boat; and at two o'clock of that morning they formed in procession upon each side of the bier, in the capacity of pall-bearers, with the Washington Greys as a guard of honor, and followed by the Common Council as mourners; they proceeded to the steamboat; and having placed a committee to remain with the body, they again marched to the Hall, politely escorted by the same company.

They then adjourned to assemble again on board of the boat, when a large deputation, together with the deputation appointed to proceed to Kentucky, accompanied the remains to the capitol at Albany.

PROCEEDINGS IN THE LAW COURTS.

UNITED STATES DISTRICT COURT.

James R. Whiting, Esq., rose and addressed the court as follows :

"May it please the court, I rise under great embarrassment, to announce to the court, the sad and mournful intelligence, which has just reached us, that Henry Clay is dead. His spirit has departed 'to that bourn from whence no traveler returns.'

"This event, though long expected, has suddenly come upon us, and presents to our serious contemplation, the subject of death. The public pulse, for a time, will almost cease to beat; the busy places of trade and commerce will be hushed, and the nation will put on her habiliments of mourning.

"A great man has fallen—gone—gone, full of years, and full of honors. His unwearied soul, taxed to its utmost powers, was always for his country's honor—his country's glory, and the benefit of mankind. His life, his being and his actions have been woven in tissues of his country's greatness, and the page of history will do him that justice which party strife has hitherto measurably denied him. Over his remains, to the credit of the nation, all men will meet to do him reverence.

"This is not the time, nor this the place, to enlarge upon his character—to speak of its strength or weakness. That he was faultless cannot be said; there is none that lives and sinneth not—no, not one. That his motives were pure, noble, lofty and patriotic, but few will deny.

"It is not inappropriate to say, that he was ready for his departure—that he died as became a man and a Christian, and that he left behind him the evidence of a good hope of an endless immortality. It is hoped, that it may hereafter be said of him, 'Blessed are the dead who die in the Lord, for their works do follow them.' In respect to his memory, therefore, I most respectfully move that this court do now adjourn."

His Honor Judge JUDSON, in reply said :

"The announcement of these sad tidings will move every American heart to the deepest sorrow. In life, HENRY CLAY was the pride and boast of the American people, and now he is no more—his name and great deeds will fill the largest page in our history, and no portion of that history will ever be read with more interest, or reflect higher honor on the country.

"HENRY CLAY has been a participator in all the great events which have given character and glory to this nation, for the last forty years. As a warm-hearted patriot and lover of freedom, he had no superior. As a statesman, upon the broadest scale, he had but few equals. As an orator, he was foremost in the rank, while his sympathies reached the oppressed of every nation.

"This is not an inappropriate place to entertain the present motion, for the early theatre of his distinction was the Bar. In our national affairs he has left the deep impress of his great mind, and especially, when dangers were thickening around us, his giant intellect devised and executed, (with others,) the system of measures which has imparted new strength and perpetuity to our union.

"As a tribute of respect to the memory of such a man, it is fit and proper that all business should be suspended in this court, and the same is now adjourned."

SUPREME COURT—CIRCUIT.

Mr. Evarts addressed his Honor, and said:

"May it please the court, since the last adjournment of the court, the rumor which reached this city yesterday, of the death of Henry Clay, has been confirmed by full intelligence of that sad event.

"I rise, sir, to move that, as a mark of respect to the memory of that eminent lawyer and statesman, this court do now adjourn. It is impossible to add, by any expression of sentiment, to the weight of sorrow which this event has brought to the hearts of our people throughout the land. The name, the character, the principles, the great public services, the labors, the fame of Henry Clay, are known everywhere; and fully understood and recognized by all his countrymen. It is, sir, as a just token of respect for his eminent character and position that I move the adjournment of the court."

His Honor Judge Edwards, in reply, said:

"Although the event which has been alluded to has been for some time expected, it has produced sorrow and gloom throughout the community. There is no man among us who, for so long a period, has acted so prominent a part in the affairs of the nation as Mr. Clay. At the time when he first came forward in public life our government was yet regarded as an experiment; but at that time the men who had carried us through the perils of the Revolution still exercised a controlling influence; and it was from the fathers of the republic that he received his first lessons of political wisdom. He no sooner appeared in our national councils than he became a master-spirit; and, at an age when most men are acquiring their political education, he became a leader. Upon all the great questions which have agitated the country for nearly half a century, his influence has been felt and acknowledged; and however others may have differed from him in opinion, no one doubted his sincerity; and all admired his earnestness, boldness, and ability. He had, pre-eminently, the courage and the strength of will which inspire confidence; and upon every question, involving our national honor, he was one of the noblest of American patriots. Owing to his vigorous constitution he continued to participate in the active duties of life until he had arrived at an age when the powers of most men are exhausted. He was fortunate in many of the circumstances of his life; and, if such an expression may be used on so melancholy an occasion, he was fortunate in the time of his death. During the closing period of his days he had withdrawn from party politics; and he had the dying consolation that his last energies had been successfully devoted to the preservation of peace, harmony, and union." The court then adjourned.

SUPREME COURT—SPECIAL TERM.

Mr. Charles P. Kirkland addressed the court, soon after its opening, and said :

"A great national calamity is just announced to us—Henry Clay is dead! Indeed, more than a national calamity, for his loss will be known and lamented in every part of the globe, where freedom has a votary, or the liberty of man a friend or an advocate; and, unless I greatly err, a grief as sincere, and a regret as lively and as deep will occupy multitudes of foreign hearts as now pervade those of his millions of countrymen. Greece, South America, Mexico, have lost their earliest friend, the most fearless and eloquent champion of their efforts for emancipation; and every man in those lands, and in all other lands, in whose bosom beats a single aspiration for freedom, will unite with us in earnest sympathy on this occasion. We are called to mourn then, not merely a loss to ourselves, but to Christendom; not merely to our institutions, but to the *cause;* not merely of an American statesman, but of a world-renowned and a world-admired apostle of liberty. No man survives, not even those who have been highest in official stations or most distinguished in war, whose name is more known and more spoken in all lands, to which civilization has extended, than his who has just been summoned from among us to immortality.

"In bidding our last farewell to HENRY CLAY, we take our leave of one, who furnished the most beautiful and most impressive illustration of the genial workings of our wonderful system of government in the bringing out and developing the individual man. With no advantages of birth, education or fortune, on the contrary, with all the depressing influences of obscurity, poverty and lowly origin, we see him, under the beneficent operation of republican institutions, rise rapidly to the zenith of human fame, and gather around him, in rich abundance, the glory and the honors of the lawyer, the orator and the statesman. What a bright example is thus presented to the young men of this country, and how are all taught by it, that no obscurity of birth, no pressure of poverty, no deficiency of early education, are here any necessary or legitimate obstruction in the pathway that leads to honor and renown.

"To the lot of this great man it fell, on at least three occasions, to be the means, under Providence, of devising, and by his commanding influence, carrying out, measures which saved our hallowed union from apparently impending dissolution. It was at these times that the greatness of his intellect, the splendor of his eloquence, and, more than all, the fervor and sincerity of his patriotism, shone out with almost superhuman brightness, and accomplished those benign results, which, without hyperbole, we may believe will extend their influence through ages of time, and will be regarded with affectionate gratitude by long successions of generations.

"But it is not as the patriot, the statesman, the philanthropist, that the immortal deceased would on this occasion and in this place, receive the solemn tribute of our respect; it is more emphatically in his character as our professional brother that we would now pay honor to his memory. And if a tribute of respect and veneration can ever properly be paid to a departed member of the American bar by his surviving brethren, there surely can be no more appropriate instance than the present. Pre-eminent as Mr. Clay was in the particulars to which I have briefly alluded, he was no less so as a lawyer. His great attainments in legal learning, and his remarkable powers of analysis, of logical arrangement and deduction, and, indeed, in the whole field of legal argumentation, were often exhibited in the highest judicial tribunal of our country, and obtained for him a place among the first of the profession. He combined with these qualities what seldom co-exists with them—the skill and tact of the advocate, and the persuasive eloquence so unusual and so effective in another department of our labors. To all this, he added as a crowning glory that delicate moral sense and elevated integrity, without which the character of no lawyer can be perfect. But, if the court please, this is not the occasion for an eulogy, and I did not rise to pronounce one. I am aware that the few remarks I have made are quite sufficient as preliminary to the motion I am about to make. And now, as a fitting though slight tribute of respect to the memory of HENRY CLAY, I move that this court do adjourn, and that an entry in the minutes accordingly be made. This motion and the feelings which dictate it will, I know, have the heart-felt acquiescence of the court and of the bar."

The District Attorney, Mr. N. B. BLUNT, said, that he rose to second the motion just addressed to the court.

"Certainly sir," he added, "on leaving this court yesterday, I did not imagine that I should to-day be called upon to participate in the official announcement of the melancholy tidings which have reached us. Long anticipated as was the event, nevertheless, to me it came with crushing, stunning force.

"Familiar for many years with his public character, enjoying his friendship, and for a brief time connected with him in immediate personal relation, the emotions which crowd upon me almost forbid language. But yesterday, as it were, pre-eminent among his compatriots, he stood the observed of all observers—to-day, he lies a cold and senseless mass—an empty casket, stripped of its treasure. The spirit of the great American commoner has fled from its earthly tabernacle—the affections which centred in him are severed, and we mourn the loss of our benefactor and friend. He was truly an impersonation of the American republic. From earliest infancy, reared under its institutions, he was an emblem of its progress, its power, and its glory. To him, as adapted to the country which gave him birth, may well be applied the eulogy pronounced upon CANNING, "He was an American through and through, American in his feelings, American in his aims, American in all his policy and projects." As WASHINGTON was the father of his country, HENRY CLAY will go down to posterity as its savior. It is fitting and proper that one who has so long been identified with the history of our country, at home and abroad, whose name and fame are imperishably connected with its welfare and prosperity, should receive the respect of a grateful people.

"I can no more at present but second the motion of my respected friend."

His Honor Judge ROOSEVELT, said,

"The court very fully concurs in the sentiments expressed by the bar, which are, no doubt, the universal sentiments of the whole community respecting the illustrious statesman who has just departed from among us. He not only was a statesman in the common sense of the term, but was a man of high, generous impulse, and noble attributes, which, in his career, were more marked than in any other instance in modern history. He was ambitious, it was true, but it was that ambition which, more than its own, sought the distinction and glory of his country. There never was a man who more enthusiastically entered into the glory of the American nation than HENRY CLAY. Whatever may have been his infirmities, they were the necessary incidents of his virtues. There was in him an ardor—a fervency of purpose—and a loftiness, which, to the eyes of all generous men, veiled his infirmities. He was at once the true statesman, and the statesman of truth. He despised falsehood in all its shapes and all its colors; and though he has parted from us, and though his mortal remains have been brought low, and are about to be consigned to the dust, we may say with the American poet,

'Truth crushed to earth will rise again.'

His spirit is now, we have reason to believe, rising on the wings of immortality to that realm on whose dominion the sun that has risen will never set." The Judge, in conclusion said, "that in honor of the memory of HENRY CLAY, I direct that the court stand adjourned for the term."

COMMON PLEAS—FIRST PART.

Mr. THEO. E. TOMLINSON, Corporation Attorney, addressing his Honor, said:

"May it please the court, it is usual, when an eminent lawyer dies, for the profession and the court to mark their respect on the public records. A distinguished lawyer, and enlightened civilian, a noble patriot has fallen. HENRY CLAY is dead! It is true we have expected his death, but it was expected as the sunset, which leaves darkness and gloom behind. It is particularly the duty of the tribunals of law, and the members of our learned profession, to pay a tribute to the great commoner, whose triumphs have been purely civic—his laurels were the laurels of peace—his triumphs the triumphs of the constitution and the law. If partisanship marked any portion of his career, it has been lost in the unbounded patriotism that marked his devotion to his whole country; so that we, the sons of this great republic, realize that in the loss of HENRY CLAY, we we have lost a father."

Mr. TOMLINSON then proposed the following resolution:

"*Resolved*, That this court, partaking of the universal sorrow which affects the nation, under its bereavement by the death of HENRY CLAY, and feeling that no eulogy can add to the glory of the great departed, feel that silence is more expressive than panegyric, and do therefore adjourn."

His Honor Judge WOODRUFF responded, with much feeling, to the address of Mr. TOMLINSON, in support of the motion—expressing the profound sensibility with which the court received the announcement; the sympathy of the court with the sentiment of deep grief which pervades the nation; the propriety of marking, by appropriate testimonials, an event which forms an important era in the nation's history,—a history in which the career of the distinguished senator, now deceased, was pre-eminently a part; and especially the propriety of pausing in our ordinary pursuits, to allow the indulgence of the feelings awakened by the sad event. With some further expressions of high admiration and respect for the eminent lawyer and statesman whose death was announced, the Judge ordered that the Court do now adjourn, and that the resolution be entered upon the records of the court.

COMMON PLEAS—SECOND PART.

Mr. DANIEL T. WALDEN, Jr., said :—

"May it please the court, for many days past the public journals have given us the melancholy intelligence that a great man was rapidly sinking to his final rest—that he, who during a long life, had fought manfully for the rights of his country in her legislative councils—who had battled, as the champion for the oppressed of other climes, was fading from the scenes of earth, and about to meet his last great enemy—yet have we hoped, and without a ray of promise, our minds have been warped by our feelings, and we would believe that he might yet be spared to that country he has so faithfully served. The electric messenger of yesterday proclaimed the dread and mournful tidings that disease had done its work—that HENRY CLAY was no more. Yes, in the federal capital, amid the scenes of his labors and his triumphs, while still in the livery of his country's service, as a senator from the state of his adoption, he has closed his eyes on earth, and,

'To wear a wreath in glory wrought, his spirit sped afar,
Beyond the soaring wings of thought, the light of moon or star;
To drink immortal waters, free from every taint of earth,
To breath before the shrine of life, the source whence worlds had birth.'

"The land is filled with lamentation--grief is in every heart, and the dark drapery of sorrow is preparing, as a poor expression of our inward woe. It is but fit that we should pause in our avocation--rest from our labor, to respect the memory of one, who, amid his public life, remained an active, industrious and illustrious member of our own profession. I move you, sir, that this court do now adjourn."

His Honor, Judge INGRAHAM, in reply, after referring briefly to the public and private character of Mr. CLAY, expressed the great regard which he had ever entertained for him as a man, a lawyer, and a statesman, and added that he was well deserving of every mark of public respect that could be shown to his memory. That he concurred in the remarks made by the gentleman who moved the adjournment, and would, in granting the motion, direct that a suitable order should be entered upon the minutes of the court.

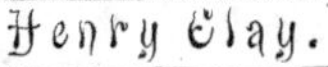

John H. White, Esq., addressed the court in substance as follows:

"May it please the court, the mournful tidings have just reached this city that Henry Clay is no more. That eloquent voice, which has so often entranced the Senate, or held spell-bound the listening throng, is now hushed in the silence of death.

"In the fullness of my feelings, it would be presumptious in me on this occasion, to attempt to do justice to his memory. I can only sit myself down, as one of a nation of mourners, and weep.

"Henry Clay needs no eulogy at my hands. His memory is enshrined in the hearts of the people, and wherever liberty has had a germination, whether among the shrines of classic Greece, in the valleys of the Chimborazo, or among the sea-girt isles of the Pacific, the name of Clay will be fondly reverenced as long as time shall last.

"In his career, so full of glorious achievements and patriotic and self-sacrificing devotion to his country, the young man may learn a most instructive lesson. Born in obscurity and poverty, without distinguished parentage; without friends, except such as he made for himself; by his own efforts and the force of his own mind, he raised himself from the humblest position in life to the highest pinnacle of renown and honor. He was, in every sense of the word, *a self-made man*, and although his early life was beset with difficulties and trials, which seemed to other minds insurmountable, yet he rose superior to them all, and for nearly half a century, he has shown to the world, that whether in the councils of the nation, or filling important diplomatic positions at home or abroad, or cultivating the social endearments of his quiet home at Ashland, he has always reflected the noblest attributes of man, and sustained in every relation of life, the proud position of 'the noblest work of God.' During the last forty years, no man has exerted a greater influence upon the destinies of this country than Mr. CLAY.

"Every page of her history, during that period, is emblazoned with his name, and though in times of party excitement, the slanderer and libeller have attempted to tarnish his fair fame, he has been spared long enough to live down all his revilers; and now, all parties, all sects, and all creeds will gather around the common altar of their country, and bowing themselves to the dust, mourn over the irreparable loss the nation has sustained.

"It is fitting, on this sad occasion, that the tribunals of justice should pay proper tribute to his memory and worth; it is fitting that we here should, for the time being, forget the excitements of the day, and laying aside our business, go forth with the multitude and weep.

"I therefore move, as a mark of respect to the memory of the illustrious deceased, that this court do now adjourn."

H. D. LAPAUGH, Esq., seconded the motion, with appropriate remarks.

His Honor Judge LYNCH, after a very feeling and eloquent address, ordered an adjournment of the court, and that the proceedings be entered upon the minutes.

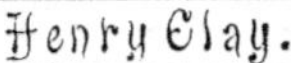

MEETING OF THE BAR.

A meeting of the members of the New York Bar was held in relation to the death of the Hon. HENRY CLAY, in the rooms of the Supreme Court. On motion, Chief Justice OAKLEY was called to the Chair, assisted by Judges DUER and CAMPBELL. HENRY E. DAVIES and JOHN J. TOWNSEND were appointed Secretaries. The following resolutions were then read and adopted :

Resolved, That in the death of HENRY CLAY, we feel, in common with our fellow-citizens, the loss of the eloquent orator, the eminent jurist, the sagacious statesman, the incorruptible patriot, the ardent advocate of American interests, and the great representative of human freedom throughout the world.

Resolved, That while we deplore the termination of his illustrious career, we rejoice that he has been so long spared to fill the measure of his country's glory; that his eloquent accents in behalf of freedom struggling against oppression are familiar to the children of classic Greece, as well as to those of our sister American republics; and that in both hemispheres it is a sufficient passport to his fellow-citizens to say, I am a countryman of HENRY CLAY.

Resolved, That a marble bust of the departed patriot be placed in the Law Library, as a durable memorial of our esteem, and in proof of the entire compatibility of the duties of a statesman and patriot with those of the lawyer; and that the members of the New York Bar will wear a mourning badge for three months, as a mark of their respect for his memory and irreparable loss.

A committee of three was appointed to carry out the last resolution.

A committee of five was appointed to co-operate with the city authorities and civic societies, in making arrangements to receive the body.

THOMAS J. OAKLEY, *Chairman*.

JOHN J. TOWNSEND,
HENRY E. DAVIES, } *Secretaries.*

BALTIMORE COUNCIL.

CITY HALL,
BALTIMORE, 7th JULY, 1852.

GENTLEMEN:—At a joint meeting of the several committees, representing the corporation and the citizens of Baltimore, appointed in connection with the obsequies of the late HENRY CLAY, convened as above, his Honor the Mayor was called to the chair, and GEORGE S. ALLEN appointed Secretary.

On motion of FRANCIS A. FISHER, Esq., a committee was appointed to prepare and submit suitable resolutions for the consideration of the meeting. Among the resolutions reported by the committee, were the following, which were adopted with unanimity.

Resolved, That the cordial thanks of this meeting be tendered to Messrs. Aldermen WM. J. BRISLEY, J. H. VALENTINE, WM. H. WRIGHT, and their associate members of the committee, for their polite invitation, tendered at Philadelphia, to accompany them to the city of New York, on the late mournful occasion of the transmission of the remains of HENRY CLAY to their final resting place.

Resolved, That although it was found impossible for us to accept the invitation, in a body, as we could have desired, we take pleasure in returning our thanks for the kindness extended toward our representative, Mr. SMITH, feeling well assured, that a similar reception must have awaited all of us had circumstances allowed us to have participated in the ceremonies at New York.

In accordance with the action of the meeting, as above indicated, we take pleasure in forwarding to you the inclosed resolutions. Permit us, at the same time, to say to you how highly we appreciate your courtesies on the occasion alluded to, and to assure you of the respect with which we remain,

Your obedient servants,

JNO. M. JEROME, *Chairman.*

GEO. S. ALLEN, *Secretary.*

To Aldermen WM. J. BRISLEY, WM. H. WRIGHT, J. H. VALENTINE, and others, representing the New York Common Council.

DEMOCRATIC REPUBLICAN GENERAL COMMITTEE.

At a meeting of the Democratic Republican General Committee, specially convened at Tammany Hall, on Thursday evening, July 1st, ROBERT J. DILLON offered the following resolution, which was unanimously adopted.

Resolved, That the Democratic Republican Committee of the city of New York, deeply sympathize in the loss which the republic has suffered in the death of our great countryman, HENRY CLAY. His eminent talents, his distinguished services, and his manly courage have won, even from his political opponents, the warmest admiration; and this Committee feel called upon particularly to express this tribute to the memory of Mr. CLAY, because he was the able and efficient supporter of the compromise measures of 1850, and because the principles upon which those measures are based are the principles of the democratic party, upon which depend their efficiency and duration.

AUG. SCHELL, *Chairman.*

JONAS B. PHILLIPS, } *Secretaries.*
JOSEPH HILTON, }

YOUNG MEN'S DEMOCRATIC GENERAL COMMITTEE.

At a special meeting of the Young Men's Democratic General Committee, held at Tammany Hall, July 2d, ULYSSES D. FRENCH offered the following resolutions, which were unanimously adopted.

Resolved, That the Young Men's Democratic General Committee of the city of New York, have heard, with deep regret, of the death of the great orator, statesman, and patriot, HENRY CLAY.

Resolved, That his course in the American Senate, side by side with the great and good men of our own party, at a time when fanaticism and disunion threatened the existence of our confederacy, has served to embalm his memory in the hearts of the whole American people. His fame is part of the history of his country; it belongs, not to a party, but to the republic.

Resolved, That this Committee will unite with their fellow-citizens in such ceremonies as may be appropriate to commemorate his death.

A communication was received from the Young Men's Whig General Committee, inviting this Committee to cooperate with them in rendering honor to the illustrious deceased; which invitation was duly accepted, and ordered to be engrossed on the minutes.

JOHN WHEELER, *Chairman.*

T. B. Glover, }
John A. Smith, } *Secretaries.*

GENERAL COMMITTEE OF DEMOCRATIC WHIG YOUNG MEN.

A meeting of this Committee was held at their rooms, in the Broadway House, to take into consideration the recent afflicting dispensation which had removed the great leader of the Whig party from their midst, and to adopt measures in regard to his obsequies.

Erastus Brooks, Esq., Chairman of the Committee of Democratic Whig Young Men for the City and County of New York, in announcing the death of Henry Clay to the members, spoke as follows:

"Gentlemen of the Committee—You have been convened at an unusual time, and for reasons so obvious in all that meets your eyes and ears, that it is not necessary for me to mention the occasion. Our chieftain is dead. At the capital of our country, in the city of Washington, amidst the scenes of nearly forty years of labor, in the cabinet and in the two houses of congress, the spirit of one whom we most dearly loved, and most profoundly respected, has taken its flight to the GOD who gave it. He died full of years and full of honors. The sweet music of his voice is hushed in the silence of death. His erect and commanding form lies prostrate in the narrow confines of the tomb. The brilliancy of his genius, the logic of his mind, the grace of his manners, the physical energy directed by a courage that never faltered, and by a will that never tired, all have been made captive by death—the King of Terrors. But HENRY CLAY lived a hero, and he died a Christian. He rests from his labors, and his works do follow him. When he was born, the constitution of our country was not adopted. Our independence had not even been achieved. He was ushered into the world, surrounded by the roar of cannon, the strife of revolution, and amidst burning struggles for liberty. His life was worthy of such a beginning, and the state of his birth honored by such a son. WASHINGTON alone was more loved as a patriot. PATRICK HENRY was more eloquent; THOMAS JEFFERSON was more fortunate, and MADISON and MONROE, Virginians all, attained, in the quiet but golden age of the republic, higher places from their country. But the mother of states and of statesmen never gave birth to one of her children whose life was more honored, or whose death is more lamented. He saw in his day our country grow, as the spreading forest oak has grown from the acorn, from four to twenty-eight millions of people. The Alleghanies were the boundaries of the country in the days of his youth; but they, too, expanded, until our American domain has stretched across the Rocky Mountains to the golden shores of the Pacific. Even the mouth of the Mississippi was not then ours. The sugar and cotton lands of Louisiana, and the vine and orange groves of Florida were the possessions of France and Spain; but now, ships from our own bays and broad-armed ports ride upon the Western ocean, while those on board contemplate and hold communion with the Eastern hemisphere, and all their oriental treasures. All this has been in the life-time of HENRY CLAY—and what an example has he left us, as countrymen, as citizens, and as friends.

"We desire, in such an hour as this, not to rob the nation of its glory, by doing homage to him as the mere man of a party. But here, in our political home, where we have party attachments, warm and enduring as our lives; and attachments which were created by our devotion to the principles of HENRY CLAY, we cannot forego the privilege of saying that he was our own political father, as he was for many, many years, the prophet and patriarch of the Whigs of the whole union. He was the father of that great American system which protects and honors American labor. He was the defender of every American interest—agricultural, commercial and social. He was known, all over the land, as the great pacificator of the country; and in three memorable struggles, when civil war threatened the land, under a good Providence, he was the instrument of creating harmony from discord, and changing the passion of sectional hate, into a sentiment of fraternal love and national respect.

"Gentlemen of the Committee—In the grave of HENRY CLAY let us bury all our personal griefs, and become once more, in the unity of a true political American faith, a band of brothers. Like our honored chief, let us know 'no north, no south, no east, no west, nothing but our country.' By defending his principles, by keeping alive his memory in our hearts, we shall learn to practice that public duty and that heroic virtue which teaches mankind that it *is better, in all our earthly aspirations, to be right than even to be successful.* We shall learn, too, from his life and his death, that the greatest political honor and the highest public service is not inconsistent with a true Christian faith, but that one may prepare himself to die even when surrounded by all the temptations and attractions of worldly power and applause.

"The glories of our blood and state
Are shadows, not substantial things;
There is no armor against Fate;
Death lays his icy hand on kings!
Sceptre and crown
Must tumble down,
And in the dust be equal made
With the poor crooked scythe and spade.

* * * * *

All heads must come
To the cold tomb.
Only the actions of the just
Smell sweet, and blossom in the dust."

MR. N. CARROLL then submitted the following address and resolutions:

GOD has removed from earth "the first of men, and the first in our hearts." Virginia, from whence sprang "the Father of his Country," gave our leader birth. Migrating in 1797, from the mother of states, he planted his feet upon the soil of her eldest daughter. While time lasts the names of Henry Clay and of Kentucky will be known and renowned; wherever liberty is loved, honor reverenced, truth revered, and virtue has its abode.

For fifty years and upward, he served his whole country, with a single eye toward the interests of each and every section. Bearing through life a spotless name, he outlived detraction and vituperation.

He devoted all his unequaled energies, during the entire period of his career, to advance the honor, the glory, and the prosperity of his native land. Wherever the spirit of freedom struggled against tyranny or oppression, his soul espoused the cause of the suffering; and that matchless eloquence, which has awed senates, and with resistless force commanded greater results than that of any other man known in our history, was ever lifted up in behalf of the persecuted of every clime and nation. He never turned aside from distress, public or private. He labored to lay, wide and deep, the foundations of the union, the perpetuity of the constitution, and the majesty as well as the sanctity of the laws. He toiled, unwearied, through long years, to establish the great and beneficent American system. His eagle eye never slept whenever peril threatened the republic. Thrice he warded from her breast the impending danger. Her honor imperiled, his voice summoned the country, and upheld her during the second war of independence. He grasped, with gigantic mind, and with abilities and genius, that never succumbed to disaster, the duties of a statesman, the bravery of a hero, and the wisdom of a sage.

While he lived, his love of country, conquering self, and every personal aspiration, led him, again and again, to sacrifice himself, without a wail or a murmur. He counted any service to his native land, at whatever cost to himself, as a proud and triumphant gain.

Looking through our history, we pause beside WASHINGTON and HENRY CLAY—these two.

Resolved, That with a stricken nation, we mourn the death of earth's greatest son.

Resolved, That we no longer can claim him as the property of party—elevated by his patriotism, his services, and his virtues to the distinction of being "the first citizen of the republic," his deathless fame passes to the keeping of immortality.

Resolved, That in this, the hour of our sorrow, from the midst of the gloom which such a death inspires, we look beyond, and see a country blessed above that of any other in the universe—free, prosperous and devoutly thankful and happy—and we remember, though many have done much toward this end, to HENRY CLAY is justly allotted the fullest meed of having most served, and thrice saved his beloved country.

Resolved, That it belongs to the Democratic Whig General Committee, and the General Committee of Democratic Whig Young Men, to proclaim the truth, that from their organization, so long as he was before the people, they never knew an hour untrue to HENRY CLAY.

Resolved, Mingling our tears with his family and kindred, we tender to them our heart-felt affection and sympathy—for our great leader and friend was so endeared to each of us, that we, too, felt that we were of his household, and that which affected or concerned him or his, grieved us alike.

Resolved, That we will cherish his fame and memory—his deeds and principles—transmitting them as the most precious legacy we can bequeath to our posterity and successors.

Resolved, That we will drape our rooms in mourning, and that the members of the Committees will wear the usual badges of mourning for thirty days.

Resolved, That a joint committee of members be appointed to make arrangements for the funeral obsequies of our illustrious champion.

Resolved, That a copy of the preamble, and of these resolutions, be furnished to his family.

Mr. DANIEL BOWLY, in seconding the resolutions, remarked—

"Mr. CHAIRMAN:—It has again become our sad office,* as the representatives of the Democratic Whig party of this city, to give expression to our profound sorrow at the loss, not only of one of its most prominent members, but of its chiefest column, which Death, with the giant hand of another Samson, has plucked away. HENRY CLAY is dead!

"Not long ago, Mr. Chairman, the veil of the temple of the great Democratic Whig party, mainly reared upon the broad, national foundation of the principles successively and successfully advocated by HENRY CLAY, was, by local variance and individual rivalry, nearly rent in twain, and tottered, even unto its fall. But, by a good Providence in the affairs of nations, and a just judgment among men, the noble structure still survives, not only the desolating hand

* In allusion to the death of DAVID GRAHAM.

of faction, but even the loss of him, its chiefest column, and towers unscathed above the base contest of sectional strife.

"HENRY CLAY is dead! yet may we not trust that this, our great national affliction, at this time, has, by a wise decree of the Ruler of national as of individual events, been so ordered that the great void made in the central arch of this, our temple, by the death of him whose deeds are above panegyric and whose life is above eulogy, may, if it cannot be filled, at least be supplied, by one whose name the voice of his fellow Whig countrymen has invoked to its conservation, until it not only restore, but preserve, in all its original proportions, that massive temple, our political faith, even unto the realization of that beautiful idea of another, its architectural type of material harmony.

"HENRY CLAY is dead! And if, Mr. Chairman, I have not been one of those who have staked the existence of a great party in the life of a single individual, I have not been the less sensible that the history of a great man is the history of a nation; and, sir, it needs no language of mine to vindicate its pages, in anticipation, from the charge of injustice to the life, the actions, and the virtues of HENRY CLAY."

The resolutions were then unanimously adopted.

A delegation from the General Committee was then announced, who, through Mr. JOHN H. WHITE, extended an invitation to the Young Men's Committee to meet them in joint session.

The invitation was accepted, and the Committee adjourned to the rooms of the General Committee.

In joint session the above resolutions were again read and adopted.

After which, a joint committee of arrangements, upon Mr. CLAY'S obsequies, was appointed, consisting of the following gentlemen :

Senior Committee,	*Young Men's Committee,*
DANIEL ULLMANN,	NICHOLAS CARROLL,
WARREN CHAPMAN,	NATHAN C. ELY,
THOMAS CARNLEY,	GEORGE W. THACHER,
ROBT. T. HAWS,	JOHN RYAN,
CHARLES F. SMITH,	S. B. ROMAINE, Jr.,
PHILIP J. MONROE,	JAMES H. MOSEMAN,
JOHN H. WHITE,	ERASTUS BROOKS, ex-officio.
JAS. KELLY, ex-officio.	

JAMES KELLY,
Chairman Dem. Whig General Committee.

WM. SHARDLOW,
GEORGE P. NELSON, } *Secretaries.*

ERASTUS BROOKS,
Chairman Gen. Com. Dem. Whig Young Men.

BERN L. BUDD
JAMES H. MOSEMAN, } *Secretaries.*

SCOTT CENTRAL COMMITTEE.

At a meeting of the SCOTT CENTRAL COMMITTEE of the city of New York, held on the 30th of June, 1852, Mr. A. J. WILLIAMSON proposed the following resolutions, which were unanimously adopted :

Whereas, By the dispensation of Providence, this great nation has been called upon to pay the last tribute of respect to the memory of HENRY CLAY; as American citizens, and as members of the Whig party, to the triumph of whose principles this great and good man devoted the best energies of his long and useful life, we feel called upon to unite our tears and sympathies with those who mourn his death; therefore, be it

Resolved, That we will join our fellow-citizens in any public demonstration of respect to the memory of the distinguished statesman—the man of his time—the pure patriot—the matchless orator, and honest philanthropist—the great commoner, whose whole life proves the sincerity of his noble sentiment: "I would rather be right than be President;" and who has so repeatedly proved his devotion to his country by his sacrifices and services—whose voice never failed to still the storm of sectional fanaticism, and allay the spirit of discord, which, from time to time, has raised its hydra-head in different portions of the republic; and whose wise and far seeing policy has been productive of such beneficial results to the whole union.

Resolved, That as members of the great Whig party, we mourn the death of HENRY CLAY as children do the loss of a good and kind father, who has watched over and guided the wanderings of our childhood and youth, and whose wise councils and patriotic teachings have placed us, in manhood, in our present proud position.

Resolved, That our respect and veneration for the man are still further increased as we look back upon the unkind and ungenerous treatment which he has so often received, without a murmur, so long as he alone was the sufferer, but who was always prompt to call back to duty all who were forgetful to their patriotism or nationality—who was always willing to sacrifice himself on the altar of his country's good.

Resolved, That the name of HENRY CLAY requires no eulogium, where freedom has a foothold or patriotism commands respect. His genius and his talents are familiar as household words, wherever the English language is spoken or civilization has penetrated. While a nation mourns his irreparable loss, generous hearts, over the whole surface of the globe, will unite in paying a tearful tribute to his memory.

Resolved, That we condole with the bereaved family and friends of the illustrious deceased, on whom this blow must fall, with even greater severity than on the nation in whose service his long life has been spent, and that as a token of our sympathy for them, and respect to the memory of the man, we will wear the usual badge of mourning for ninety days, and that our meeting rooms be decorated in a becoming manner for the same period.

ROBERT T. HAWS, *Chairman.*

J. F. FREEBORN,
G. W. BLUNT, } *Vice-Chairmen.*

W. L. SHARDLOW,
A. J. WILLIAMSON, } *Secretaries.*

FIRST WARD SCOTT AND GRAHAM ASSOCIATION.

At a regular meeting of this Association, the Hon. J. PHILLIPS PHŒNIX introduced the following resolution, which was unanimously adopted:

Resolved, That this Association has heard, with the deepest sorrow, the death of the patriot and statesman, HENRY

CLAY. For half a century he has been our distinguished champion at home and abroad; knowing "no north, no south, no east, no west," his gigantic mind has ever been devoted to the best interests of his country. It may truly be said, "Our country mourns the loss of her noblest son."

JOHN H. WHITE, *President.*

JOHN GRIFFIN,
JOS. A. GARDNER, } *Secretaries.*

FIFTH WARD SCOTT AND GRAHAM CLUB.

At a meeting of this Association, held on Wednesday evening, June 30th, the following preamble and resolutions were unanimously adopted:

Whereas, It has pleased an all-wise Providence to remove from our midst, the sage, patriot and statesman, HENRY CLAY, whose life, for the last fifty years, has been devoted to the interests of the country, and whose whole history has proved his declaration, "that I would rather be right than be President;" therefore,

Resolved, That we condole with our fellow-citizens, throughout our extensive country, for the great loss sustained in the councils of the nation, in the death of the SAGE OF ASHLAND.

Resolved, That although we deeply deplore the death of HENRY CLAY, we are cheered in the knowledge that he ended his long and useful life in the bright hopes of the future, and that his example will always be the guide, and ought to be the aim, of every American.

JOHN B. FRINK, *President.*

JOHN L. GIEB, *Secretary.*

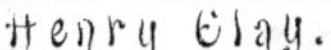

FIFTH WARD COMMITTEE.

At a regular meeting of the Whig Committee of the Fifth Ward, held July 1st, on motion, the following resolutions were unanimously adopted :

Whereas, This Committee has received intelligence of the death of HENRY CLAY, and whereas, the members of this Committee have long cherished the most profound feelings of respect and love for that great patriot, and deem his death a calamity falling heavily upon themselves, their party, and their country ; therefore, be it unanimously

Resolved, That the members of this Committee deeply deplore the death of HENRY CLAY, and while trusting the inscrutable wisdom of Divine Providence, and bowing with submission to His solemn and irrevocable decree, they regard the death of that departed patriot as one of the greatest national misfortunes that could have fallen upon the American people.

Resolved, That although death may have ended his counsels, his labors and his virtues, the feelings of the members of this Committee remain unaltered and unalterable; and that they, in common with their countrymen, will ever reverence HENRY CLAY as the embodiment of all that was noble and patriotic.

Resolved, That the members of this Committee, as a tribute of respect, wear the usual badge of mourning for thirty days.

THOMAS E. SMITH, *Chairman.*

WM. H. CANNIFF, *Secretary.*

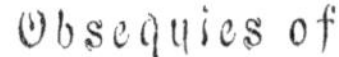

TENTH WARD LUNDY'S LANE CLUB.

At a regular meeting of the Tenth Ward Lundy's Lane Club, held on Thursday evening, July 1st, the following preamble and resolutions were unanimously adopted:

Whereas, This Club has heard with profound sorrow the melancholy tidings that America's noblest son has fallen—that he, who was almost the idol of the Whig party—who, from early manhood to the grave, devoted his talents and his energies to the advancement and preservation of the great interests of his country—whose love of liberty led him to labor for its establishment in the southern republics as well as on the classic soil of Greece, and who was at all times willing to sacrifice himself for that country by standing forth as its pacificator in the dark and perilous hours of its history; that this man, the statesman, the patriot and the orator, has fallen; therefore

Resolved, That in common with all friends of liberty, we mourn the loss of its noblest advocate, and as members of the Tenth Ward Lundy's Lane Club, we will unite in any demonstration which may take place to commemorate the death of our late beloved leader.

Resolved, That the patriotic services of the late senator of Kentucky, are recorded upon almost every page of our country's history; and when that history ceases to be read, or ceases to be known, then, and then only, will be forgotten the name and fame of HENRY CLAY.

ROBT. MACOY, *President*.

M. S. DUNHAM, *Secretary*.

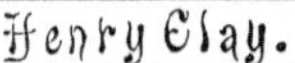

THIRTEENTH WARD CHIPPEWA CLUB.

A regular meeting of the Thirteenth Ward Chippewa Club was held on Wednesday evening, June 30th, when the following resolutions were unanimously adopted :

Resolved, That we have heard with profound regret the decease of the pure patriot, the wise statesman, and the firm friend of his country, Hon. HENRY CLAY, and while we bow in submission to the dispensation of an overruling Providence, which has called him from the scenes of his labor, full of honors and of years, and we express the fear that we shall never look upon his like again, we cannot but hope that his bright example, as a devoted friend to the constittuion and the laws, will stimulate his countrymen to follow in the path which he has marked out for them, in order to promote the prosperity and happiness of the land which he loved to his latest breath.

Resolved, That this Club and the Whigs of the Thirteenth Ward, be requested, (in case of a public demonstration,) to meet in front of this hall, on the day set apart for the funeral of HENRY CLAY, and march in procession under the Clay Club banner of this ward.

AUG. MORAND, *President.*

GEORGE F. COACHMON, *Secretary.*

SIXTEENTH WARD WHIG COMMITTEE.

At a meeting of the Sixteenth Ward Whig Committee, held on Thursday evening, July 1st, the following preamble and resolutions were unanimously adopted :

Whereas, Intelligence of a great national calamity—the death of that noblest of patriots, the greatest of statesmen, the purest of men, HENRY CLAY—has been received by this Committee; therefore,

Resolved, That while we deeply deplore the loss we are called upon to lament, we feel that his example has been left inscribed upon our national history, for us to follow in the exercise of candor, truth, sincerity, forbearance and conciliation, one toward another, for the sake of peace, concord and harmony, and the success of Whig principles.

Resolved, That we will unite in any demonstration which may be called forth by reason of the nation's bereavement, as may be designated by the Common Council of our city.

WILLIAM CRUSSELL, *Chairman*.

H. H. WHEELER, *Secretary pro tem*.

NARRATIVE OF EVENTS

FROM

ALBANY TO KENTUCKY,

INCLUDING THE

Funeral Solemnities at Lexington.

BY A DELEGATE FROM THE CLAY FESTIVAL ASSOCIATION.

THE funeral cortege, consisting of the Senate Committee, the delegation of the Clay Festival Association, and the family and Kentucky friends of the deceased, as mourners, escorted by the corporate authorities of Albany, the officers of the railroads, a deputation of citizens, and the Burgess Corps, left Albany on Tuesday morning, 6th July, at 9 o'clock, in a special train, by the western railroad.

The funeral car was elegantly and tastefully decorated, bearing befitting and touching inscriptions—the whole train was heavily hung in deep mourning.

From the place of leaving the eye met everywhere mute evidences of the general feeling. Country seats and farm-houses hung out their sable banners. All along the road were seen the sad, upturned faces of all ages, sexes, and conditions. School-houses, with their pupils assembled in front, reverentially and silently gazing upon "the last of earth" of the leading spirit of the immortal line of post-revolutionary patriots.

SCHENECTADY.—An imposing spectacle was presented to the eye. As the train advanced toward this old republican city, their way was through a dense, orderly crowd, increasing until we reached the depot,—and here the whole population seemed to have congregated. Bells were tolling; minute-guns were fired from several stations; the road hung across with black cloth; all the buildings, in sight, wearing the same sombre hue; the national colors at half mast, and bands playing funeral marches. We were joined by the Mayor and a deputation of citizens. The professors and students of "old Union" were observed among the throng—many of them, as well as the old and young of the inhabitants, seemed deeply affected.

AMSTERDAM.—The station was heavily draped, as well as the American flags, numerously displayed. The sound of bells, guns firing, and the gathered people, in sorrowing silence, gazing at the sarcophagus, as if they would penetrate the casings and cerements to behold the features of the beloved dead.

FONDA.—The draperies here were very heavy, and but faintly expressed the manifest grief of the large crowd,—among whom were observed many aged men and women. A requiem from the band—the bells tolling, and the booming of the cannon, echoing and re-echoing through the hills and valleys of that beautiful region.

CANAJOHARIE.—The uninterrupted scenes of the morning repeated. The shadowy folds of colors, clothed in crape, and the dark hangings of the adjacent buildings—all classes clustered in silent awe, and passing regularly, in deep files, the funeral car.

Little Falls.—The largest number of persons that had ever been collected at this place, awaited the arrival of the train. The ladies and children—most sincere mourners—had deputized an eloquent speaker, in their behalf, to present bouquets of white flowers—immortelles and evergreens, draped with black, while a wreath, circling pure white flowers, was their offering to the mighty dead.

Fort Plain, St. Johnsville, Fultonville, Mohawk and Herkimer, at the Palatine Bridge, all through the valley of the Mohawk, were presented the noblest tributes to the virtues, to the greatness, and to their enduring memory of the illustrious statesman. A large portion of the almost countless masses, gathered at all the stopping places through this section, had journeyed from ten to one hundred miles, by all modes of conveyance, to testify, by their presence, that although Henry Clay lived no more on earth, his example, his principles, and his public services, were immortal.

Utica.—Several thousands were assembled. A deputation of their leading citizens waited on the Senate Committee. From this city, as well as from all the principal places on the route, the authorities and special delegations joined in the honored tribute. The very atmosphere had become oppressive. It was laden with the universal woe of a stricken land. The eye everywhere rested upon the emblems of national sorrow, or upon the reverential throng that had made one immense procession from the bed of a Christian hero's death. The ear heard only lamentations; the gloomy tones of funeral bells; the dirges of many bands; and stationed cannon, that each minute caught the other's echo. It was, in truth, a burdened air, but there was this sweetness in it, that if envy or jealousy had hindered his just living reward, at the hands of his countrymen—he had survived these, and was now bearing, to his long home, universal appreciation and affection. The whole land bowed their heads before the general loss; which would have been awhile averted if prayer could have stayed the hand of time—a calamity as vast as the boundaries of the UNION he had mainly helped to cement together, as the fearless and all-powerful republic. This—and his whole life meted out in the service to his country—bore testimony, from his grave to heaven, of a nation's lasting gratitude for all that he had done and suffered in their behalf.

ROME.—Another delegation was received. Among the crowd was a remnant of the most powerful tribe of North American Indians; their bearing indicated the deepest reverence. Did they remember, in him, the champion who thrice sacrificed the electoral vote of a great southern state, to his sense of duty, in rescuing the mighty tribe of Cherokees in that state, from the wrong which would otherwise have been perpetrated?

SYRACUSE.—The train waited here an hour. At the hotel the Senate Committee and the various deputations attendant on them, were presented to the authorities and to numbers of the citizens. The Albany Burgess Corps were here relieved. They are a gallant and renowned company, who had so far performed most arduous duty; files of them passing to either side of the funeral car at each stopping place, and by every means in their power preserving the decorum and solemnity of the occasion.

ROCHESTER.—The pressure was very great. Not less than ten thousand were in and around the depot—besides the multitude in the thronged street through which the train had to pass. Another military detachment, the corporate and other delegated authorities from this place, as well as from all places beyond, including Buffalo, here joined the train.

AUBURN.—The same array of upturned faces—the deep silence—the unuttered grief. There was a stern solemnity —a deep pondering of the thoughtful, reverential multitude; the tolling of bells—the minute-guns—the lowered flag of the union—the heavy draperies of black.

GENEVA.—Another crowd—a rustic band—cannon—the houses dressed in mourning—the honest weeping of their inmates, who had loved him well,—American flags bearing the names of " CLAY and FRELINGHUYSEN," that had not looked upon the light of day since they had seen service in that memorable conflict of opinion in 1844. As the train left the place a woman was seen, overpowered with grief, kneeling, and with upstretched hands imploring Heaven's blessing upon the final repose of her nation's savior.

CANANDAIGUA.—Again an ardent and devoted throng of friends, of all classes and of all parties. A deputation, headed by FRANCIS GRANGER, waited on the Senate Committee, and in low tones expressed their sense of the country's bereavement.

BUFFALO.—So numerous had been the receptions, so manifest the eager, yet respectful anxiety of each place along the route—not to be resisted—that the cars would tarry awhile, it was impossible to make a rapid journey. The train was upward of thirteen hours in passing from Albany to the City of the Lakes. As they approached Buffalo a thousand flashing lights were seen. Her authorities and people, remembering his inestimable national services, and his unwearied efforts to improve and make secure the navigation of all the great water highways of the country, upon the success of which their general and individual prosperity mainly depended, had made extensive preparations for a general demonstration. Their entire Fire Department, with their torches, apparatus and banners—all their citizen soldiery, civic societies, the orders of Freemasons, Odd Fellows, and United Americans, joined in the ceremonies. The long procession moved through the principal streets; many of the houses and all the public buildings appropriately decorated, and it was approaching midnight when the remains reached the shore, and were placed on a cenotaph on board the steamer. Amidst the firing of guns, the tolling of the bells of the churches and public buildings, of all the steamers and shipping in the harbor, and away from the thousands who attended the remains of HENRY CLAY to her shores, the "Buckeye State" bore her holy charge over the waters of Lake Erie.

LAKE ERIE.—The night was clear—the air and the waters were hushed, as those whose duty it had been to sustain the painful scenes of *that* trying day of travel through the heart of the Empire State, sought repose to be the better able to endure the fatigues yet awaiting them.

But before these retired to rest, they gathered in silence around the cenotaph, upon which their great countryman was laid. He slept well on the bosom of the vast lake, that had borne him oftentimes in glory and triumph to glad and expectant throngs of ardent partisans. It was now carrying him for the last time toward his far off home,—a nation's wail, echoing from shore to shore; the grief of the universal heart. Upon a bed of countless flowers, with wreaths of laurel—of cypress—the ivy and the oak leaf—lit up by an hundred lights—he rested—great in life—greatest in death.

OHIO.

CLEVELAND.—The wharf was reached at nine o'clock, Wednesday morning. Then came his old friends and neighbors, the Lexington Committee, and their silent, tearful greeting. Nearly all of them were men advanced in years. Who can describe the deep grief, the agony with which they realized, to quote their own language, that "the soul of their city, the sun and centre of their social life, had set forever."

These gave place to the Governor of Ohio, the Cleveland Committee, with deputations from Columbus, Dayton, Zenia, Cincinnati, other parts of the state, and from Louisville. They were received in the main saloon of the steamer. The tall and imposing form of Gov. WOOD, bending with the weight of emotion, approached the Senate Committee, and paused, and with broken voice, he addressed Judge UNDERWOOD. The solemn sight of many men gathered there, who had long known the American statesman—his dear friends and intimates—his colleagues in the Senate, and those who had devoted years of their lives to his service—so still they were that their sobbing was distinctly heard. "Sir," said the governor, "in behalf of Ohio I greet this sad company. The noble state I represent was strongly attached to the illustrious man, whose remains are now about to pass through the midst of her people, and which she desires to receive and pass through her territories, with heart-felt homage and reverence. Not even Kentucky, whose proud distinction it will be to possess his ashes, entertains for the memory of this patriot and great American statesman, deeper veneration—not more ardent affection when living—than Ohio, who now, so full of sorrow, receives his noble corse."

Judge UNDERWOOD, in vain, essayed to reply. The eloquence of manly tears, the silent pressure of the hand of GOV. WOOD, who had affected in like manner all his hearers, was the most fitting response. Marshaled by this honorable escort, the body was placed in a car, appropriately decorated, provided by the railroad companies, and the numerous cortege of the family, mourners, committees and authorities, joined the train. Its passage was through a dense throng of uncovered heads. Before noon they had stopped at various places, and at every one they met assemblages of Ohians, that had journeyed many miles to take a last look of one who had always received their support. Thrice had the vote of this most important of the western states, been given to him.

COLUMBUS.—The shadows were indicating the approach of evening as the train neared the capital. The state and city authorities, the military, fire department, orders and societies, had been marshaled to receive the dead CLAY, and these, in numerous procession, carried him through the principal streets to the resting place provided for him. At an early hour, on Thursday morning, the sad retinue left Columbus. The houses throughout the whole city, were very generally dressed in mourning. From Columbus to Cincinnati, the assemblages were frequent, besides the crowds at the various stations. A deputation, styled the Dayton Committee, joined the company. The approach to Cincinnati was through a highly cultivated region, and everywhere along the route, was exhibited tokens of the general feeling.

CINCINNATI.—The committee of this city and the marshals were presented to the Senate and other committees at the depot. Here they received the body, and through miles of this beautiful city, the procession moved, passing on every side the elegant decorations, upon which had been lavished the taste of a munificent people. The procession was very beautiful, admirably arranged, and the crowds of thousands upon thousands filling the streets, and from every window, seemed to utter "God bless you," as the funeral car passed them. Innumerable busts and pictures, draped with wreaths or covered with crape—transparencies, inscriptions, and mottoes, in every street, spoke to the gazers the tribute of the heart from the Queen City of the West to her beloved champion. Hundreds of guns were fired from many points, answered from the United States military depot at Newport—all the bells of the city were tolling, and thus heralded, the extended line at length reached the steamer Ben. Franklin. Upon a cenotaph in her bow, elevated aloft, open on all sides to the public view, they deposited the body of HENRY CLAY. The steamer was nearly covered with mourning. As far as the eye could reach, there was a sea of heads upon the levee. Amid these solemn funeral voices of chimes, and the echoing cannon, the steamer left the shores,—tarried for an instant at Covington, which had also poured out her people, and whose houses were very generally dressed in mourning. When he had last visited Cincinnati, as many people smote the air with a louder noise than artillery, in their countless cheers—and now there came in the pauses of the booming sound—the deeper, lower tone of lamentation.

The party that left Cincinnati, consisted of the Senate Committee, Sergeant-at-Arms, deputation of the Clay Festival Association of the city of New York, joined to the Senate Committee, the Dayton Committee, the Young Clay Guard of Cincinnati, numbering some one hundred remarkably fine looking men, all similarly dressed in funeral uniform; the Cleveland and Columbus Committees; authorities of the states and cities through which the body had passed; the Louisville and Frankfort deputations, and the Special Committee of Arrangements from Lexington.

THE OHIO RIVER.

North Bend.—The neglected and already dilapidated tomb of the lamented Harrison was eagerly regarded. For him the mighty Kentuckian had been ruthlessly thrust aside, yet how gallantly and with what utter self-abnegation did the latter forget his own wrongs in a patriot's duties. It was impossible not to draw parallels—not to remember the dissimilar careers of these two, and yet, in each case, from the bed of a painful death, went up fervent prayers for the welfare of their country, and the maintenance and preservation of the Union and the Constitution.

Lawrenceburg.—The firing of cannon, colors at half mast, and the uncovered throng upon the bank of the river, these were the reverential tributes of her inhabitants.

VEVAY.—The same tokens—the same gathered crowds; and now the heavens were putting on like demonstrations in deep clouds, with her lightnings and her thunders—the sky replying to the earth. The rain soon poured down in torrents, and yet each place we neared had turned out their people, who silently stood, in many instances uncovered, upon either shore, as the steamer passed on her way.

RISING SUN.—Guns were heard for some time before the boat came in sight, and the tolling of bells. As the Ben. Franklin made the turn that brought her in full view, the whole river front of the place was observed to be dressed in deep mourning—the national flags trailing. Near the shore were observed, standing in a semi-circle, thirty-one ladies, dressed in white, with black veils upon their heads, and one dressed in deep mourning, each with bouquets of flowers—" the Sisterhood of the States"—mourning their loss, and Kentucky clothed in sable, as the nearest sufferer in the common calamity. The gentlemen were drawn up, *uncovered*, in that pitiless storm, in deep files behind this touching group. Looking around, the scene had become infectious; the whole escort on board were moved to tears.

CARROLTON, MADISON, WEST PORT.—Each of these places paid their tribute. As the sun was setting, the clouds broke over the bow of the boat shedding over the cenotaph a sea of light, and resting there as a ray of glorious promise; while in the rear, spanning the Ohio, was seen a rainbow of surpassing beauty. It was painfully still, as all on board, gathering either on the hurricane deck, in front, or upon the guards at the stern, gazed with deep emotion upon these eloquent and sublime omens of nature.

The night had advanced, but still the minute-guns took up their sentinel duty, and their sound reverberated from hill-side to hill-side, awakening in each heart the knowledge that the Friend of the West was passing by their homes to his tomb.

INDIANA.

The boat made the wharf at New Albany, just before daylight, on Friday morning. The American flags flapped heavily against their staffs, and dimly seen through the fog was Louisville; and the early notes of preparation for the approaching solemnities were heard from the same quarter.

At six o'clock, the steamer Ben. Franklin, having left the Indiana side, delivered to the Louisville authorities the precious remains, that now, for the first time, touched Kentucky ground.

KENTUCKY.

LOUISVILLE.—The body was removed to the designated place, from whence it was afterward more formally received Again the clouds formed, and just at nine o'clock, a flash of lightning, vivid and glaring—was followed by one crash of thunder as if all the artillery of the skies had congregated there. The signal gun for the starting of the procession followed this. The dense mass of vapor gradually broke away, and the clear sunlight lit up the funeral streets, which, for miles through which it passed, was one *continuous* drapery of black. Many of the streets were dressed from side to side, and from corner to corner. The ladies of Louisville were very generally robed in black, and every male citizen wore crape upon the arm.

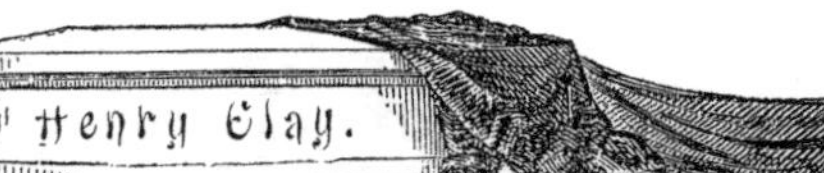

There was but one expression upon every face—the woe of a people lamenting the death of their father.

The cortege filed on through the lines of the procession to the cars, which were prepared by the railroad company, and appropriately decked in mourning. It was with extreme difficulty, and then only by the exertion of force, that the anxious crowd were induced to fall back from the funeral car, while many, with uncovered heads and weeping eyes, were mutely testifying their abiding regard.

Through these closed thousands the cars slowly took their way. It was the last day of that sad but yet glorious journey. He was being borne now through his own people. The state that he had brought up from her obscurity to the first rank of states, whose name, in connection with his, was now immortal, was summoning, from far and near, her prosperous inhabitants to join with the multitude then journeying, from all parts of her territory, toward his final resting place. And thêy were coming, old, young, and middle-aged—the women of Kentucky, whose hearts were lifted up for him, because he always loved his country and her honor—the children whose first syllables had lisped his name,—and that unfortunate race in whose behalf had been his first essay in public life, and also among his latest, to ameliorate and improve their condition, felt that they too had suffered in the bereavement which deprived them of their most powerful advocate.

At every little stopping place we saw preparations for the journey, and clusters of all ages, sexes, and colors, and invariably the aged and the youth in tears.

FRANKFORT.—The route was necessarily slow and tedious. The afternoon was advanced when the train reached Frankfort. They stopped in front of the State House, covered, from the basement to the roof, with black. The adjoining houses, and every point the eye rested upon, displayed similar decorations. Immediately in front of the State House was drawn up a line of remarkable men; those who had known him through years of trial, and with whitened heads and streaming eyes, they were there to render up a life long experience to his fame, to his honor and to his inviolable faith and truth. At their head was Governor POWELL, and the state and civic authorities; and beside them the masonic and other orders, and the various civic societies, with a multitude from the adjoining country.

LEXINGTON.—The cortege reached Lexington at sundown. As far as the sight, dimmed with tears, could reach, there was one sea of heads. The mission of the Senate Committee was ended. Gathered in their car were the various deputations—first the sons of Kentucky—her distinguished men—who had been, to the great dead, through many years of his life, as brothers—then that sad group from the far off city of New York, who represented thousands that bore toward him the affection of kindred, the governor and the authorities of the state. On the hushed air broke the tremulous voice of Judge UNDERWOOD, the surviving colleague of HENRY CLAY, in the United States Senate.

"Mr. Chairman, and gentlemen of the Lexington Committee:—Mr. CLAY desired to be buried in the cemetery of your city. I made known his wish to the Senate after he was dead. That body, in consideration of the respect entertained for him, and his long and eminent public services, appointed a committee of six senators to attend his remains to this place. My relations to Mr. CLAY as his colleague, and as the mover of the resolution, induced the President of the Senate to appoint me the chairman of the committee. The other gentlemen comprising the committee, are distinguished, all of them, for eminent civil services, each having been the executive head of a state or territory, and some of them no less distinguished for brilliant military achievements. I cannot permit this occasion to pass without an expression of my gratitude to each member of the Senate's Committee. They have, to testify their personal respect and appreciation of the character, private and public, of Mr. Clay, left their seats in the senate, for a time, and honored his remains by conducting them to their last resting-place. I am sure that you, gentlemen of the Lexington Committee, and the people of Kentucky, will ever bear my associates in grateful remembrance.

"Our journey, since we left Washington, has been a continued procession. Everywhere the people have pressed forward to manifest their feelings toward the illustrious dead. Delegations from cities, towns and villages have waited on us. The pure and the lovely, the mothers and daughters of the land, as we passed, covered the coffin with garlands of flowers, and bedewed it with tears. It has been no triumphal procession in honor of a living man, stimulated by hopes of reward. It has been the voluntary tribute of a free and grateful people to the glorious dead. We have brought with us, to witness the last sad ceremony, a delegation from the Clay Association of the city of New York, and delegations from the cities of Cincinnati and Dayton, in Ohio. Much as we have seen on our way, it is small compared with the great movement of popular sympathy and admiration which everywhere burst forth in honor of the departed statesman. The rivulets we have witnessed are concentrating; and in their union will form the ocean tide that shall lave the base of the pyramid of Mr. CLAY's fame forever.

"Mr. Chairman, and gentlemen of the Lexington Committee, I have but one remaining duty to perform, and that is, to deliver to you, the neighbors and friends of Mr. CLAY, when living, his dead body for interment. From my acquaintance with your characters, and especially with your chairman, who was my schoolmate in boyhood, my associate in the legislature in early manhood, and afterward a colaborer, for many years, on the bench of the Appellate Court, I know that you will do all that duty and propriety require, in burying him, whose last great services to his country were performed from Christian motives, without hopes of office or earthly reward."

As he closed, the chairman of the Lexington Committee, Chief Justice ROBERTSON, sharing the emotions of all present, and himself deeply affected, replied:

"Senator UNDERWOOD, Chairman, and Associate Senators of the Committee of Conveyance:—Here, your long and mournful cortege, at last ends—your melancholy mission is now fulfilled—and, this solemn moment, you dissolve forever your official connection with your late distinguished colleague of Kentucky.

"With mingled emotions of sorrow and of gratitude, we receive from your hands, into the arms of his devoted state and the bosom of his beloved city, all that now remains on earth of HENRY CLAY. Having attained, with signal honor, the patriarchal age of seventy-six, and hallowed his setting sun by the crowning act of his eventful drama, a wise and benevolent Providence has seen fit to close his pilgrimage, and to allow him to act—as we trust he was prepared to act—a still nobler and better part in a purer world, where life is deathless. This was, doubtless, best for him, and, in the inscrutable dispensations of a benignant Almighty, best for his country. Still, it is but natural that his countrymen, and his neighbors especially, should feel and exhibit sorrow at the loss of a citizen so useful, so eminent, and so loved. And not as his associates only, but as Kentuckians and Americans, we, of Lexington and Fayette, feel grateful for the unexampled manifestations of respect for his memory, to which you have so eloquently alluded, as having everywhere graced the more than triumphal procession of his dead body homeward from the national capital, where, in the public service, he fell with his armor on and untarnished. We feel, Mr. Chairman, especially grateful to yourself and your colleagues here present, for the honor of your kind accompaniment of your precious deposit to its last home. Equally divided in your party names, equally the personal friends of the deceased, equally sympathizing with a whole nation in the Providential bereavement, and all distinguished for your public services and the confidence of constituents,—you were peculiarly suited to the sacred trust of escorting his remains to the spot chosen by himself for their repose. Having performed that solemn service in a manner creditable to yourselves and honorable to his memory, Kentucky thanks you for your patriotic magnanimity. And allow me, as her organ on this valedictory occasion, to express for her, as well as for myself and committee, the hope that your last days may be far distant, and that, come when they may, as they certainly must come, sooner or later, to all of you, the death of each of you may deserve to be honored by the grateful outpourings of national respect which signalize the death of our universally lamented CLAY.

"Unlike BURKE, he never 'gave up to party what was meant for mankind.' His intrepid nationality, his lofty patriotism, and his comprehensive philanthropy, illustrated by his country's annals for half a century, magnified him among statesmen, and endeared him to all classes, and ages, and sexes of his countrymen. And, therefore, his name, like WASHINGTON'S, will belong to no party, or section, or time.

"Your kind allusion, Mr. Chairman, to reminiscences of our personal associations, is cordially reciprocated—the longer we have known, the more we have respected each other. Be assured that the duty you have devolved on our committee shall be faithfully performed. The body you commit to us shall be properly interred in a spot of its mother earth, which, as 'THE GRAVE OF CLAY,' will be more and more consecrated by time to the affections of mankind.

"How different, however, would have been the feelings of us all, if, instead of the pulseless, speechless, breathless CLAY, now in cold and solemn silence before us, you had brought with you to his family and neighbors, the *living man*, in all the majesty of his transcendent moral power, as we once knew and often saw and heard him. But, with becoming resignation, we bow to a dispensation which was doubtless as wise and beneficent as it was melancholy and inevitable.

"To the accompanying committees from New York, Dayton and Cincinnati, we tender our profound acknowledgments for their voluntary sacrifice of time and comfort to honor the obsequies of our illustrious countryman.

"In this sacred and august presence of the illustrious dead, were an eulogistic speech befitting the occasion, it could not be made by me. *I* could not thus speak over the dead body of Henry Clay. Kentucky expects not me, nor any other of her sons, to speak his eulogy now, if ever. She would leave that grateful task to other states and to other times. His name needs not our panegyric. The carver of his own fortune, the founder of his own name; with his own hands he has built his own monument, and with his own tongue and his own pen he has stereotyped his autobiography. With hopeful trust his maternal commonwealth consigns his fame to the justice of history and to the judgment of ages to come. His ashes he bequeathed to her, and they will rest in her bosom until the judgment day; his fame will descend, as the common heritage of his country, to every citizen of that Union, of which he was thrice the triumphant champion, and whose genius and value are so beautifully illustrated by his model life.

"But, though we feel assured that his renown will survive the ruins of the capitol he so long and so admirably graced, yet Kentucky will rear to his memory a magnificent mausoleum—a votive monument—to mark the spot where his relics shall sleep, and to testify to succeeding generations, that our republic, however unjust it may too often be to *living* merit, will ever cherish a grateful remembrance of the *dead* patriot, who dedicated his life to his country, and with rare ability, heroic firmness, and self-sacrificing constancy, devoted his talents and his time to the cause of Patriotism, of Liberty, and of Truth."

At the close of this address, the procession was formed, led by a cavalcade of horsemen, preceding the hearse, which was followed by the Senate Committee, and the deputation from the Clay Festival Association, in carriages, as mourners; the Clay Guard, of Cincinnati; the deputation of fourteen, from Dayton, Ohio; the seventy-six, from Louisville, and the citizens in the rear—their march being under the funeral arches, and through the sombre street—lined by the silent multitude—toward that place known to every inhabitant of the republic, and throughout the civilized world, as the home of the great commoner.

Who can fittingly speak of the agonized group awaiting, at Ashland, the arrival of the dust of him, who had been husband, father and the beloved master? That wife, who for fifty-three years and upward, had been his faithful partner,—sharer of his triumphs and of his many trials; whose saint-like virtues had secured to her the affection and veneration of all classes, in the place where she was so well known; herself more than threescore years a sojourner on earth, having survived her parents and all her daughters, with gallant sons mouldering in the tomb, bending beneath the weight of this, her speechless sorrow; bowing with years, and broken in health, amid surviving children, grandchildren and kindred, and gathering around them, the old and young of their servants, awaited there the remains of her peerless husband.

Guided by the many torches, the train moved through the grounds, designed and laid out under his supervision. It was in truth a solemn—a holy scene. Under the dark shadows of the spreading grove, treading on a lawn where the wild flower, the myrtle and the laurel were strangely mingled, they bore him toward that portal which had last seen him depart near the close of the preceding year, impelled again to cross the mountains, and to tread the Halls of Council, because there had come to him a rumor of threatened resumption of hostilities, against the peace, the concord, the happy prosperity of the country and the Union, the gods of his earthly idolatry. There the fell destroyer smote his lordliest victim. He had left his honored home, the owner of a nation's love, and possessed of the esteem and respect of all Europe. He was now being borne lifeless into those halls, and on the air was heard a peoples' lamentation, as they mourned the loss of their nearest friend and greatest benefactor.

They gently laid him beneath his roof tree, and in that room where he had for half a century received the homage of countless thousands, representing all classes and callings—the gifted and the great of either sex—coming from every country, and traveling from all directions, to Lexington, that they might thus, in person, pay tribute to the worth, the genius, the patriotism, and surpassing excellence of the private and public character of the illustrious host.

Beside the bier were gathered his sons, some of his grandsons, and nephews; behind these the family servants—not forgetting old Aaron and Duke—each of whom were the seniors, one by nearly a score of years, of their deceased friend and master.

Slowly and reverentially his honored bearers departed from the house of mourning; sad and thoughtful faces peered through the gathering darkness, as they sought to penetrate the then gloomy looking demesne, of that which was to each beholder sacred ground. The memory of Ashland and of Mount Vernon, will be, to American minds, the Meccas of the heart, so long as this Union shall endure, from generation to generation, to the latest posterity. And so they still slowly departed, looking back until even the very shadows folded themselves into the night, some wearied with deep feeling and trying, touching scenes spread over days of fatiguing travel, crowded with events, through which they had journeyed, toward this garden of "the dark and bloody ground," to lay in the tomb the BAYARD of their country's fame and honor.

The Clay Guard, of Cincinnati, solicited the honor of watching over his remains—this, the last night before sepulture. It was granted to them, and so arranged that they relieved each other—the alternate hours until daylight.

In the deep hours of the night—alone with him and her God—the widow knelt beside her husband's corse. For that hour it was directed that she should not be disturbed. In that hour what other heart knew her thronging memories of joys and sorrows, save the spirit of the dead she longed to join. In 1844, when he was the victim of a thousand schemes to track his way and prevent his election to the presidency, she had, on the night that knew his defeat, knelt beside his living form, and inclosing him within the strong arms of affection, uttered those words, never to be forgotten, "My husband, this ungrateful people can never truly appreciate you while living; thank God, they have left you in the bosom of your family, and in this, your dear Ashland." They had commenced together the struggles of life. Together they had planned their home—together they had arranged their grounds, and with their own hands had planted the young shoots of what now were the stately trees, that in the intense stillness of that night, were soughing and sighing nature's dirge for their dead owner. Life had opened to them full of the bright hope and promise that belong to youth, energy, and commanding abilities. She had seen him leap into a dazzling greatness, reflecting honor and dignity upon his native land, lifting his young state to the front rank of her compeers, and conferring prosperity upon his country and her citizens, while he gave stability and permanence to the institutions and laws of the land, and cemented together the Union, as he ardently desired, prayed for, and labored ceaselessly to accomplish, from end to end—from centre to circumference. And he bore all these accumulated and thickening honors with such dignity, and all his high offices so truly great while in their active discharge, and so meekly when away from them, and in the midst of his family and friends, that he was there always so simple and unaffected, these clung to him with intensity beyond description, and hung about his heart, as the shield that warded from it all the envenomed arrows, that through so many years were showered at that mark. There was born to them, in this happy home, eleven children—six daughters and five sons. Where were they now? No daughter survived on whose breast that aged head could rest. Their eldest born was worse than dead, living for many years a confirmed lunatic; and yet another son, whose sanity is not always reliable; and how deep had been their joint sorrow when their accomplished and beautiful daughter-in-law, Julia, the wife of their son Henry, had been prematurely laid in her grave, and then found too that there they had buried that son's heart. She saw then, that son of promise, named after his father, crimsoning the ground of Buena Vista, with his blood. It was but a little while before that the aged pair had wept beside the honored tomb, at the capital of the state, where Kentucky, in proud grief, surrounded by thousands of her gallant men, had laid him beneath the sculptured marble. That day her husband's corse had been borne past that son's tomb. All the past, painfully extended, and seemingly interminable winter, she had been wrung with that hopeless grief which attends loving and suffering natures, necessarily separated from one another. Her own life was whiling away, and each had the additional pang of knowing that other's illness, and yet realizing the impossibility of ever being again together during life.

"Why," said she, "should I grieve, or mourn, or weep? He has departed, possessed of a nation's love. He died as he had wished to die—in the full hope of the humble but trusting Christian. It is but a short time—a few months—perhaps a year—not longer—and we will be united forever." In that dread hour, who shall say the years that lone matron lived were not a decade? Through her thronged mind passed the remembrances of a life-time. She has the sympathy and regard of millions, and in that watch of the dead, she was companioned by the thoughts or dreams of countless thousands, who remembered what event the morrow was to commemorate in history. "The peace of our Lord, which passeth all understanding, be with her and remain with her always."

Saturday, July 10.

Long before the day had fairly broke, every avenue of approach to the city was crowded by those who came up to render their last tribute to him who had always, living, received their measureless devotion. For three days the current had set that way. Each public and private house was overflowing. The whole city teemed with their visitants. It was computed that nearly one hundred thousand

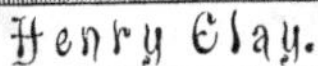

persons, of all classes and sexes, had come together on that memorable occasion. The multitude who could find no other resting-place, slept in the market, and in the court house. Every barn, stable and out house, was filled with tired occupants.

At an early hour, those appointed to meet at Ashland, had gathered together within the house. The pall-bearers, his oldest and most distinguished friends in Kentucky, the Senate Committee, and the deputation of the Clay Festival Association, with his family and kindred. In front were arranged the deputations from other states, from the Masonic fraternity, and a dense crowd were in a semi-circular array before the porch. Upon a bier, cushioned with flowers, and immediately in front of the door, they laid the iron coffin that inclosed the body of HENRY CLAY. Upon it shone a clear, cloudless sun. Upon the breast of it reposed the civic wreaths of the Clay Festival Association; the wreath of immortelles; the laurel wreaths from Baltimore and Philadelphia, and bouquets from Washington, Wilmington, Trenton and Little Falls; while strewed around were the floral offerings of every principal place, from the national capital to the grave.

It was as bright a day in 1844, toward the close of that year, but nature had put on her sere and yellow leaf, when that same spot, and that same lawn, were witnesses of a great and solemn spectacle. The State of Kentucky came to the Sage of Ashland—her electoral college, her state authorities and congressional representatives, her citizens from the most distant places within her limits, the daughters of Kentucky and the military companies of Frankfort and Lexington. Then, as now, that immense audience were bathed in tears. Upon that green, the same Judge

UNDERWOOD, then President of the College of Electors, now Chairman of the Senate Committee, having in charge the remains of HENRY CLAY, was their spokesman. Then he thus closed his speech: "In the shades of Ashland, may you long continue to enjoy peace, quiet, and the possession of those great faculties which rendered you the admiration of your friends and the benefactor of your country. And when, at last, death shall demand its victim, while Kentucky will contain your ashes, rest assured, that old and faithful friends, those who, knowing you longest, loved you best, will cherish your memory and defend your reputation."

"The Mill boy of the Slashes;" the youthful devotee of the Fathers of the country; the eloquent advocate of emancipation in Kentucky before this century had commenced, or the constitution of his state had been framed; the dauntless foe of oppression and tyranny everywhere; always the champion of American interests; the great commoner; the author of the war of 1812; the negotiator of the peace of 1815, and the convention with Great Britain; the benefactor of the South American republics, he "had looked abroad and called a new world into existence;" the savior of his country in the Missouri compromise; the friend of Greece in the burning eloquence of 1824, while Speaker; their able advocate as Secretary of State, securing the assistance of Russia, through which thus closed their struggle, and through the same power procuring the acknowledgment, by Spain, of the Independence of South America; restoring the peace of the country by the compromise of 1833; exposing, by his own self-sacrifice, the dangerous tendencies of fanaticism aimed at the lawful institutions of the country; preserving peace with France in 1835; his

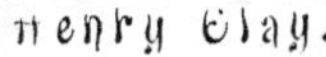

almost numberless acts of public service during fifty years; closing that series of self-sacrifices by offering up his own life as the costly price at which the country saw the "slavery issues" finally adjusted and settled, in 1850; and before that great drama of his life had closed, the two leading political divisions had solemnly indorsed those principles as their common chart, by which the ship of state should be hereafter conducted.

From that solemn bed of death to his own sweet home, millions had attested their love. Dying on the 29th of June, his body rested on that Sabbath, which was at once the Lord's day, and the anniversary of the nation's Holy-day of Independence. And on that day every minister of GOD solemnly attested to his hearers the greatness and the goodness of the dead; and every orator, the next day, when the anniversary was celebrated, paused, and in befitting language eulogized the life and public services of HENRY CLAY. Through thousands of miles that the continuous procession had journeyed, on every side the mourning multitude had passed, and the eye everywhere rested upon the dark draperies of woe; wending their slow way between funeral arches, and inscriptions, and mottoes, and paintings, and busts, and statues, and monumental columns erected on the instant,—all these decked in honor of the friend of mankind. Men, women, and children, even of the tenderest years, all bore, in their saddened features and tear-stained faces, those most eloquent testimonials of his worth. From Washington to the tomb was one votive offering of wreaths of oak, immortelles, the cypress, the ivy and the laurel—bouquets of flowers of every species, and in wondrous profusion. These alone, if it had been possible to collect them, would have piled a monument. It was no unfrequent sight to witness youth and beauty bend and press their lips upon his sable shroud. Old men would pause beside his iron case, and burst into uncontrollable sobs. Early manhood and middle age, that had banked their hopes in him, and clung to him as their chieftain and leader, to the last moment resisting the assured certainty that they were no more to listen to that silver voice, nor hang upon its tones, with speechless woe at length realized, that for the future, his memory, and the preservation of his patriotic principles were their future charge.

His late colleagues in the senate—that revered band of chosen intimates, who were honored as his pall-bearers, the New York delegation, and his family and kindred, grouped near the porch and within his dwelling; on the porch stood the minister of God, at whose hand he had received the sacrament, when last he was alive, within those halls—the same minister who had baptized him, his children that were left to him, and the children of his dead son, Col. Clay—while all around the eye rested on his near friends and neighbors, who were there assembled, and yet, without these, lines of people from many states, and the far off counties of his own.

The funeral services were performed by the Rev. Edward F. Berkley, Rector of Christ Church, Lexington. Never, perhaps, did that impressive service fall upon the ear more solemnly than then. And then the preacher lifted up his voice and thus addressed the people:

"My Friends:—A Nation's griefs are bursting forth at the fall of one of her noblest sons.

"A mighty man in wisdom—in intellect—in truth—lies in our presence to-day, insensible, inanimate and cold.

The heart which once beat with a pure and lofty patriotism—shall beat no more. The renowned Statesman, who was learned in the laws of diplomacy and government, will never again give his counsel in affairs of State. And the voice which was ever raised in behalf of truth and liberty, is silenced forever!

"Indulge me in a remark or two, whilst I speak of him; and in consideration of the personal comfort of this immense assembly, my words shall be few.

"This is neither a proper place nor a fit occasion to dwell on the peculiar and striking incidents of his public life; and I mean to say a few words only of his character as viewed in connection with religion.

"We have not come here to weave a garland of praises for the brow of the fallen statesman, nor to throw the incense of adulation upon the urn which incloses his ashes; but we have come here to pay the last offices of respect and affection, to a neighbor and a friend; and to draw, from the visitation which has stricken down one of the mightiest of our mighty men, such lessons as are calculated to teach us 'what shadows we are, and what shadows we pursue.'

"Our venerated friend has been before the public eye for half a century; and for nearly the whole of that period in the occupancy of high public places. He has done the State great service. He combined in his character such elements as could make him no other man than he was, except, that he might have been as great a soldier as he was a Statesman and Orator. But the crowning excellence of all his virtues, was this—he was a Christian.

"As he was eminently open, candid, and honest, in his long public career, so was he deeply sincere in his adoption, as the rule of his life, of the principles of our holy religion.

"Although the suns of seventy summers had shone down upon him before he made a public profession of CHRIST, yet, when he did make it, he did it, not mechanically, and as a matter of course, because he was an old man—he did it heartily, and upon conviction, because he felt himself to be a sinner, and because he felt the need of a Savior! And when he came to make the inquiry, What shall I do? and it was told him what he ought to do—he did it gladly—he made haste to fulfill the purposes of his heart. And his great mind being brought to the investigation of the pure and simple doctrines of the Cross, new beauties, in a new world broke in upon him, of the existence of which, to their full extent, he had never dreamed before. And I know, that in times when he lay under the hand of disease, and of great bodily infirmity, here at home, he clung to those doctrines, by a lively faith, as the highest consolations of his soul.

"Although he had his Church preferences, yet the power and influence of the teachings of Christianity, rightly understood, gave rise to sympathies in his nature, which extended to all Christian people.

"Surrounded as he was, by the allurements and fascinations of a high public place, nevertheless, he strove to walk in the pure and perfect way; and by a steady maintenance of the principles which bound him to religion and to GOD—like the eagle, with his eye fixed upon the sun, his course was onward and upward!

"And these principles, which our illustrious friend found so comforting and consoling in life, did not forsake him when he had nothing else on earth to cling to.

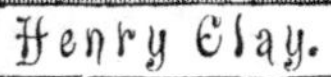

"In reference to some of his last hours, a lady, connected with him by family, who recently spent several days at his bedside, writes: 'He is longing to be gone, and said something of this kind to me, which caused me to ask him, if he did not feel perfectly willing to wait until the Almighty called him. He replied, O, my dear child, do not misunderstand me—I supplicate Him continually for patience to do so. I am ready to go—no, not *ready*, but *willing*. We are none of us *ready*. We cannot trust in our own merits, but must look to Him *entirely*.'

"The writer adds: 'He is the most gentle, patient, and affectionate sick person I almost ever saw—thanks you for every thing, and is as little trouble as he can possibly be.'

"And this is the power of religion upon a vigorous and discriminating mind—a mind fully capable of meeting all the great emergencies which have ever arisen in its collisions with other great minds, at the bar, in the senate, and upon the forum.

"And O, the recollection to mourning friends, and to a mourning country is of the most consoling interest, that, as in his life, by his genius and wisdom, he threw light, and peace, and blessing, upon his country; so, in his death, the Glorious Giver of grace and wisdom, threw light, and peace, and blessing upon him—borne upward, as he was, by the aspirations to heaven—of a million hearts.

"But his earthly career is run. Full of age and full of honors, he goes down to earth, to ashes and to dust. A man of extraordinary genius. A man of the highest practical wisdom—possessing the largest powers of true eloquence—a pure patriot—a sincere Christian, and a friend of his race.

"His friends will grieve for him—the Church has lost

him—his country will bewail him—and hereafter, when the passing traveler shall come to Ashland, and look for the bland, agreeable and hospitable host, *he will not find him here!* His aged wife, who, for more than fifty years, has grieved with him in his sorrows, and rejoiced with him in his public success, shall go down unto the grave, mourning—and men, in every civilized nation of the earth, will shed a tear at the fall of such a man. But he is gone to a brighter and a better world. Whilst this memorial shall remain of him here, that he was as simple and sincere in his religion, as he was great in wisdom and mighty in intellect.

"God is no respecter of persons. Neither genius, nor wisdom, nor power, nor greatness can avert the fatal darts which fly thick and fast around us. If public services of the highest value—a fair fame which reaches to the utmost habitations of civilized man, and an integrity as stern as steel, could have done this—a nation had not been in tears to-day.

"But the great and the humble—the useful and the useless—the learned and the ignorant—the mighty and the mean—the public and the private man—must all, alike, lie down in the cold chambers of the grave! Death is the common leveller of men and of nations. Temples and monuments, which have been erected to perpetuate the achievements of statesmen and of heroes in past ages, have been ruined and robbed of their grandeur by the insatiable tooth of time—not a vestige remains of the glory that once covered the earth, and not a stone to mark the spot where the master of the world was laid.

"And this is the end of man! This, the obscurity and oblivion to which he shall come at last! But his end may be worse than this, if he had no hope in the blessed SAVIOR's death. For, whoever confides in the world for the bestowment of true happiness—whoever trusts to its gains, its pleasures, or its honors, to bring him peace at the last, will find himself miserably imposed upon, and grievously deluded. He will find that this misplaced confidence will involve him in ruin, as inevitable, as it will be—eternal!

> 'Lean not on earth! 'twill pierce thee to the heart:—
> A broken reed at best, but oft a spear!
> On its sharp point, peace bleeds, and hope expires.'

"If we aspire to a true, a deathless immortality, let us not seek it in the praises of men, or in the enrollment of our name upon the page of history—for these all shall perish!—but let us seek, by obedience to GOD, and a recognition of the claims of religion, to have our names written in the Lamb's Book of Life. This, and this only, will guarantee an immortality as imperishable as the heavens, and as certain as the Life of GOD.

"The observation is almost universal, that 'all men think all men mortal but themselves.' And yet there is nothing more surely reserved for us in the future, than disease and dissolution. And these too, may, and very often do, come when we are least expecting a disturbance of our plans.

"The statesman falls with plans of future glory yet unaccomplished;—the poet expires in the midst of his song, and the magic of his muse lingers on his dying lips;—the sculptor drops his chisel before he has taught the marble to breathe,—and the painter his pencil, while the living figures on his canvass are yet unfinished;—the sword slips from the hand of the warrior, before the battle is won,—

and the orator is silenced, while the words of wisdom are yet dropping in sweetest accents from his lips.'

"'I said ye are God's, and children of the Most High, but ye shall die like men.'

"No consideration can purchase a moment's respite, when the decree shall go forth, 'this night thy soul shall be required of thee!' whether it be uttered at the doors of the stately mansion, or at the cot of the lowly poor. And not to be wisely and well prepared to hear this summons, is destructive of the best interests of the soul. Happy they who have made a friend in God. Happy they who have done, and they who do this in early life—the failing of which, in his case, our revered friend so often himself regretted—thrice happy they in whom greatness and goodness meet together. Imperishable joys shall be awarded to them. They shall shine as stars in the firmament forever and ever. In each successive generation their 'memory shall be blessed,' and their 'name be had in everlasting remembrance;' and, 'their conflicts o'er, their labors done,' the ransomed spirit shall escape from the prison that confines it to the earth, and the King of Kings shall bind upon their victorious brow, wreaths of unfading glory, in that blest place—

> 'Where pain, and weariness, and sorrow cease,
> And cloudless sunshine fills the land of peace.'

"Our great friend and countryman is dead! He has no more connection with the living world, and we are about to bear his honored remains to the beautiful spot, where our own dead lay, and around which our memories love to linger. What to him, I ask you, are now the policy, or the politics of the country? What to him, now, are the nice points upon which turn the honor of the State? What to him, now, is the extension of empire?—the rise or fall of nations?—the dethronement or the establishment of kings? His work is done, and well done. As it is with him, so shall it shortly be with every one of us. Then,

> 'So live, that when thy summons comes, to join
> The innumerable caravan, that moves
> To the pale realms of shade, where each shall take
> His chamber in the silent halls of death—
> Thou go not, like the quarry slave at night,
> Scourg'd to his dungeon; but sustained and soothed
> By an unfaltering trust, approach thy grave
> Like one who wraps the drapery of his couch
> About him, and lies down to pleasant dreams.'

"One word more. The distinguished subject of our present attention, has fallen a martyr to his country. The cause of his sickness and his death originated in his last great efforts in securing the passage, through Congress, of certain measures, known as THE COMPROMISE. In more senses than one, may he receive the heavenly welcome, 'Well done, good and faithful servant.' His love of country—his enthusiasm in any cause in which her interests were involved—his great and singular powers—his wonderful and controlling influence over even great minds, marked him as *the* man of the age, and adapted him, in a peculiar manner, to act and to lead in grave questions of government.

"And if, in the future, any one section of this great republic should be arrayed in hostility against another; and any cruel hand shall be uplifted to sever the bonds which unite us together as a common people—the Genius of Liberty shall come down in anguish and in tears, and throwing herself prostrate before his tomb, implore the Mighty

Ruler of nations—for the preservation of our Institutions, and the protection of our Liberty, and of our Union—to raise up from his ashes, another CLAY!"

At the close of this address, for some moments the pressure of the crowd around the bier was so great as to render it almost impossible to place the coffin in the hearse.

The procession from Ashland was then formed:

The Senate Committee.
Delegation of the Clay Festival Association.

PALL BEARERS.	CORPSE.	PALL BEARERS.

The Family and Officiating Clergyman.
Clay Guard, of Cincinnati.
Dayton Committee.
The Seventy-six, of Louisville.
Citizens.

Upon reaching the head of Main street, the military, masonic fraternity, and the various associations received the body in open order and uncovered. The procession was then formed in the following order:

GEN. PETER DUDLEY,
OF FRANKFORT,
GRAND MARSHAL.

Col. H. C. PINDELL and WILLIAM G. TALBOTT,
SPECIAL AIDS.

Marshals Dunlap, Goodloe and Beard.

The Military, in sections of six, with reversed arms, muffled drums, colors furled, and draped in mourning.

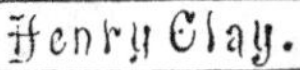

Officers of the Army and Navy of the United States.
Committee of Arrangements.

Marshal Postlethwaite.

Committee of the Senate of the United States, Judge UNDERWOOD, of Kentucky; Gen. LEWIS CASS, of Michigan; Gov. HAMILTON FISH, of New York; Gen. SAMUEL HOUSTON, of Texas; Governor JAMES C. JONES, of Tennessee; and Commodore ROBERT F. STOCKTON, of New Jersey.

Committee of the Clay Festival Association of New York; JOSEPH M. PRICE, ALFRED G. PECKHAM, D. L. PETTEE, JOSIAH P. KNAPP, DAVID WEBB, and NICHOLAS CARROLL, with them the venerable Governor METCALF, of Kentucky.

Clay Guard of Cincinnati, consisting of over one hundred Young Men.

Dayton Committee.

The Seventy-six from Louisville.

The Deputation from Frankfort, with other Committees from various places.

Committee of the city of Lexington, sent to receive the body

Marshal C. W. Kennedy.

Masonic Fraternity.

PALL-BEARERS.		PALL-BEARERS.
B. W. DUDLEY,	CORPSE.	BENJ. GRATZ,
M. T. SCOTT,		D. VERTNER,
GEO. ROBERTSON,		CHILTON ALLAN,
E. WARFIELD,		R. HAWES,
CHARLES CARR,		GARRETT DAVIS,
ROGER QUARLES,		C. S. MOREHEAD.

[The funeral car, which had been made under the direction of the citizens of Lexington, was of excelling taste in the design, exceedingly rich in material, and elegant in execution; of quadrangular shape, lined with velvet and satin, overhung with black crape, a large silver urn of classic mould upon the top, surmounted with a massive eagle of the same material, with outstretched pinions, grasping in his talons a bundle of arrows, the whole drapery, as well as the netting, covering the eight splendid white horses, heavily fringed with silver bullion. Each horse was led by a black groom, in the funeral costume of the Moors.]

Officiating Clergyman and Family, consisting of
THOMAS HART CLAY, Wife and Children;
JAMES BROWN CLAY and Wife;
JOHN M. CLAY; HENRY CLAY, Jr., *now* HENRY CLAY, the eldest son of the late Col. CLAY;
THOMAS SMITH and Wife, with the younger orphan children of Col. CLAY,
[Whose guardians they are, as well as close kindred.]
Mrs. SUSAN CARTER, and other nieces and nephews of Mr. and Mrs. CLAY.
[Infirmity prevented Mrs. CLAY from leaving Ashland.]
Reverend Clergy of all denominations.

Marshal C. W. Dudley.

Governor and Heads of Departments of the State of Kentucky.
Committees of Cities, Towns and Counties of the State of Kentucky.

Marshal S. D. Bruce.

Mayor and Council of the City of Lexington.
President and Directors of Lexington Cemetery Company.
Trustees and Faculty of Transylvania University.

Marshal C. D. Carr.

Judges, Members of the Bar, and Officers of the Fayette Circuit Court.

Judges of the Superior and Inferior Courts of Kentucky, and Officers.

Judges of the United States Courts, and Officers.

Members and ex-Members of the Congress of the U. S.

Marshal Silas P. Kenney.

Independent Order of Odd Fellows, in sections of six.

Sons of Temperance, in sections of six.

Marshals R. W. Bush and M. B. Gratz.

Fire Companies, in sections of six.

Members of the Senate and House of Representatives of the State of Kentucky.

Teachers of Schools.

Marshal Isaac Shelby.

Citizens on Foot, in sections of six.

Marshals Clifton Wier and R. P. Todhunter.

Citizens and Strangers in carriages, two abreast.

Marshals Robert Bullock and J. H. Shropshire.

Citizens and Strangers on Horseback, in sections of four.

This section was very numerous, and presented an imposing array of equestrians, besides the noblest specimens of the celebrated race of Kentuckians.

From Ashland to the Cemetery, every house was clothed in mourning. At nearly every crossing, heavy and tasteful draperies were transversely stretched from corner to corner—frequent displays of the national colors at half mast, and cased in crape—the large court house and public square covered with a sable mantle—the monument erected to the memory of WILLIAM T. BARRY, in the square, also covered with black cloth. The street, through which the procession passed, was clothed with black from end to end—and lined with a dense crowd. Every window was filled, and each roof bore its burden of spectators. The population of Lexington is some nine thousand, and when it is remembered that it was estimated an hundred thousand strangers were there, the mind can conceive readily the sublime spectacle that immense mass, embracing, literally, every age, sex, condition and color, presented. Each male and all the children uncovered as the body passed, and every countenance displayed the deepest sorrow and sympathy. Where else, in all the universe, could such a scene be witnessed? A whole country mourning the loss of their benefactor—a nation's tears bedewing his grave, and the grateful memory of the republic building his immortal monument.

As the line approached the cemetery, still other thousands were seen crowding every slope, hillock, and down into the vale where he was to be temporarily entombed. A gun had announced the march of the procession—and then, simultaneously, the muffled drum—the dirge-like music—the chiming of the bells, and continuous discharge of minute-guns, during the hours that elapsed between the commencement and the close of the ceremonies, smote the hot and dusty air, which breathed everywhere, the heavy atmosphere of oppressed hearts, these pulsating with a common suffering grief, that pervaded the land, and hung like a pall over the public mind—the inquiry, passing unanswered, from lip to lip, "who shall supply his place—who now is our sure reliance, when the country he defended is in danger?"

Slowly through the graveled way, the mourning train passing within the cemetery grounds, the beloved dead was carried to his tomb. There the services of the Episcopal Church were closed by the rector. "Ashes to ashes—dust to dust," and the hollow sound reverberated with more power over the hearts of those present than would the loudest thunder. The Masonic Fraternity, the Family, the Senators and the New York Delegation, alone remaining near the bier; the Grand Master, assisted by the Grand Lodge of Kentucky, took charge of the corpse, and performed their highest masonic ceremonies in honor of the illustrious member of their Order.

Governor JONES laid ANN S. STEPHENS' wreath of immortelles around the head; JOSEPH M. PRICE placed the wreath of oak and cedar, the offering of the Clay Festival Association of the city of New York, over his breast, and deposited, at the same time, and on that holy spot, which had been the home of love, and truth, and patriotism, the seal ring of one of the members of the Committee, and other mementoes of his comrades—and then the coffin was closed from mortal sight. By the generous permission of the Grand Lodge, who fully appreciated their sacred mission, the Committee of the Clay Festival Association, with the Masonic Fraternity, bore the remains of HENRY CLAY to the vault prepared for their reception, and laid him beside his mother and his kindred. Plucking from within that tomb, oak leaves, with a silent prayer that their end might be like his, at peace with GOD and man, and a vow that while life remained, they would cherish his memory and seek to preserve his immortal principles—devotion to the honor, welfare and happiness of the country, and the perpetuation of the Union, that sad train slowly withdrew—the iron bound door closed behind them —the mouth of the tomb was sealed, and in the same order the marshaled host passed back their sad and thoughtful way—

"Rest thee—there is no prouder tomb."

The procession had dispersed, but the gloom remained visible in every face, and the crowd silently dispersed toward their homes. At sundown the bells tolled, and thirty-one minute-guns were fired, and thus were closed, at his own home, the ever-memorable obsequies of the "First Citizen of the Republic!"

In the eloquent language of the Lexington Observer: "All the crowds which we have seen, sink into insignificance when compared to this. Were it not that no display, however grand—that the collection of no multitude, however numerous—that the exhibition of no sorrow, however deep and general—could have been commensurate with the genius, fame and services of the illustrious dead —we would say that the occasion was worthy of any man. Other places paid the same honors to the remains of our great statesman, but it was felt that *here* was the place where he originated his immortal career, and that, at least in proportion to our limited population, should be the marks of respect. And never did we have more cause to be proud of our city, county, and state.

"But our task is done. The patriot sleeps calmly in the 'city of the dead,' but he lives in the hearts of the people, and will live whilst human liberty has a votary. He was so decided a partisan, that in life he had many foes. But now that death has closed the scene, his virtues and his powers will be acknowledged by all. Perhaps, the history of human greatness does not exhibit such a remarkable career. We doubt if in intellectual conflict he was ever foiled, if left to choose his own position. And this too, as he said, commencing with but a limited education. Perhaps no man has gone through a stormier political life. His friends always relied implicitly upon him against the most gigantic opponents—never did he disappoint their confidence. Hence, to the last, never was a man surrounded by such devoted friends; and the sad procession on Saturday attested the hold he had upon the whole country. A child of the people—leaning alone upon the prayers of an humble but devoted mother, and the protecting care of a beneficent Providence, he made for himself a fame more enduring than marble, more precious than the sordid advantages of power; placed himself before the world as its master-spirit; died amid a nation's tears, and has his name embalmed in a nation's memory."

On Sunday, by appointment,—some of them having to leave immediately thereafter,—Mrs. CLAY received the delegates of the Clay Festival Association, in the drawing-room, at Ashland. There were portraits of Mr. and Mrs. CLAY; of their children, and of her brother and father, with a very large original picture of Gen. WASHINGTON and his family. Beneath the portrait of Col. CLAY, hung his sword, worn in the fatal field of Buena Vista. There was the massive glass vase, which had been presented to him by the people of Pittsburg, and it was with water from that vase he had been baptized. There too were the splendid silver vases—the one presented by the ladies of Tennessee, and the other, and perhaps the most beautiful vase ever executed in this country, from the Gold and Siver Artisans of New York. Here Mrs. CLAY was presented to the delegation by her son, JAMES B. CLAY, now a resident of St. Louis, who recognized among them familiar friends of his father and himself. Mrs. CLAY was evidently suffering from great depression, and this interview affected her still more. She was surrounded by devoted friends and honorable servitors of her husband from a far off Atlantic city, who had come there on the most mournful duty of their lives. They were afterward shown through the house, and they especially lingered in his library and sitting room. In the former were countless tokens of the affection and regard that had been showered upon him by his loving countrymen and countrywomen. Among other things were canes enough for an entire community, embracing every variety that could be imagined—the costly and the massive—the antique and curious, and the grotesque. The delegation were shown through the grounds, and bore with them each a cane from those which had been presented to the illustrious dead, the offering and generous gift of the executors. They gathered sprigs of myrtle and of laurel—plucked some flowers, and tufts of moss and sod—and then "with a last lingering glance," reluctantly returned to Lexington. A portion left at dawn the next morning, while the senators, who tarried a few days, and those of the Clay Festival Delegation, who remained, were invited to meet "the Old Guard, of Kentucky," at the hospitable and princely mansions of two of their number.

This narrative is closed with a synopsis of his will. After bestowing all his personal effects, unconditionally, upon his wife, LUCRETIA CLAY, constituting her executrix, and Judge THOMAS A. MARSHALL and JAMES O. HARRISON, his executors, devises his estate among the members of his family with great equity, and provides for the gradual

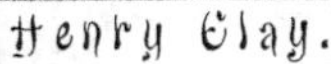

emancipation of his slaves. Those born after January, 1850, to be free—the males at twenty-eight, and the females at twenty-five—the last three years' earnings, previous to their manumission, to be reserved as a fund for their benefit in their new homes in Liberia.

Ashland remains the property of his wife, during her life, then to be sold, and the proceeds disposed of among his children.

He devises to his friends as follows:

"I give to my friend, Dr. B. W. DUDLEY, the gold snuff-box, presented to me by Dr. HUNT, late of Washington City.

"I give to my friend, HENRY T. DUNCAN, my ring, containing a piece of the coffin of General WASHINGTON.

"I give to my friend, Dr. W. N. MERCER, my snuff-box, inlaid with gold, said to have belonged to PETER the Great, Emperor of Russia."

The will, with noble appreciation of the faith of those he intrusted with the fulfillment of his wishes, provides that no security shall be required from them.

The following order and testimonial of appreciation was laid before your Committee.

COMPANY D, WASHINGTON GREYS.

SPECIAL ORDER.

NEW YORK, JULY 3, 1852.

This company having been detailed as the Guard of Honor over the remains of Hon. HENRY CLAY, the members are directed to assemble at the armory, THIS DAY, Saturday, at 11 o'clock precisely, in full uniform, gray pantaloons, without knapsacks, and with white gloves, crape on the left arm.

JAMES LITTLE,
Commandant.

CHAPIN, *Orderly.*

Regular Quarterly Meeting, COMPANY D, WASHINGTON GREYS, held at their Armory, 13th July, 1852.

LEMUEL W. SERRELL, moved that Orderly Sergeant JOHN R. CHAPIN, and ex-orderly RICHARD P. CLARK, be appointed to draft suitable resolutions of thanks, for the attentions received by this company during their late visit to Albany.—Carried.

After retiring, the committee presented the following:

Whereas, Having returned from the melancholy duty, which had fallen to our lot, of escorting the remains of the late HENRY CLAY to the seat of the State government, and feeling duly sensible of the honor conferred upon us, and of the unremitting kindness and attention which awaited us on all hands, and feeling anxious, as soon as possible, to express the gratitude which actuates us, therefore, be it

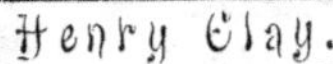

Resolved, That the thanks of this company are eminently due, and are hereby tendered to the Common Council of this city, and its Committee of Arrangements, for the honor conferred in selecting COMPANY D, for guard and escort duty over the body of the late HENRY CLAY.

Resolved, That we tender our sincere and heart-felt thanks to the officers, members and ex-members of the Albany Burgess Corps, for the unremitting attention paid to us by them, while in Albany.

Resolved, That we also feel sensibly the honor conferred upon us by Governor HUNT, in reviewing this company, and by the very eloquent and affecting remarks addressed to us by him.

Resolved, That the thanks of COMPANY D are due to Col. FRISBIE and Staff, and the ALBANY REPUBLICAN ARTILLERY, for the escort on our arrival and departure; and finally, we extend the expressions of our warmest feelings of remembrance and gratitude to the citizens of Albany, and to all with whom we were brought in contact, while there, for the universal good feeling and kindness with which we were treated.

JAMES LITTLE, *Commandant.*

LEMUEL W. SERRELL, *Secretary.*

FRIDAY, JULY 9th.

This day, your Committee held their first meeting, after their return from the capitol of the state, where they had placed the remains of the honored dead, in the keeping of the corporate authorities of Albany, upon whom the mournful and honored duty devolved of rendering their testimony of homage to the memory and virtues of the illustrious deceased.

On motion, the following resolutions were unanimously adopted:

Resolved, That the Common Council of the city of New York will solemnize the death of the Hon. HENRY CLAY, by a civic and military procession.

Resolved, That TUESDAY, July 20th, be designated as the day for the public funeral solemnities in honor of the memory of the lamented HENRY CLAY.

Resolved, That our fellow-citizens generally, and the different societies, trades and associations, and Fire Department of this city and adjoining counties, are requested to unite in this testimony of respect to the illustrious dead; and all societies and associations intending to co-operate, are requested to communicate with the Committee, at the chamber of the Board of Assistant Aldermen, from Wednesday, the 14th, to Saturday, the 17th inst., from 12 to 5 o'clock, P. M., each day, in order to make the necessary arrangements to carry out the views of the Common Council, in an appropriate manner.

Resolved, That the army and navy of the United States, on this station, are requested to co-operate with us in making the necessary arrangements, and that the Committee on Military be requested to communicate with the commanders of the different stations.

Resolved, That no banner, bearing political devices or inscriptions, shall be admitted in the procession.

Resolved, That in order to render more effective the action of the Committee, Special sub-committees be appointed with power, to direct and carry into effect the duties specially delegated to them.

The chairman then announced the following

SPECIAL SUB-COMMITTEES.

On Military,

Messrs. BARKER, SMITH and TAIT.

On Civic Societies and Associations,

Messrs. TWEED, WARD and ANDERSON.

On Fire Department,

Messrs. VALENTINE, McGOWN and BOYCE.

On Programme,

Messrs. COMPTON, TROTTER, WOODWARD, WRIGHT and BARD.

On Invitations,

Messrs. SMITH, BRISLEY and TROTTER.

On selecting an Orator,

Messrs. BRISLEY, TWEED and BARKER.

TUESDAY, JULY 13.

The Committee met pursuant to adjournment. Numerous communications and delegations were received from civic societies and associations, expressing a desire to participate in the funeral solemnities in honor of the departed statesman.

Brigadier-General WILLIAM HALL, was selected as the Grand Marshal of the day.

The Light Guard, Capt. E. VINCENT, was selected to act as GUARD OF HONOR to the funeral car.

Subsequently, the Committee on Invitation, issued the annexed circulars to a number of the corporate bodies and distinguished gentlemen in the United States, as well as to many of the citizens of this city.

CITY HALL,
NEW YORK, JULY 14, 1852.

DEAR SIR:—The undersigned, on the part of the Joint Committee, appointed by the Common Council of this city, to make the necessary arrangements for solemnizing the obsequies of the late Honorable HENRY CLAY, on the 20th instant, respectfully invite you to be present on that occasion, and unite with the Common Council and citizens of New York, in this testimony of respect to the illustrious deceased.

Yours, very respectfully,

WESLEY SMITH,
WM. J. BRISLEY,
JONATHAN TROTTER,

Committee on Invitation.

CITY HALL,
NEW YORK, JULY 14, 1852.

The undersigned, on behalf of the Joint Committee of the Common Council of the city of New York, to make the necessary arrangements for solemnizing the obsequies of the late Honorable HENRY CLAY, on the 20th instant, respectfully invite you to participate on that occasion, as PALL-BEARER, in uniting with the Common Council and citizens, in paying respect to the illustrious deceased.

Yours, very respectfully,

WESLEY SMITH,
WM. J. BRISLEY,
JONATHAN TROTTER,
Committee on Invitation.

From the time of the announcement that the obsequies of the revered HENRY CLAY would be solemnized in a public manner, the citizens, civic and military associations, political societies, officers of the army and navy, members of the bar, and in fact the whole population seemed to vie with each other who should perform the best service, or render the greatest tribute of respect to the memory of the man whom the whole nation, with one voice, devoutly lamented.

To which the following replies have been received.

WASHINGTON, JULY 15, 1852.

GENTLEMEN :—I regret that my official engagements, at Washington, will not allow me to accept your invitation, to be present at the "solemnizing the obsequies of the late Hon. HENRY CLAY, on the 20th instant," at New York, and,

Have the honor to remain,
Gentlemen,
Your ob't serv't,

WINFIELD SCOTT.

Messrs. W. SMITH, W. J. BRISLEY and J. TROTTER, &c., &c.

ALBANY, JULY 19, 1852.

GENTLEMEN:—Please accept my acknowledgments for the honor you have done me in inviting me to attend the obsequies of the late HENRY CLAY, which are to be solemnized in your city to-morrow.

I sincerely regret that my official engagements do not permit me the melancholy satisfaction of uniting with the Common Council and citizens of New York, in the proposed demonstration of grief for the loss, and respect for the memory, of the departed patriot.

Very respectfully,
Yours, &c.,
WASHINGTON HUNT.

WESLEY SMITH, WM. J. BRISLEY, JONA. TROTTER, Esq's., Committee.

TROY, N. Y., JULY 19, 1852.

GENTLEMEN:—I have the honor to acknowledge the receipt of your invitation, on the part of the "Joint Committee," to unite with the Common Council and citizens of New York, in "solemnizing the obsequies of the late Hon. HENRY CLAY."

It would afford me sincere gratification to participate with you, in this public demonstration of respect to the memory and distinguished services of the illustrious deceased, and in the hope that I might still be able to accept the invitation with which you have honored me, I have deferred replying to your communication until this day. But I regret exceedingly to find that pressing private engagements, as well as official duties, will compel me to

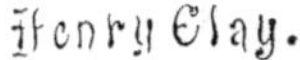

forego the pleasure of being with you on an occasion of such universal interest.

I am, gentlemen,
With great respect,
Your ob'dt servant,
JOHN E. WOOL.

Messrs. SMITH, BRISLEY, and TROTTER, Committee on Invitation.

WASHINGTON, JULY 16, 1852.

GENTLEMEN—I deeply regret that my engagements here will deprive me of the power of uniting with you on the 20th inst., in solemnizing the obsequies of the late Hon. HENRY CLAY.

In common with all the citizens of this republic, I entertain the highest respect and veneration for the memory of the illustrious deceased. His character as a statesman and patriot now forms a part of the rich inheritance of his country; and his great example will continue, through all future time, to influence the character of posterity, and liberalize and nationalize the hearts and minds of future American statesmen.

I have the honor to be, gentlemen,
Very respectfully,
Your ob'dt serv't,

JAS. SHIELDS.

Messrs. WESLEY SMITH, WM. J. BRISLEY, and JONATHAN TROTTER,
Committee on Invitation.

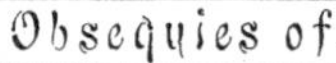

WASHINGTON, 15TH JULY, 1852.

GENTLEMEN:—I have the honor to acknowledge the receipt of your invitation, to unite with the Common Council and citizens of New York, on the 20th inst., in solemnizing the obsequies of the late Honorable HENRY CLAY.

It would afford me a mournful pleasure to join in this public demonstration of respect to the memory of the illustrious dead; but I find that my public duties here, forbid that I should consult my inclination by accepting your invitation.

I am, gentlemen, very respectfully,
Your ob'dt servant,
N. K. HALL.

To WESLEY SMITH, WM. J. BRISLEY, and JONA. TROTTER, Esq's., Committee.

WASHINGTON, JULY 16, 1852.

GENTLEMEN:—I received yesterday the invitation with which, as the Joint Committee of the Common Council of the city of New York, you have honored me, to be present at the solemnization of the obsequies of the late Honorable HENRY CLAY, on the 20th instant. The high personal admiration which I have always entertained for the lofty patriotism, elevated character, and brilliant genius of Mr. CLAY, would prompt me to avail myself of every opportunity of testifying my reverence for his memory.

It is therefore, with unfeigned regret, that I feel compelled, by the pressure of my duties here, to refrain from uniting with the Common Council and citizens of New

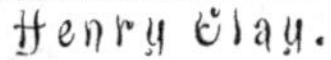

York in their most appropriate testimony of respect to the illustrious deceased, whose loss our whole country so deeply deplores.

Very respectfully,
Your ob't servant,
J. A. BAYARD.

Messrs. WESLEY SMITH, WILLIAM J. BRISLEY, and JONATHAN TROTTER,
Committee on Invitation.

PORTCHESTER, 19TH JULY, 1852.

GENTLEMEN :—I have just received your favor of the 14th inst., inviting me to unite with the Common Council and citizens of New York, in solemnizing the obsequies of the late Hon. HENRY CLAY, and I regret that it will not be possible for me to be present.

The great talents of our late eminent fellow-citizen; his distinction as an orator and a statesman, and the high rank which he has always held among the prominent men of his day, give to every man, of true American feeling, a deep interest in the perpetuation of his fame as a part of the property of the country. With this feeling of respect for the departed statesman, it is a source of sincere regret to me that I cannot unite with the Common Council and citizens of New York, in paying a last tribute to his memory.

I am, gentlemen,
Very respectfully,
Your ob't servant,
JOHN A. DIX.

Messrs. WESLEY SMITH, WM. J. BRISLEY, and JON. TROTTER, Committee.

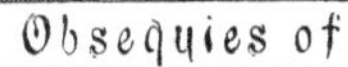

City Hall,
Philadelphia, July 14, 1852.

Gentlemen:—I was directed by the Committee of Councils of the city of Philadelphia, appointed to receive the remains of the late Henry Clay, to express to you their acknowledgments for your polite invitation to visit your city on the late mournful occasion, and to thank you for the very kind and hospitable manner in which they were treated whilst there.

With great respect,
JOHN PRICE WETHERILL,
Chairman.

Alderman Cornell, Esq., and Associates of Board of Aldermen, N. Y.

Council Chamber,
July 17, 1852.

Gentlemen:—We are directed by the Councils of Philadelphia, in forwarding you the inclosed resolution, to express to you their thanks for your very kind and polite invitation. Accept, on behalf of ourselves and our colleagues, the assurance of our high respect and esteem.

Yours, very truly,
THOMAS SNOWDEN,
President of Common Council.

William Morris, *President of Select Council.*

Messrs. Wesley Smith, Wm. J. Brisley, Jon. Trotter, Com. on Invitation.

Council Chamber,
July 17, 1852.

Resolved, That the invitation extended by the Committee of Councils of New York to the Mayor and members of

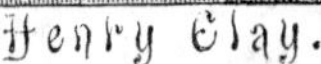

Councils of this city, to visit that city, on Tuesday next, to participate in the funeral ceremonies, to be observed there in commemoration of the death of HENRY CLAY, be accepted, and that the Presidents of Councils be directed to express our appreciation of the kindness thus offered.

[Extract from Minutes of Councils.]

Attest, CRAIG BIDDLE,
Clerk of Common Council.

EDMUND WILCOX, *Clerk of Select Council.*

MAYOR'S OFFICE,
BROOKLYN, JULY 19, 1852.

GENTLEMEN:—I have the pleasure to acknowledge the receipt of your note of the 14th inst., inviting the Common Council of Brooklyn to unite with the Common Council and citizens of New York, in solemnizing the obsequies of the late Hon. HENRY CLAY, deceased. The Common Council have unanimously accepted your invitation, but owing to arrangements having been made for a discourse to be delivered by the Rev. Doctor Cox, on the 20th inst., it may not be possible for them to be present with you.

Very respectfully, yours,
CONKLIN BRUSH, *Mayor.*

To Messrs. WESLEY SMITH, WM. J. BRISLEY, and JON. TROTTER, Committee.

TROY, JULY 17, 1852.

GENTLEMEN:—By order of the Common Council of this city, I reply to your invitation to us to attend, on the 20th inst., the solemnization of the obsequies of HENRY CLAY, which invitation, our Board has, by resolution, accepted.

I regret to be obliged to say, that before receiving (yesterday) your note of invitation, I had made such business arrangements for Tuesday and Wednesday next, as render it utterly impossible for me to be present with you, to do honor to the memory of a man whom, living, I so highly regarded.

Very respectfully, yours,

GEO. GOULD,

Mayor of Troy.

Messrs. WESLEY SMITH, WM. J. BRISLEY, JON. TROTTER, Committee.

HARTFORD, JULY 17, 1852.

GENTLEMEN:—Your polite note of invitation, to the Mayor and Council, "to be present and unite with citizens of New York in solemnizing the obsequies of the late Hon. HENRY CLAY," was received on the 16th inst.

It will be a mournful pleasure to join in the ceremonies in honor to the memory of one of the greatest patriots and statesmen of the age.

A delegation of the Council will be in attendance on the 20th inst.

Yours, respectfully,

EBENEZER FLOWER, *Mayor.*

Messrs. WESLEY SMITH, WM. J. BRISLEY, JON. TROTTER, Com. on Invitation.

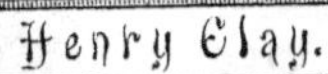

NEW HAVEN, JULY 17, 1852.

GENTLEMEN:—I have received your favor of the 14th, in behalf of the Joint Committee of the Common Council of the city of New York, inviting the Mayor and Common Council of the city of New Haven to unite with you in solemnizing the obsequies of the late HENRY CLAY, on the 20th inst.

It would afford me a mournful pleasure to pay that last tribute of respect to the illustrious statesman and patriot, but my engagements will not allow me to be present.

I will communicate your courteous invitation to the Common Council, and hope some of them will be able to accept.

Please, gentlemen, accept for yourselves, and the Common Council whom you represent, my thanks, in behalf of the Common Council of New Haven, for your friendly courtesy, and assurances of my high personal consideration.

With great respect,
I am truly yours,
A. N. SKINNER,
Mayor of the city of New Haven.

Messrs. WESLEY SMITH, WM. J. BRISLEY, JNO. TROTTER, Committee.

OFFICE OF THE CLERK OF THE COMMON COUNCIL,
HUDSON, JULY 17, 1852.

GENTLEMEN:—At a meeting of the Common Council of the city of Hudson, held this evening, the Mayor having presented and read your invitation, to attend the funeral solemnities in testimony of respect to the memory of the

Hon. HENRY CLAY, to take place in your city on the 20th inst., it was unanimously resolved to accept the same.

I am requested to say, that in accordance with said resolution, the Mayor and Council of our city will be in attendance at the *Astor House*, on Tuesday morning next, at which place you can communicate with them, and assign to them such place in the ceremonies of the day as the Committee on Invitation, or of Arrangements may think proper.

Very respectfully, yours,

WILLIAM BRYAN,

Clerk of Common Council.

To WESLEY SMITH, WM. J. BRISLEY, JON. TROTTER, Committee on Invitation.

WASHINGTON HEIGHTS, JULY 16, 1852.

GENTLEMEN:—I received your note last evening, announcing my selection to deliver a eulogy on the life and character of Mr. CLAY, on the 20th inst. Although I could have desired some longer time for preparation on so momentous an occasion, I will, however, essay the attempt. It will at least be an honor to fail on so glorious a theme.

With great respect,

Your obed't servant,

N. BOWDITCH BLUNT.

Hon. WM. J. BRISLEY, WM. M. TWEED, ISAAC O. BARKER, Committee.

---

141 HENRY STREET,

NEW YORK, JULY 19, 1852.

GENTLEMEN:—I have the honor to acknowledge the receipt of your letter of the 12th inst., and the information that the Special Committee of the Common Council, to make arrangements for the obsequies of the late Hon. HENRY CLAY, have selected me to offer a prayer prior to the delivery of the oration which is to be pronounced on the occasion.

It will be highly gratifying to me to unite with the authorities and with our fellow-citizens, in this proposed tribute of respect for the memory of our illustrious patriot, and to perform the service requested from me on that occasion.

Permit me to add, that this reply to the invitation would have been earlier, but for my absence from home when your letter was received, and it has but now come to my hands.

Very respectfully,
Your ob'dt servant,
JOHN M. KREBS.

Messrs. WM. J. BRISLEY, WM. M. TWEED, and ISAAC O. BARKER, Committee.

---

239 BROADWAY, 13TH JULY, 1852.

DEAR SIR:—Your favor, informing me of my appointment as GRAND MARSHAL on the occasion of the obsequies of the late Hon. HENRY CLAY, is received. I feel the honor conferred on me by your choice, and accept the position. I shall be pleased to meet the Committee as soon as possible, as there is but a short time to complete the detail of the necessary arrangements.

I am, very respectfully,
Yours,
WM. HALL.

JOHN H. CHAMBERS, Esq.

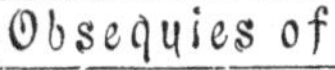

ASTOR HOUSE,
NEW YORK, JULY 15, 1852.

SIR :—I have the honor to acknowledge the receipt of your note of the 15th inst., apprising me that the Committee, appointed by the Common Council, have selected the LIGHT GUARD to act as Guard of Honor in the obsequies to be observed in honor of the late Hon. HENRY CLAY.

I pray you will convey my acceptance to the Committee, and likewise to assure them of my high appreciation of the compliment they have conferred upon my command.

I am, very respectfully,
Your ob'dt servant,
ED. VINCENT,
Commanding Light Guard.

JOHN H. CHAMBERS, Esq.

NEW YORK, JULY 17, 1852.

GENTLEMEN :—I had this day the honor of receiving, through you, an invitation from the Joint Committee, to unite, as PALL-BEARER, with the Common Council and citizens, in paying respect to the illustrious deceased.

In accepting this invitation, allow me, gentlemen, to express my unfeigned acknowledgments for the distinguished position your Committee have been pleased to assign me in the solemnities of that occasion; and at the same time to assure them of the consolation they have afforded to the countless friends of the deceased by their judicious and very liberal arrangements. The tears of a grateful people

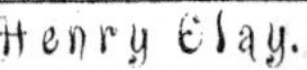

may well and deservedly be shed over the remains of a statesman so eminently endowed—whose services have been performed without fear and without reproach—and whose long life has been spent in an untiring devotion to the interests of his country and the liberties of mankind.

I have the honor, to be, gentlemen,
Faithfully and truly, your friend,

A. R. LAWRENCE.

Aldermen WESLEY SMITH, WM. J. BRISLEY, JON. TROTTER, Committee.

NEW YORK, JULY 20, 1852.

GENTLEMEN:—I returned to the city this morning, and have the honor to acknowledge your invitation to attend as a PALL-BEARER, and join with the Common Council and our fellow-citizens, in paying the last tribute of respect to the late Hon. HENRY CLAY. I beg to assure you that I esteem your invitation a distinguished compliment, and will present myself to your Committee at the appointed time.

I have the honor to be,
With great respect,
Yours, &c., &c.,

J. PHILLIPS PHŒNIX.

Hon. WESLEY SMITH, WM. J, BRISLEY, JON. TROTTER, Com. on Invitation.

NEW YORK, JULY 16, 1852.

GENTLEMEN:—The honor conferred on me by you, to officiate as a PALL-BEARER, in the funeral procession of the late Hon. HENRY CLAY, is accepted with melancholy pleasure.

I am, gentlemen,
With sincere regard,
Yours, &c., &c.,
G. H. STRIKER.

WESLEY SMITH, WM. J. BRISLEY and JON. TROTTER, Esq'rs., Committee.

NEW YORK, JULY 17, 1852.

GENTLEMEN:—I very much regret that, owing to my arrangements to be absent from the city on the 20th, it will not be in my power to accept your esteemed invitation to attend on the solemnization of the obsequies of HENRY CLAY, deceased, whose memory so well deserves the respect of the nation at large. I beg of you to excuse my necessary absence on the occasion, and believe me to remain,

Yours, most truly,
M. ULSHOEFFER.

Messrs. WESLEY SMITH, WM. J. BRISLEY, JON. TROTTER, Committee.

FORT WASHINGTON, JULY 16, 1852.

GENTLEMEN:—I have your invitation to participate as PALL-BEARER, on the occasion of solemnizing the obsequies of the late Honorable HENRY CLAY. I regret the event that has thrown the nation into mourning. I will take part, on the 20th instant, in paying respect to the illustrious deceased.

Respectfully, gentlemen,
Your obedient servant,
THOS. O'CONOR.

Aldermen WESLEY SMITH, WM. J. BRISLEY, JON. TROTTER, Committee.

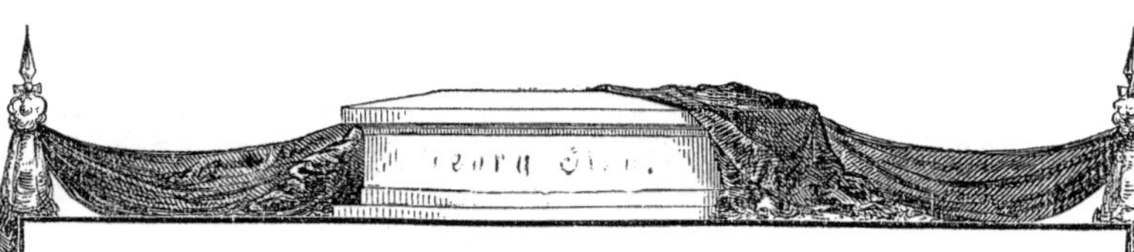

NEW YORK, JULY 19, 1852.

GENTLEMEN :—I have received the invitation with which you have favored me, to attend as a PALL-BEARER, in solemnizing the obsequies of the late HENRY CLAY, and accept h same.

I am, very respectfully,

Yours,

WM. B. ASTOR.

WESLEY SMITH, WM. J. BRISLEY, JON. TROTTER, Esq'rs., Committee.

FRANKLIN SQUARE, JULY 17, 1852.

GENTLEMEN :—I beg to acknowledge the receipt of your kind invitation of the 13th inst., to assist as PALL-BEARER in solemnizing the obsequies of the late Honorable HENRY CLAY, on the 20th inst., and to say, that I thankfully accept the same.

I remain, gentlemen,

Yours, respectfully,

JAMES HARPER.

Messrs. WESLEY SMITH, WM. J. BRISLEY, JON. TROTTER, Com. on Invitation.

NO. 22 BREVOORT PLACE.

GENTLEMEN :—I have just received your invitation to act as PALL-BEARER, on the 20th inst., in paying respect to the illustrious deceased, the Hon. HENRY CLAY.

With great respect,

I have the honor to be,

Yours, truly,

W. N. BLAKEMAN.

Messrs. WESLEY SMITH, WM. J. BRISLEY, JON. TROTTER, Committee.

67 Wall street, July 19, 1852.

Gentlemen:—Your note of the 13th, inviting me as Pall-Bearer, in solemnizing the obsequies of the late Hon. Henry Clay, owing to my absence from the city, did not reach me until Sunday evening. This is my apology for not having sooner answered your invitation.

In case you have not filled the place designed for me, I accept your kind invitation to participate in the mournful tribute of respect to the departed statesman. I will be in attendance.

Yours, respectfully,

ROBT. H. MORRIS.

Messrs. Wesley Smith, Wm. J. Brisley, Jon. Trotter, Committee.

GRAND LODGE OF THE STATE OF NEW YORK,

OF THE ANCIENT AND HONORABLE FRATERNITY OF FREE AND ACCEPTED MASONS.

The Grand Lodge was specially convened by the M. W. Grand Master, for the purpose of adopting suitable measures for rendering a tribute of respect to the memory of our late illustrious brother, the Hon. and M. W. Henry Clay. The Grand Lodge was opened in due form.

Rt. W. Joseph D. Evans, Deputy Grand Master, presiding, after stating the object of the meeting, in a few eloquent and feeling remarks, delivered the following address;

Brethren:—We have met in sadness! The principal object of this call for a special meeting of the Grand Lodge of the State of New York, is to consider what course we ought to pursue in giving honor to the memory

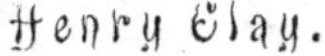

of our late illustrious brother, the Honorable, the Most Worshipful HENRY CLAY, one of the most distinguished men and finished orators the world ever knew.

We are called upon to mourn the loss of a great man, a finished gentleman, a beloved brother. We but sympathize with the whole world while deploring the death of HENRY CLAY. The magnitude and efficiency of his intellectual powers were not confined to the narrow limits of the Western Hemisphere; far, far over seas, and over land, extending to every clime, penetrating every country, city, town and hamlet, the power of his mighty intellect, and the benevolence of his magnanimous heart, will leave their influence so long as there is a responsive heart to beat a consonant note for national freedom and universal love.

As a statesman, he has a place upon one of the highest pinnacles of "Freedom's Temple." His nobleness of character has been the admiration of every man. His boldness in the cause he deemed just amazed his friends and astounded his opponents, and gave efficiency to his efforts.

As an orator he was surpassed by none, upon whatever rostrum he was placed, whether in the senate chamber, at the bar, or before the people; he held all who heard him, spell-bound by the rich intonations of his voice. His graceful attitude, his faultless gestures, his illumined countenance, and above all, his perfect *rhetoric;* no figure out of place, no imaginative thought but defined its aptitude without an explanation. Never, while indulging in those lofty flights of intellectual inspiration, did he collapse his wings and fall fluttering to the level of a common mind; always maintaining his position, he soared even higher and played with "fancy's gems," and "stooped to touch the loftiest thought."

As a Mason, he stood among us as a high and honorable brother—a Mason, good and true. No one among us could possess his heart and be otherwise. It is in this capacity he has so entwined himself around the Mason's heart. As a man and a statesman he commands our admiration. As a philanthropist and Mason he insures our veneration and love.

Initiated into the Order at twenty-two years of age, he continued an active and zealous Mason, and was elevated to the high position of Grand Master over the Ancient Free and Accepted Masons of Kentucky; since then he has given frequent instances of his firm attachment to the institution. He was not only an honorary member of one of the Lodges under this jurisdiction, but there are members of the craft, now present, who have in their possession evidences of his fondness for Masonry.

It is but a few years since, while on a visit to this city, he expressed a wish to see the BIBLE* on which the great WASHINGTON took the oath of office as President of the United States; that wish was gratified, under due and appropriate ceremonies. Although these manifestations of his veneration for the Order may be brought down to a very recent date, yet it could not be expected, in the nature of things, that he would continue to be what we term an active member of a Lodge.

The multiplicity of his engagements, public and private, which must necessarily have been heavy, forbade it. We were nevertheless bound to him, and he to us, by the Mystic Tie, and shall ever revere and cherish his name as one of the brightest ornaments of our Order, while there is a link of that chain remaining, which binds the brotherhood to-

* The property of St. Johns' Lodge, No. 1, of this city, of which HENRY CLAY was an honorary member.

gether with a sincere affection. And then too, he was an old man—this enunciation is startling. HENRY CLAY old! Could we realize the fact!—the silver cord was loosening, yet we saw no wavering of mind, no declension of intellectual vigor; but elastic, clear and firm to the last, the Godlike spirit struggled to sustain the frail, crumbling tenement which inclosed it. It is true he was beyond us in years, yet he seemed to grow with our growth, and to feel as we felt, so that we could not perceive that his majestic frame gave evidence of declining years.

Then, in speaking of him, we would call him *Henry* CLAY—*Harry* of the West—Mill *Boy*. These familiar expressions indicate a companionship which bring others upon a level with ourselves, and are used toward those who are younger, or of our own age, consequently we schooled ourselves to look upon him as one of us. Alas it is true, he was physically an old man—he was born in the midst of our revolutionary struggle, rocked in its cradle, and nurtured into manhood by the Goddess of Liberty. He was a brilliant link which bound the present generation to the birth of our National Independence.

He has gone! The crumbling tenement has fallen—the spirit is released. The voice which aroused a nation is hushed in death. His manly form lies mouldering in the silent tomb; but the soul, the immortal soul, has taken its everlasting flight and returned to the GOD who gave it, there to possess its beatific enjoyments. We have but his memory left. It shall flourish—fresh and perennial—its home, the heart of every true Mason.

At the close of the address, M. W. WM. H. MILNOR, Esq., P. G. M., offered the following preamble and resolutions, which were unanimously adopted :

Whereas, It has pleased the Supreme Architect, to call from his earthly labors, our illustrious brother HENRY CLAY, in a ripe old age, full of honors, and with mind unshaken, it is meet and proper, that we, his brethren, should render to his memory the tribute of our love. *We leave to others,* who, laying aside all party feeling, and forgetting all sectional difficulties, are clustering around his bier, to eulogize him as a statesman, wise and enlightened, a patriot, pure and incorruptible. We would, in humble submission to the Divine will, approach as Masons, and cast a chaplet upon his tomb, a tribute to his many virtues, as a brother of the Mystic Tie.

Distinguished for truthfulness of character which despised petty intrigue and deceit, for gentleness of deportment, which won the love of high and low—for charity of heart, which embraced all within its circle,—he lived a pure minded and consistent Mason, and leaves us a bright example of what a true Mason should be.

Resolved, That in fulfillment of these views, and as an expression of the regard which this Grand Lodge feels for our deceased brother, the Lodges within this jurisdiction be clothed in the emblems of mourning for ninety days.

Resolved, That we sympathize with the aged widow and family of our deceased brother, and trust that *that strength,* which cometh only from above, will be vouchsafed them.

Resolved, That a carefully engrossed copy of the address of the R. W. Deputy Grand Master, together with the preamble and resolutions, be sent to the family of our late brother HENRY CLAY.

At a subsequent meeting of the Grand Lodge, a communication was received from the Committee on Invitation, soliciting the Masonic fraternity to unite with the Common Council and the citizens of New York in solemnizing the obsequies of the illustrious deceased. Whereupon the following resolutions were adopted:

Resolved, That this Grand Lodge accept the invitation of the Committee of the Common Council, and will cordially participate in the obsequies on the 20th inst., in testimony of respect to the memory of our distinguished brother HENRY CLAY, and that the R. W. Grand Secretary be directed to communicate the same to the Committee of Arrangements of the Common Council.

Resolved, That a committee of ten be appointed, with power, to make every necessary arrangement for carrying the foregoing resolution into effect.

The Grand Lodge again assembled on the 20th, at one o'clock, when the procession was formed, in Masonic order, under direction of the Grand Marshal, R. W. WM. H. UNDERHILL, and his aids. The Grand officers appeared in full regalia, enshrouded with the emblems of mourning; the Officers of Lodges with their rich regalia and jewels, and the brethren clothed with white aprons and gloves; the whole presenting an imposing and beautiful appearance. The procession then moved, preceded by the Grand Lodge banner, which was heavily draped in mourning, and a very full and efficient band of music, to the position assigned them in the line, at the head of the civic bodies, and after passing through the whole route, returned to the Lodge room, when the Grand Lodge was closed in due form.

JOSEPH D. EVANS,
Deputy Grand Master.

JAMES W. POWELL, M. D.,
Grand Secretary.

NEW YORK STATE SOCIETY OF CINCINNATI.

GENTLEMEN:—The Cincinnati Society accepts your invitation to be present and unite with the Common Council and citizens of New York, in solemnizing the obsequies of the late Hon. HENRY CLAY, and I inclose you the order for assembling the members of the Society for the above purpose, which I have issued as their president.

I am, gentlemen,
Very respectfully,
Your ob't servant,
ANTHONY LAMB.

Messrs. WESLEY SMITH, WILLIAM J. BRISLEY, JON. TROTTER.

GENERAL ORDER, NEW YORK STATE SOCIETY OF CINCINNATI.—The Committee appointed by the Honorable the Common Council of this city, to make arrangements for solemnizing the obsequies of the late Hon. HENRY CLAY, on the 20th inst., have invited our Society to be present on that occasion, to unite with the Common Council and citizens of New York in this testimony of respect to the illustrious dead.

And, as it is our duty, as descendants of the patriots of the Revolution, to testify our respect for the memory of this illustrious statesman, who has rendered such important services to the nation; therefore,

The members of the Society will assemble at the City Hall, on Tuesday, the 20th inst., at 12 o'clock, with the usual badge of mourning, for the aforesaid purpose.

Gen. ANTHONY LAMB,
President.

EDWARD P. MARCELLIN, *Secretary.*

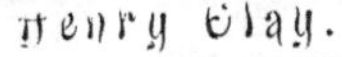

NEW YORK HISTORICAL SOCIETY.

MONTHLY MEETING.

The Hon. LUTHER BRADISH, President, in the chair.

Hon. J. W. BEEKMAN, in some brief and touching remarks, brought to the notice of the Society the death of the Hon. HENRY CLAY, an honorary member of this Society, and moved the appointment of a Committee to take suitable measures for testifying the sense of the members of the Society in regard to that melancholy event. The Chair appointed the following gentlemen as such committee: Hon. JAMES W. BEEKMAN, CHARLES KING, LL. D., and J. R. BRODHEAD, Esq.

At the next meeting, the Hon. JAMES W. BEEKMAN, from the Committee, appointed to prepare resolutions in memory of HENRY CLAY, a member of the New York Historical Society, in presenting their report, said:

Since the June meeting of the Society, death had stricken down several of the chiefest among its members. During the summer recess, HENRY CLAY has ceased from among men, and a name, which has long thrilled every American bosom with pride and love, has become a name of history.

What can I tell you of HENRY CLAY that is not already known by heart by us all?—of the man who had rather be right than be President; who, everywhere and under all circumstances, loved his country first and himself last; who grappled, at the very beginning of his public actions, in 1797, with that most unpopular, yet most important of subjects, negro slavery—exposing its evils, and, at every hazard to himself, striving to root it out of the soil of Kentucky;—who founded the Colonization Society, and never spared an effort to mitigate the hugest evil that threatens his country.

I might remind the Society of Mr. CLAY's successful efforts in the legislature of Kentucky, to preserve the Common Law to her courts of justice. An attempt, well nigh successful, was made to prohibit reference to any precedents of the British Reports in legal proceedings. Four-fifths of the Assembly wished Kentucky removed as far from Great Britain in jurisprudence as in geography. Mr. CLAY saw the importance of this outbreak of prejudice, and its danger to the Commonwealth, and turned the tide of ignorance and passion by his single might. His control over his auditory was most absolute and astonishing. Holding the rough backwoodsmen in rapt astonishment,—now bathing them in tears, and now convulsing them with laughter; and all about mere dry disquisitions on the Common Law. When he concluded, says an eye-witness, scarce a vestige of opposition remained.

The eloquence of CLAY was not merely the oratory of ancient Greece, that "swayed the fierce democracy at will;" but was as powerful in debate as before a popular assembly. On one occasion pre-eminently he measured weapons with WEBSTER. Both were in their prime. In 1824, the tariff was once more before Congress. CLAY advocated amendments which WEBSTER opposed. Then were wars such as giants wage. The eloquence of WEBSTER was described as the majestic roar of a strong and steady blast, pealing through the forest; but that of CLAY was like the tones of a celestial harp,—sometimes thrilled as by angel's fingers, and swept anon as by the furies of the storm. Mr. WEBSTER was defeated, and, by the close vote of 107 to 102,

Clay vindicated his American System, and established it as the policy of the country for many years.

Twice Mr. Clay, under Providence, was the means of averting dire calamities. Once in 1821, he accompanied the Missouri Compromise, with such personal toil and anxiety as well nigh cost his life. Again, in 1850, when the series of national measures, which great men of all parties in Congress labored to accomplish, were on the anvil, Henry Clay was foremost in the work. Here he laid down his life; for it is not too much to say that in his old age the night long labors of the forum wore him out. Striving for his country, compromising every thing but honor for her good, he fell;—not the less glorious because he fell—not on the battle field, but on that intellectual arena where Americans decide the destiny of their nation by the contest of minds, as they remedy their grievances by the arbitrament of the ballot-box. To the statesman, far more fitly than to the warrior, apply the Roman words:

"Dulce et decorum est pro patria mori."

On behalf of the committee charged with that duty, I respectfully submit for adoption by the Society, the following resolutions:

Resolved, That while the whole people of the United States mourn the death of Henry Clay as a national bereavement, the New York Historical Society laments it as the loss of one of its most honored members.

Resolved, That the life of Henry Clay, the orator, the advocate, the ambassador, the statesman, ever devoted to his country's service, and shortened by his ardent labors in times of her extremity, presents, for imitation in after days, a rare pattern of lofty intellect and a noble heart.

Resolved, That although the State of New York might well adopt the words of one of her own eminent sons, "I envy Kentucky, for when HE dies she will have his ashes;" the memory of CLAY and the record of his great deeds are of the world, and his fame finds its materials in the archives of universal history.

Resolved, That a copy of these resolutions, duly attested by the seal of the Society, and signed by the President and Secretary, be transmitted to the family of the deceased.

Rev. F. L. HAWKS, D.D., LL. D., said, he was unwilling that the question should be taken without saying a few words; and he did so, not in the hope that he could add anything to the reputation of the illustrious HENRY CLAY, but because he knew him intimately, and bore many recollections which endeared his memory. He was, indeed, a wonderful man. His extraordinary power of eloquence, was natural; it resulted from the strong feelings of a warm and honest heart. This was the secret of the hold he possessed over those who knew him. He ever had their affection. He had said that he could not add to the glory of his name; but there was one feature in his character to which he might properly call the notice of Americans. There were those in other lands who asserted, and were willing to believe, that religious feeling was eminently defective in this country, and they would improve it by introducing the system existing among themselves, of making religion rest upon legislative enactments, more than upon our reason and honest convictions. Now, he believed that our fathers who emigrated hither, were at least as religious as any equal number they left behind them; they laid their foundations in religion—it was the basis of their subsequent prosperity. This religious feeling exercised a large influence, and was the cause of the order which prevailed, generally, in this country, shown in the quiet submission to law, and acquiescence in the will of the majority. Occasional outbreaks among twenty-three millions of people, were of course to be expected, but they certainly furnished exceptions to the rule, not the rule itself. He would illustrate by a single historical fact. Upon our acquisition of territory on the shores of the Pacific, they could remember how quickly people from all parts of the Union hastened to the new found El Dorado. Many of these came from parts of the country widely separate, and were different in manners—knowing nothing of each other, but this, that they had the privilege of being Americans, and under a free constitution. In an incredibly short time, before the general government could interpose to furnish them, they formed a plan of government for themselves—moved thereto by the habits of order in which they had been trained, (and religious habits were at the bottom of it) they formed a constitution, and established order. Now, take an equal number of men of any other part of the earth, and place them under such circumstances, and he felt assured that anarchy and confusion would have been the result. This fact showed that they possessed sufficient religious feeling to know that GOD willed order, and they acted on it. Now, the feature to which he had alluded, was the religious close of Mr. CLAY's life. Here was one of our greatest statesmen—one who guided public opinion in a large degree—one over whom his countrymen literally wept, and who, was perhaps more personally beloved than any other servant of the republic; and what was the closing scene? Why, as his mind ran over the events of his honored and useful life, bright as they were, he could but feel that the last was the brightest. He died as a Christian; and America could say of this one of her noblest sons, that he had so lived that his country could honor him, and so died, that selfishness only could regret his departure to happiness.

Rev. Dr. VAN PELT also, in a few eloquent remarks, alluded to the character, virtues, and especially to the religious feelings of the illustrious deceased.

SOCIETY OF CINCINNATI, MASS.

A meeting of the MASSACHUSETTS' STATE SOCIETY OF CINCINNATI, was convened for the purpose of expressing their sympathy for the loss the nation had sustained in the death of HENRY CLAY, and of manifesting their high appreciation of the character of the honorable deceased. After the object of the meeting being stated by the President, it was voted that FRANKLIN PIERCE, CHARLES S. DAVIES and Col. SECOR, be a committee to report resolutions on the death of HENRY CLAY.

The Committee, by their Chairman, after a beautiful speech from Gen. PIERCE, on the resolutions, made their report.

Resolved, That the Society of the Cincinnati of Massachusetts, in common with the people of this entire country, deeply deplore the death of the Hon. HENRY CLAY, and that as in life, his brilliant genius and ardent patriotism have commanded universal admiration, so in death, the grateful memory of his eminent services in the councils of the nation, for almost half of a century, will be sacredly cherished while the Union shall endure.

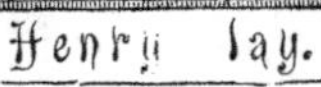

Resolved, That the foregoing resolution be forwarded by the President to the widow of the great statesman and patriot, with the Society's sincerest sympathy.

ADAMS BAILEY, *Secretary*.

TO THE CITIZENS OF HOBOKEN.

Whereas, By the dispensation of an all-wise Providence, the greatest statesman, the purest patriot and the most eloquent civilian of the age, who by his devoted services for more than half a century has endeared himself to the people, and commands the admiration of the world, was removed from our midst on the 29th of June last, and

Whereas, We deeply sympathize with the great Whig party of the United States, under the irreparable loss it has sustained by the death of its illustrious advocate, the Hon. HENRY CLAY, whose public obsequies have been arranged to take place in the city of New York, on Tuesday, the 20th inst.; therefore, be it

Resolved, That we condole with our fellow-citizens, under this great affliction, and earnestly request that, as far as practicable, they close their places of business, and suspend their labors on that day, and also drape their houses and public buildings in mourning.

Resolved, That cannon be fired every five minutes during the movement of the procession, in Hoboken, and the church bells be tolled for two hours.

Resolved, That the members of the Committee wear crape on the left arm for two weeks, as a token of respect; and that they will meet at the Town Hall, (except they are engaged with the military,) one hour before the time arranged for the formation of the line, with those of our citizens who wish to join in the *cortege*. Also,

Resolved, That we cordially invite all our citizens, without distinction of party, to meet with us at the time and place designated, and assist us in paying a last tribute to departed worth.

Whig Executive Committee.

ISAAC V. BROWER, HAZELTON WALKLY,
DAVID M. DEMAREST, JAMES STEVENSON,
WILLIAM MITCHELL.

JOHN M. BOARD, *Chairman.*

JOHN W. VAN BOSKERCK, *Secretary.*

FIRE DEPARTMENT.

Special meeting of Engineers and Foremen, held at Firemen's Hall, on Thursday evening, July 15th, 1852, ALFRED CARSON, Esq., Chief Engineer, in the chair. Roll called, and ninety-one officers present.

The chairman having stated that he had called the meeting for the purpose of laying before them the joint resolution, as passed the Common Council of the city of New York, extending an invitation to the Fire Department to participate in the funeral obsequies to the late Hon. HENRY CLAY.

On motion, the invitation was accepted, and the Chief and Assistant Engineers were appointed a committee to make the necessary arrangements.

ALFRED CARSON, *Chief Engineer.*

JESSE THOMAS, *Secretary.*

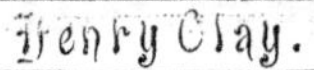

I.O. OF O.F.

CITY OF NEW YORK, JULY 17th, 1852.

GENTLEMEN :—Your invitation, on the part of the Honorable the Common Council, addressed to the Grand Lodge of Southern New York, to unite with the citizens of New York, in solemnizing the obsequies of the late Hon. HENRY CLAY, and paying a last testimony of respect to the illustrious deceased, was received on Thursday, the 15th inst. A special meeting of the G. L. was convened last evening, and after a full interchange of opinion between its members, it was generally concurred in, that owing to the short time allowed for the necessary arrangements, together with the engagements entered into by many of its members to turn out with other bodies, it would be impossible to get a sufficient number of the members together, to make our turn-out, a "testimony of respect." Under these circumstances, the Grand Lodge has no alternative, though it is with the deepest regret, but most respectfully decline the invitation so kindly tendered.

Yours respectfully,

JOHN J. DAVIES, *Grand Secretary.*

AMERICAN INSTITUTE.

At a regular meeting of the American Institute, the following resolutions were unanimously adopted :

Resolved, That the members of the American Institute have heard of the death of the Hon. HENRY CLAY, of Kentucky, with feelings of the deepest regret, and desire to unite their sympathies with their countrymen throughout

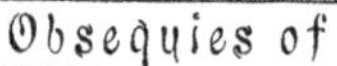

the Union, in deploring the loss our most eminent statesman.

Resolved, That it is peculiarly appropriate for the American Institute, an association formed for the purpose of promoting national industry, to cherish the memory of the great champion of the American System.

Resolved, That the members of this Institute remember, with feelings of gratification, the early visits to, and the deep interest manifested by Mr. CLAY, in the welfare of this association, of which he was one of the oldest honorary members, and desire on this occasion to express their heart-felt testimony to the long continued public services; the purity of the motives, and the exalted patriotism which distinguished the life and career of the departed senator.

Resolved, That a copy of these resolutions be forwarded to the family of Mr. CLAY.

ROBERT LOVETT, *Vice President.*

HENRY MEIGS, *Recording Secretary.*

NEW YORK TYPOGRAPHICAL SOCIETY.

At a regular meeting of this Society, the following preamble and resolutions were adopted:

Whereas, Our country has been bereft of one of her purest patriots and wisest statesmen, in the loss of HENRY CLAY, whose name and history are so dear and sacred to us all; therefore,

Resolved, That the members of the New York Typographical Society would mournfully mingle their feelings of sorrow with their fellow-citizens throughout the Union, and attest their sense of respect for the illustrious dead, by placing upon their records this mark of esteem for the

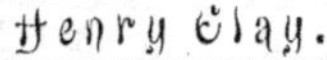

memory of him who "knew no north, no south, no east, no west," nothing but his country.

Resolved, That a copy of the foregoing resolutions be transmitted to the family of the lamented deceased.

DANIEL GODWIN, *President pro tem.*

E. M. SKIDMORE, *Secretary.*

ORDER OF UNITED AMERICANS.

The Grand Chancery of the Order of United Americans was called together by the Grand Sachem, to make the necessary arrangements for participating in the solemnities of the 20th of July.

The G. C. of the C. then read the following communication from the Grand Sachem:

NEW YORK, JULY 12, 1852.

To the Honorable the Chancery, State of New York:

It has become my painful duty to inform you, officially, of the death of one of our country's most distinguished and honored sons, the better portion of whose life has been devoted to her service, and the loss of whom our common country mourns as truly a national calamity.

HENRY CLAY is dead!

He closed his active and eventful life at the city of Washington, on Tuesday, the 29th day of June last. His remains, in charge of a Congressional Committee, passed through our city to its final resting-place, at Ashland, and rested here, at the Governor's Room, City Hall, on the anniversary of our national birthday.

The Common Council of our city have resolved to perform the obsequies to his memory by a military and civic procession, on the 20th of the present month, as a fitting testimonial of the love and respect of a free people for the memory of one of such exalted patriotism, and who has rendered our country such distinguished and valuable service. I make this official announcement, trusting that your honorable body will take such measures for the participation by our patriotic Order in the solemnities of that occasion, as in your wisdom may seem proper.

W. W. OSBORN, *Grand Sachem.*

After the communication was read, it was

Resolved, That this Chancery will unite, in its official capacity, with the Common Council and our fellow-citizens in the obsequies to the late HENRY CLAY, and that the several Chapters, under this jurisdiction, and our brethren of other States, be invited to join with us on that occasion.

NEW YORK, JULY 15th, 1852.

DEAR SIR :—The Order of United Americans having appointed a committee to make arrangements for uniting with the Honorable the Common Council in obsequies to the honor of the late HENRY CLAY, I have the honor to solicit from your Committee the usual place assigned to our order on previous occasions of this nature, in the line of procession.

Our number will probably amount to about two thousand men, making all allowance for those that may be drawn off in the ranks of the military and fire department.

Your ob't servant,

THOS. R. WHITNEY,

Chairman Com. of Arrangements.

Alderman WILLIAM M. TWEED.

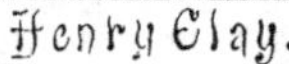

NATIONAL ACADEMY OF DESIGN.

GENTLEMEN :—I have the honor to inform you, that at a special meeting of our academicians, associates, honorary members and students, and of the artists generally, the national bereavement in the decease of that eminent and beloved statesman and citizen, the Hon. HENRY CLAY, was communicated, and resolutions were entered upon our journals, expressive of an exalted admiration of his matchless genius; of our gratitude for his long and unrivalled public services, and of an earnest sympathy with the sorrowing millions of our countrymen.

We subsequently united with the Common Council and the people of our city, in the last tribute of respect to the illustrious dead.

Your obedient servant,
T. ADDISON RICHARDS,
Cor. Secretary, N. A.

To the Committee of Arrangements on the obsequies of the late HENRY CLAY.

NEW YORK, JULY 14th, 1852.

GENTLEMEN :—I am instructed by the Clay Festival Association, to notify your Honorable Body, that the Association intend to take part and participate in the ceremonies of the 20th inst.

Please to communicate, if convenient, what position, or place, will be designated for the Association in the procession.

Respectfully, your ob't servant,
M. R. BREWER, *President.*

To the Committee of Arrangements.

NEWBURG, JULY 15, 1852.

DEAR SIR:—Having seen by the papers that you intend to honor the memory of the illustrious HENRY CLAY, by a funeral procession, in your city, on the 20th inst. A meeting of the Clay Club was called for last evening, at the Orange Hotel, for the purpose of making suitable arrangements to participate in the honor of paying respect to the greatest of statesmen. Among other proceedings the following was had:

Resolved, That the Clay Club, of Newburg, attend the funeral obsequies of the Hon. HENRY CLAY, on Tuesday next, and that the Chairman be requested to communicate with the Chairman of the Board of Aldermen, informing him of the passage of the resolution, and also requesting a place in the procession on that mournful occasion.

I am, with great respect,
Yours, &c.,
R. D. KEMP, *Chairman*.

R. T. COMPTON, Esq., President Board of Aldermen.

PORT WARDENS' OFFICE,
JULY 15, 1852.

GENTLEMEN:—I have the honor herewith to hand you a copy of the minutes of the Board of Port Wardens, and also to acknowledge the receipt of your polite note of the 14th inst.

Very respectfully,
Your ob'dt servant,
W. W. STORY, *Master Warden*.

Messrs. WESLEY SMITH, WM. J. BRISLEY, JNO. TROTTER, Committee.

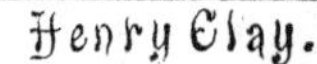

PORT WARDENS' OFFICE,
JULY 15, 1852.

Resolved, That this Board, entertaining the highest regard for the great public services of the late Hon. HENRY CLAY, will unite with the Honorable the Common Council, in testifying their respect to his memory, and will attend in a body on the 20th inst.

Resolved, That a copy of the above resolution be furnished the Committee of Arrangements, signed by the Master Warden and Clerk of this Board.

[Copy of minutes.]

W. W. STORY, *Master Warden.*

ROBERT T. NORRIS, *Clerk.*

CADETS OF TEMPERANCE.

NEW YORK, JULY 14, 1852.

GENTLEMEN:—In accordance with your request, the Mount Vernon Section, No. 1, Cadets of Temperance, of this city, herewith express to you their wish to unite in the ceremonies of the obsequies of the late Hon. HENRY CLAY, to be held on the 20th inst. We presume our position in the line will be noticed in the programme of the day.

Yours, very respectfully,

JOSEPH T. REED,
Chairman Com. of Arrangements.

To the Special Committee of the Common Council
on the obsequies of Honorable HENRY CLAY.

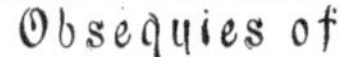

MECHANICS' SECTION, No. 2.

NEW YORK, JULY 17, 1852.

In accordance with the request of the Special Committee of the Common Council, the Mechanics' Section, No. 2, of the Order of Cadets of Temperance, of the State of New York, hereby give notice of their wish to participate in the funeral obsequies of the late Hon. HENRY CLAY, on Tuesday next, and that they wish to be assigned a place in the line with Mount Vernon Section, No. 1, Cadets of Temperance.

Respectfully,

CHARLES PAYNTON,

Chairman.

To the Committee of Arrangements, funeral obsequies of HENRY CLAY.

YOUNG MEN'S DEBATING SOCIETY.

The Young Men's Debating Society of the city of New York, most respectfully notify your honorable Committee that we have made all the necessary preparations, and desire joining in the mournful pageant on the 20th inst.

Therefore, any position which you may be pleased to assign us in the procession, will be gratefully acceded to.

Yours, most respectfully,

THOMAS J. MUNDAY,

Chairman of Committee of Arrangements.

To Committee on Civic Societies and Associations.

Your Committee embrace this opportunity of tendering their sincere acknowledgments to the officers and members of the First Division, New York State Militia, also, to the officers and members of the various companies from adjacent cities, for their prompt and efficient services upon this melancholy occasion. This great arm of protection to our national institutions paraded in such immense numbers, as at once to establish their high appreciation of the character of the illustrious deceased, and to command the gratitude of the Common Council of New York, and the admiration of the whole country.

The following orders of the various companies, were laid before the Committee, from the

MILITARY DEPARTMENT.

First Division, New York State Militia.

DIVISION ORDERS.

New York, July 15th, 1852.

This Division will parade on Tuesday next, the 20th of July instant, for the purpose of uniting with the public authorities and our fellow-citizens, in rendering funeral honors to the late lamented Henry Clay.

The Division line will be formed on Broadway, the left resting on Chambers street, at half-past 2 o'clock, p. m., precisely.

Brigadier General Spicer will detail a suitable detachment from his command, to fire minute-guns from the Battery during the procession, and will make requisition upon the Commissary General for the necessary ammunition.

Brigadier General Hall will direct a troop of horse for escort duty, to report to the Major General, at his quarters, at two o'clock ; and a troop of horse for guard duty, to the Division Inspector, upon the Parade ground, at the same hour.

Broadway, from Chambers street to Astor place, is designated as the Parade ground of the Division, from two o'clock, P. M. until the commencement of the procession.

Commandants of Regiments will send their standard and camp colors to the City Hall, on Monday next, at eight o'clock, A. M., to be draped with appropriate emblems of mourning, under the direction of the Committee of Arrangements.

Officers will wear the usual badges of mourning upon their left arm and sword-hilt.

The Division Staff will assemble at the quarters of the Major General, at two o'clock, P. M.

Commandants of Brigades, Regiments and Companies, are directed to report, and return to court martial, the names of any officers, non-commissioned officers, or privates, who may leave the ranks during the parade, without the permission of their officers.

By order of

CHAS. W. SANDFORD,
Maj. Gen. Commanding.

R. C. Wetmore, *Division Inspector.*

First Brigade, New York State Militia.

BRIGADE ORDERS.

NEW YORK, JULY 15th, 1852.

The foregoing Division orders are promulgated for the information and government of this Brigade, and, in compliance therewith,

This Brigade will parade on Tuesday next, the 20th July, inst., for the purpose of rendering funeral honors to the late Hon. HENRY CLAY.

The Brigade line will be formed on the Fifth avenue, right on Washington Parade ground, at half past one o'clock, P. M., precisely.

The Veteran Corps of Artillery, Capt. Raynor, is hereby detailed to fire minute-guns from the Battery during the procession. Capt. Raynor will make requisition on the Commissary General for the necessary ammunition.

The Brigade Staff will assemble at the quarters of the Brigadier General, at one o'clock, precisely.

By order of

CHARLES B. SPICER,

Brigadier General.

C. H. SMITH, *Acting Brigade Maj.*

Third Brigade, New York State Militia.

BRIGADE ORDERS.

NEW YORK, JULY 14th, 1852.

This Brigade will parade in full uniform, in compliance with the above Division order. The line will be formed at 2 o'clock, P. M., precisely, on Broadway, east side, right resting on Walker street. The Staff will meet at the General's quarters, at quarter before 2 o'clock, P. M.

By order,

WILLIAM HALL,
Brigadier General.

Fourth Brigade, New York State Militia.

BRIGADE ORDERS.

NEW YORK, JULY 15th, 1852.

Pursuant to Division orders of this date, this Brigade will parade on Tuesday next, the 20th of July, instant, for the purpose of uniting with the public authorities and our fellow-citizens, in rendering funeral honors to the lamented HENRY CLAY.

The Brigade line will be formed on Broadway, the left on Chambers street, at two o'clock, P. M.

Commandants of Regiments will send their standards and camp colors to the City Hall, on Monday next, at 8 o'clock, A. M., to be dressed in mourning.

Officers will wear the usual badges of mourning upon their left arm and sword hilt.

Henry Clay.

The Brigade Staff will assemble at the quarters of the Brigadier General, at half-past one o'clock, P. M.

Commandants of Regiments and Companies are directed to report, and return to court martial, the names of any officers, non-commissioned officers, or privates, who may leave the ranks during the parade, without the permission of their officers.

By order of

JOHN EWEN,

Brig. Gen. Commanding.

E. J. HAWLEY, *Act. Aid-de-Camp.*

Third Regiment, New York State Militia.

REGIMENTAL ORDER.

NEW YORK, JULY 16th, 1852.

In compliance with Division and Brigade orders, this Regiment will parade, mounted, and in full uniform, on Tuesday, the 20th inst., at one o'clock, P. M., to participate in the funeral solemnities of the late Hon. HENRY CLAY.

The line will be formed on Fifth avenue, left on Fifteenth street.

The usual badges of mourning, will be worn. Troops will join in squadrons, at half-past one o'clock.

By order of

WILLIAM MENCK,

Lieut. Col. Com.

H. H. GUNTER, *Adjutant.*

E. LYON, *Serg. Major.*

Fourth Regiment, New York State Militia.

REGIMENTAL ORDER.

NEW YORK, JULY 16th, 1852.

Pursuant to Division and Brigade orders, this Regiment will parade as Cavalry and Light Artillery, (Artillery in white pantaloons,) on Tuesday, the 20th July, instant.

The line will be formed in Broadway, opposite Union square, left on Fifteenth street, at 1 o'clock, P. M.

Officers will wear the usual badges of mourning on the left arm and sword hilt.

By order of

CHAS. YATES, *Colonel.*

N. COLES, *Adjutant.*

H. SMITH, *Serg. Major.*

Sixth Regiment, New York State Militia.

REGIMENTAL ORDER.

NEW YORK, JULY 15th, 1852.

The Brigade orders are hereby promulgated for the information and government of this command.

It is becoming in citizens of all classes and professions to mourn the loss of a great and good man, especially one so highly esteemed, and possessing so thoroughly the respect and admiration of his countrymen, as HENRY CLAY. The authorities of our city having appointed Tuesday, the 20th inst., to do honor to the memory of the illustrious deceased; for the purpose of joining the solemnities of this mournful occasion, pursuant to Division and Brigade orders, this Regiment will parade on that day, fully uniformed and equipped—white pants (without knapsack,) and with the usual badge of mourning. Line will be formed in Broome street, right on Crosby, at half-past one o'clock, P. M. Commandants of companies will report their respective commands to the Adjutant fifteen minutes previous to that time, also the non-commissioned staff. The band, color-bearer and general guides will report to Captain Gregory, at the Mercer House, at a quarter before one o'clock, P. M.

Field and Staff will report to the commanding officer, on the Parade ground, at quarter past one o'clock, P. M.

By order of

JOHN G. WELLSTOOD,

Lieut. Col. Comd'g.

WM. CHALMERS, *Adjutant.*

Twelfth Regiment, New York State Militia.

REGIMENTAL ORDER.

NEW YORK, JULY, 16th, 1852.

The above Brigade orders are promulgated for the use of the Regiment.

In obedience, the regiment will assemble in Chambers street, right resting on West Broadway, on Tuesday next, the 20th inst., fully armed and equipped, at half-past one o'clock, P. M., at which hour the regimental line will be formed.

Adjutant Stearns will see that the standards and camp

colors of the regiment are sent to the City Hall, on Monday morning next, at 8 o'clock, to be draped in mourning.

The Court of Appeals, for the above parade, will be held at the Mercer House, on 29th of August next, at 8 o'clock, P. M. Commandants of companies will make their returns within ten days after the parade.

By order of

H. G. STEBBINS, *Colonel.*

CORNELIUS CARNES, *Serg. Major.*

Board of Marshals,

NEW YORK, JULY 16th, 1852.

At a meeting of the Board of Marshals for the funer al obsequies of the late Hon. HENRY CLAY, held at the Mayor's office on the evening of the 15th, the following bill of dress was adopted :

Black coat and pants, with white vest.

Chapeau, without ornament, trimmed with crape.

Scarf—black satin, trimmed with crape.

Crape knot on left arm.

Dress sword, scabbard covered with black velvet, and hilt with crape mourning knot.

Black body-belt worn over the coat.

Light spurs.

Black saddle cloth, trimmed with deep fringe, and cord festooned in front.

Russet bridle, with black fringe, and crape knot on the foretop and nose piece.

Black kid gloves.

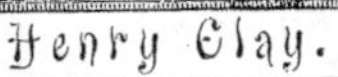

Baton—white, with gilt balls on the ends, trimmed with black crape.

The following articles will be furnished by the Committee of the Common Council.

The scarf, gloves, sword mountings and baton. The use of horse equipments and chapeaux.

Marshals will send their swords, for mounting, to Child & Wemmell, 31 Park row, immediately on receipt of this order.

They will also order their chapeaux from Mr. Ira Todd, 178 Broadway.

Horse equipments will be procured of C. Francis, 39 Bowery.

Marshals wishing to use their own saddles and chapeaux will cause the saddles to be sent immediately to Mr. Francis, to have the saddle-cloth fitted; and their chapeaux to Child & Wemmell to be draped.

The chapeaux and horse equipments that are furnished, will be returned as soon as convenient, after the parade.

A meeting of the marshals will be held at the Mayor's office, on Monday, 19th inst., at half-past 7 o'clock, P. M.

WILLIAM HALL,
Grand Marshal.

JAMES F. HALL, *Secretary.*

MONDAY EVENING, JULY 19th, 1852.

The Board of Marshals met at the Mayor's office, pursuant to previous notice; the Grand Marshal in the chair.

The minutes of the previous meeting were read and approved.

The Grand Marshal stated the regulations for the parade, and assigned the Aids their respective divisions.

Adjourned to meet at the Grand Marshal's quarters, No. 16 White street, at half-past one o'clock, P. M., tomorrow.

WILLIAM HALL,
Grand Marshal.

JAMES F. HALL, *Secretary.*

OBSEQUIES OF THE LATE HON. HENRY CLAY.

MARSHAL'S ORDER.

NEW YORK, JULY 20th, 1852.

The different orders, societies, associations, &c., intending to participate in the ceremonies of the day, will report to the Aids of the Grand Marshal, on the right of the respective divisions, at a quarter-past two o'clock, P. M., precisely. Columns will form, six abreast, march in close order. Marshals will cause this order to be strictly enforced. The aids will assemble at the Grand Marshal's quarters, No. 16 White street, at half-past one o'clock, P. M.

By order,

WILLIAM HALL,
Grand Marshal.

JOHN W. AVERY, *Aid.*

The various sub-committees having completed their arrangements, and every thing now being in entire readiness for solemnizing the obsequies in a manner comporting with the character and standing of the deceased, and commensurate with the wealth and dignity of this city, the Committee on Programme, assisted by the Grand Marshal, reported the following

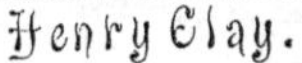

PROGRAMME OF ARRANGEMENTS

FOR THE

FUNERAL CEREMONIES

IN HONOR OF THE LATE

HON. HENRY CLAY.

The Joint Committee, appointed by the Common Council of the city of New York, to make the necessary arrangements for solemnizing the obsequies of the lamented HENRY CLAY, have adopted the following Programme of Arrangements for the occasion.

GENERAL WILLIAM HALL

HAS BEEN UNANIMOUSLY SELECTED AS

Grand Marshal

Of the day, who has appointed the following gentlemen as his Aids.

WM. L. MORRIS,
JOHN W. AVERY,
JOHN J. CISCO,
FREEMAN CAMPBELL,
MEDAD PLATT,
J. B. MONTGOMERY,
A. A. BREMNER,
JAMES F. HALL,
SAMUEL OSGOOD,
WM. T. CHILD,
JOHN A. BUNTING,
WM. L. MORRIS, Jr.,
WM. B. DINSMORE,
CLARKSON CROLIUS,
G. H. STRIKER,
SAMUEL ROGERS,
HENRY B. COOK,
J. J. KELLY,
ELIJAH F. PURDY,
ROBERT SMITH,
WILLIAM DODGE,
J. C. BURNHAM,
JAMES CONNER,
ADAM P. PENTZ,
JOHN W. STYLES,
ROBERT B. BOYD,
JOHN T. OGDEN,
ERASTUS GROVER,
WM. H. UNDERHILL,
SYLVANUS S. WARD,
Dr. H. F. QUACKENBOSS,
RUFUS E. CRANE,
JAMES ACKERMAN,
G. H. LYNCH,
JORDAN MOTT,
R. H. SHANNON.

The procession will move from the Park, at 3 P. M., precisely, and will proceed down Broadway, around the Park to Chatham street, through Chatham street to the Bowery, up the Bowery and Fourth avenue to Union square; around Union square to Broadway, and down Broadway to the Park, in front of the City Hall, on passing which point each division will be under the orders of its respective Marshal.

The solemnities at the Hall, at the close of the procession, will be as follows:

1. Prayer by the Rev. Dr. JOHN M. KREBS.
2. Funeral Oration, by N. B. BLUNT, Esq.
3. Benediction by the Rev. Dr. BENJAMIN J. HAIGHT.

The arrangements of the day will be under the command of the Grand Marshal.

The several persons having charge of the church and fire alarm bells in the city, are requested to cause the same to be tolled, from the hour of 3 o'clock, P. M., until the close of the procession.

The owners and masters of vessels in the harbor, and the proprietors of the various public buildings in the city, are requested to display their colors at half mast, from sunrise to sunset.

It is also respectfully requested, that our fellow-citizens close their several places of business during the moving of the procession.

They are also requested, whether in the procession or not, to wear the usual badge of mourning on the left arm.

The several orders, societies, associations, trades, and other bodies, are requested to assemble at such places as they may respectively select, and repair to the places of rendezvous, by 2 o'clock, P. M.

The different divisions, in the following programme, will be designated by a white banner, with the appropriate number of each in black.

ORDER OF PROCESSION.

First Division.

TROOP OF CAVALRY, as escort to the Grand Marshal,
Under command of Capt. JOSHUA A. VARIAN.

Band.

GENERAL WILLIAM HALL,
GRAND MARSHAL.

Col. JOHN W. AVERY,	Col. WILLIAM DODGE,
Major JAMES CONNER,	FREEMAN CAMPBELL, Esq.,
JOHN J. CISCO, Esq.,	JAMES F. HALL, Esq.

SPECIAL AIDS.

First Division, New York State Militia.

Including the Military Corps from other cities, and the whole under the command of

MAJOR GENERAL CHARLES W. SANDFORD,

As a military escort, in reverse order.

STAFF.

Division Inspector.........Colonel WETMORE.
Division Judge Advocate....Colonel WARD.

Division Engineer..........Colonel MORELL.
Division Quartermaster.....Lieut. Colonel SANDFORD.
Division Paymaster.........Major BIBBY.
Aid-de-Camps ....Majors TOMES and SCHENCK.
Volunteer do ....Majors RICHARDS and KANE.
Division Hospital Surgeon..Dr. L. A. SAYRE.
Division Assistant do. ..Dr. WOODWARD.

THE HUDSON BRIGADE OF HOBOKEN,

Under the command of General E. V. R. WRIGHT.

Aid-de-Camp........Major HARRISON,
Wash'n Volunteers..Capt. SPEAR,
Wright Rifles....... " RILEY,
Jer. City Continentals " POLLARD,
Highwood Guard......Capt. BROWER,
National Guard....... " TUTHILL,
Hoboken Rifles........ " NEIMAN,
Washington Blues..... " HARRIS.

FOURTH BRIGADE,

Commanded by Brigadier General JOHN EWEN.

Brigade Major......ROBERT TAYLOR,
Judge Advocate.....N. B. LA BAU.
Aid-de-Camp........E. LE GAL,
Quartermaster.........H. EAGLE,
Paymaster............G. A. SMITH,
Engineer..............E. J. HAWLEY,
Volunteer Aid-de-Camp........JOHN H. ABRAHAM.

Band.

SIXTY-NINTH REGIMENT.

Colonel.........CHARLES S. ROE,
Lieut. Colonel..MICHAEL DOHENY,
Major..........JAMES C. MCBIRNEY,
Quartermaster..J. C. O'BYRNE,
Assis't Surgeon..W. M. GILES,
Company A.....Captain LEONARD,
" B..... " NEWMAN,
Company C...... Captain MCCOURT,
" D....... " TOBIN,
" E....... " RYAN,
" F....... " GORMAN,
" G....... " GREEN,
" H....... " JUDGE,
" I........ " COAKLEY,
Company K..............Captain HINCHMAN.

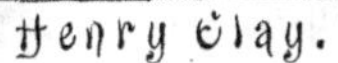

Band.

TWELFTH REGIMENT.

Colonel..........HENRY G. STEBBINS,
Lieut. Colonel...E. B. HART,
Adjutant.........J. B. STEARNS,
Paymaster.......F. W. COOLIDGE,
Quartermaster ...T. C. FIELDS,
Surgeon..........A. BURDETT,
Engineer.........J. LIVINGSTON,
Chaplain.........J. T. DALY,
Sergeant Major..C. CARNES,

Light Guard*.....Capt. VINCENT,
Garde Lafayette.. " LECLERC,
Independ. Guards. " CAIRNS,
Lafay'e Fusileers.. " FRENCH,
Baxter Blues...... " WATERBURY,
City Blues........ " JOHNSON,
City Musketeers.. " PALMER,
Tompkins Blues... " BESSON,
Baxter Guard..... " DYCKMAN,

New York Riflemen................Captain JOHNSON.

* This Company paraded as Guard of Honor to the funeral car.

Band.

ELEVENTH REGIMENT.

Lieut. Colonel..JAS. H. WATERHOUSE,
Major ....D. C. HYDE,
Adjutant ....S. R. PINCKNEY,
Paymaster.......KEYSER,
Surgeon.........DR. VAN CORT,
Engineer........H. ROBINSON,
Chaplain........STEWART,
City Guards.....Captain MCARDLE,

Continentals......Capt. HELM,
Irish Am. Guards.. " BRADY,
Montgomery " .. " MURPHY,
City Rifles........ " TANGIER,
Wash'ton Guards.. " RINGHAUSEN,
State Rifles....... " VAN VULTY,
National Riflemen. " ELLIS,
Brigade Lancers... " CLANCEY.

Band.

TENTH REGIMENT.

Colonel.............W. HALSEY,
Lieut. Colonel......THOMAS JONES,
Major ....G. J. SMITH,
Adjutant............HENRY A. SMITH,
Paymaster...........E. M. DODGE,
Quartermaster ......THOS. E. SMITH,
Company A.........Capt. W. HUSEN,

Company B.........Capt. JACHRLING,
" C......... " FANTH,
" D.........Lieut. WILLETS,
" E.........Capt. MCGRATH,
" F......... " DODGE,
" G......... " WARREN,
" H........ " BECHER,

Artillery—National Grays..................Capt. RAYNOR.

THIRD BRIGADE,

Commanded by Col. B. C. Ferris.

Act'g Brigade Maj. Geo. W. Smith,
Surgeon.......... H. J. Quackenboss,
Judge Advocate... J. J. Lerocque,
Engineer.......... E. W Leavitt,
Brigade Paymaster.... J. R. Smith,
Brigade Quartermaster. G. Harriot,
Assis't Quartermaster.. Smith,
Aid-de-Camp.......... J. J. Northop.

Band.

NINTH REGIMENT.

Lieut. Colonel... Charles Sweeney,
Major........... Charles E. Shea,
Adjutant........ J. McDonough,
Paymaster...... John Colgan,
Quartermaster... T. O'Brien,
Surgeon......... W. O'Donnell, M.D.
Chaplain........ Peter Hogg,
Dragoons....... Capt. Kerrigan,

Company A.......... Capt. Coffey,
" C.......... " Mackey,
" D.......... " Phelan,
" E.......... " Cavanagh,
" F.......... " Daly,
" G.......... " Dolan,
" H.......... " Murray,
" I.......... " Kelly.

Band.

EIGHTH REGIMENT.

Colonel........... Thomas F. De Voe,
Lieut. Colonel..... Moses E. Crasto,
Adjutant.......... R. P. Clark,
Paymaster......... D. V. Freeman,
Quartermaster .... J. Matthieson,
Surgeon's Mate.... J. Aitken, Jr.,
Engineer.......... A. Winham,
Chaplain.............. P. Trainor,
Company A...... Capt. Lyons,
" B...... " Mandeville,
" C...... " Forshay,
" D...... " Little,
" E...... " Chamberlin,
" F...... " Quin,

CAVALRY.

Company I.......... Capt. Patterson, | Company J............. Capt. Varian.

Band.

SEVENTH REGIMENT.

Colonel........... Abraham Duryee,
Lieut. Colonel..... Lefferts,
Acting Adjutant... Pond,
Paymaster......... Carpenter,
Quartermaster..... Allen,
Surgeon .... Higgins,
Engineer.......... Launitz,
Chaplain.......... Brainard,

Company 1........ Capt. Pressinger,
" 2........ " Shaler,
" 3........ " Price,
" 4........ " Riblet,
" 5........ " Creighton,
" 6........ " Nevers,
" 7........ " Monroe,
" 8........ " Shumway,

Troop of Cavalry.................... Capt. Watts.

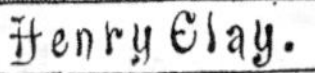

SECOND BRIGADE,

Commanded by Col. ANDREW WARNER.

Major and Inspector..ROBERT H. BOYD,
Judge Advocate......WM. H. PAINE,
Hospital Surgeon....ALEX. B. MOTT,
Engineer............B. E. MANIERRE,
Quartermaster..STEPHEN PAUL,
Paymaster......WILLIAM MATTHEWS,
Aid-de-Camp...JAMES L. DAYTON,
Volunteer "....GEO. H. PENNIMAN,

Band.

SIXTH REGIMENT.

Colonel...........THOMAS F. PEERS,	Company A..........	Capt.	CORDELL,
Lieut. Colonel....J. G. WELLSTOOD,	" B..........	"	ELLIS,
Adjutant.........WILLIAM CHALMERS,	" C..........	"	SEUFERT,
Surgeon..........JAMES ALCOCK,	" D..........	"	ALLAIRE,
Surgeon's Mate...WM. W. JACKSON,	" E..........	"	PINCKNEY,
Quartermaster....CHARLES HARRISON,	" F..........	"	FINCH,
Paymaster........MARK LEVY,	" G..........	"	LALOR,
Engineer........J. M. TRIMBLE,	" H..........	"	GREGORY.

Band.

FIFTH REGIMENT.

Lieut. Colonel..U. SCHWALZWAELDER,	Company A.......	Capt.	WESTFALL,
Major..........OTTO KLOPPENBURGH,	" B........	"	HEITMAN,
Adjutant.......FRED. ESENWEIN,	" C........	"	FINCKE,
Surgeon........FRANCIS MILLER,	" D.......	"	BAACD,
Surgeon's Mate.FRANCIS H. LOSS,	" E........	Lieut.	DOHRMAN,
Quartermaster..H. FUNKE,	" F........	Capt.	ROTTGIER,
Paymaster......HENRY A. CASSENEER,	" G.......	"	BETJEMANN,
Engineer.......HENRY RANCH,	" H.......	"	EWALD.

Band.

FOURTH REGIMENT.

Colonel.............CHARLES YATES,
Lieut. Colonel......ED. C. CHARLES,
Major...............DAN. W. TELLER,
Adjutant............NATHANIEL COLES,
Quartermaster......JAMES F. COX,
Paymaster,..........W. H. GUNTHER,
Surgeon's Mate.....BEZALEEL HOWE,
Engineer...........THEO. TIMPSON,
Chaplain...........J. RENWICK, Jr.

CAVALRY.

Company A, Hussars,	Capt.	LOUIS,
" B, "	"	LUERSSON,
" C, Dragoons	"	ARENT.

ARTILLERY.

Company B..........	Capt.	FERBER,
" C..........	"	FINK,
" D..........	"	FORBES,
" E..........	"	FAY,
" F..........	"	HIRCKEN.

FIRST BRIGADE,

Commanded by Brigadier General CHAS. B. SPICER.

Brigade Major.....CHARLES H. SMITH,
Judge Advocate...LUCIUS PITKIN,
Hospital Surgeon..HOMER BOSTWICK,
Engineer.........JOHN BROUGHAM,
Paymaster........CHARLES F. WOOD,
Aid-de-Camp.....DAN'L H. SPICER,
Voluntary Aid-de-Camp.............C. J. GUILLEMOT.

Band.

THE SEPARATE BATTALION.

Major............F. L. HAGADORN,
Adjutant, Acting..M. TOMPKINS, JR.,
Quartermaster.....JOHN LAWRENCE,
Paymaster........W. HAGADORN, JR.,
Surgeon..........C. BRUENINGHAUSEN,
Surgeon's Mate...JOHN E. GALLAER.

Company A..........Capt. BLAKE,
" B.......... " MEYER,
" C.......... " O'BRIEN,
" D.......... " KAPPES,
" E.......... " BLAKE.

Band.

SEVENTY-FIRST REGIMENT.

Colonel............A. S. VOSBURGH,
Lieut. Colonel......W. P. MOODY,
Major.............S. S. PARKER,
Quartermaster......P. J. PARESEN,
Paymaster ....HENRY W. FISHER,
Chaplain..........GEO. W. WARNER,
Engineer and Adj't..T. B. JOHNSTON.

Company A......Capt. HAGADORN,
" B...... " WHEELER,
" C...... " LITTLE,
" D...... " SMITH,
" E...... " WOODWORTH,
" F...... " GLOVER.

Band.

THIRD REGIMENT.

Lieut. Colonel.......WM. MENCK,
Major...............C. MARTIN,
Adjutant............E. LYON,
Paymaster...........JOHN FINCK,
Quartermaster.......PHILIP ZEIGER,
Surgeon.............J. P. MUMFORD,
Engineer............F. DICKEL,
Chaplain............S. STANFIELD,
Company A..........Capt. DUCKER,

Company B.....Capt. BRISER,
" C..... " WUBBENHORST,
" D..... " FROELICK,
" E..... " ROTTMAN,
" F..... " MEYER,
" G..... " BECHTEL,
" H..... " KELLER,
" I..... " WICTHEN,
" K..... " HERF.

Henry Clay.

Band.

SECOND REGIMENT.

Colonel ....JOHN A. BOGART,
Lieut. Colonel......JOSEPH CRAIG,
Major...............J. W. BRAISTED,
Adjutant............JOHN RAY,
Paymaster...........S. A. DARLING,
Quartermaster......JAMES BECK,
Chaplain...........JAMES FRAZER,
Surgeon............WM. BECK,
Assis't Surgeon.....JAMES F. FRAZER,
Engineer...........JOSIAH P. KNAPP.

Company A.........Capt. CASTLE,
" B.........." EAGLESON,
" C.........." DARROW,
" D.........." JOHNSON,
" E.........." McKENZIE
" F.........." MANSON,
" G.........." LUTZ,
" H.........." ROBERT,
1st Comp. Gov. Blues " CASSALIER

Band.

FIRST REGIMENT.

Colonel.............JOHN B. RYER.
Major...............WM. FORSYTHE,
Adjutant............ISAAC C. HUNT,
Paymaster..........A. HAGENLORKER,
Quartermaster.......S. B. RYER,
Surgeon............H. TRAPHAGEN.

Company A......... Capt. KOEN,
" B.........." RASCHE,
" C.........." STORMS,
" D.........." KENNEDY,
" E.........." LUBEC

Second Division.

Gen. WM. L. MORRIS, Aid to Grand Marshal.

Col. JOHN B. MONTGOMERY, }
WILLIAM MORRIS, Jr., Esq., } *Aids.*

Band.

Officiating Clergymen,
Orator of the Day,
In carriages.

Funeral Car,*

DRAWN BY EIGHT GRAY HORSES, APPROPRIATELY CAPARISONED.

LIGHT GUARD, CAPTAIN VINCENT,

AS A GUARD OF HONOR.

* The funeral car was of magnificent design, and neatly executed, by EDWARD H. SENIOR, Esq. It was constructed in the form of a temple, upon a scale of massive grandeur, and presented a mournfully gorgeous appearance. It was nearly square, and stood about fifteen feet high. Upon a raised centre, on the platform, was a large gilt urn, of classic mould, bearing the simple inscription—"HENRY CLAY," and overhung with crape, supported from the beak of a splendidly carved gilt eagle, representing America protecting the ashes of her beloved son. At each corner of the car, a tapering Corinthian column, wrapped in crape, supported the canopy. Upon the top of the canopy, a dais of sky blue velvet, entwined with black satin, and trimmed with gold lace and stars, supporting an American eagle in a drooping position, emblematical of the Nation's grief. The whole car was surrounded with evergreens, and a chaplet of the same was thrown around the urn. The national banner, heavily shrouded with funereal draperies, and half furled around the flag staff, occupied each corner, their folds forming a fitting shroud for the urn within. The skirting of the whole drapery was contrastingly ornamented with heavy gold bullion. To the rear part of the car was attached a banner of white silk, upon which the following inscription, beautifully embroidered in black silk, appeared:

"Hearts which glow for freedom's sway,
Come and mourn for HENRY CLAY."

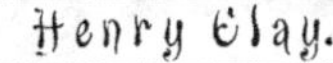

The following gentlemen were selected as Pall-Bearers :

A. R. Lawrence,
James Kelly,
Isaac Newton,
John Robbins,
Robert Hyslop,
Jacob Bell,
J. A. Westervelt,
Anthony Compton,
Willis Hall,
Gideon Ostrander,
William Smith,
Henry Shaw,
John Dimon,
Andrew Mills,
William B. Astor,
W. F. Havemeyer,
Thomas Owen,
Gilbert Cleland,
G. H. Striker,
George Law,
C. W. Lawrence,
D. Austin Muir,
Frederick Pentz,
Michael Ulshœffer,
James Harper,
Robert H. Morris,
Peter Cooper,
Thomas O'Conor,
Stephen Allen,
Alex. Stewart,
Jeremiah Dodge,
C. S. Woodhull,
Isaac M. Phyfe,
J. Phillips Phœnix,
W. N. Blakeman.

Mayors of New York, Brooklyn, Williamsburgh, Jersey City and Newark.

The Common Councils of the cities of New York, Philadelphia, Brooklyn, Williamsburgh, Jersey City, Newark, Paterson and adjoining cities, in the following order :

The Board of Aldermen,
Preceded by their Sergeant-at-Arms, and headed by their President.

The Board of Assistant Aldermen,
Preceded by their Sergeant-at-Arms, and headed by their President.

Officers of both Boards.
Committee of the Common Council of the City of Philadelphia.
Common Council of the City of Brooklyn.
Officers of the Common Council of the City of Brooklyn.
Mayor and Common Council of the City of Williamsburgh, with their officers.
The Common Council of Jersey City, with their Clerks, Marshal, and others.
The Common Council of the City of Newark, with their Clerk and other officers.
Committee on the part of the village of Jamaica.
Ex-Presidents of the United States.
His Excellency Governor Hunt and Suite.
Heads of Departments of the State.
Senate and Assembly of the State of New York.
Members of the Senate and House of Representatives of the United States.
The Commanding Officer of the First United States Military District, and his Aids.
Officers of the Army of the United States.
Commodore W. D. Salter, Commander of the Navy Yard and Station of New York, with the Officers of the Navy of the United States, and Civic Officers of the Navy Yard.
New York State Society of the Cincinnati.

Third Division.

Col. John W. Styles, Aid to Grand Marshal.
Medad Platt, Esq., Aid.

Band.

Ex-Members of Congress and of the State Legislatures.

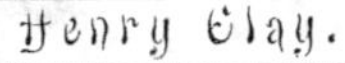

Ex-Mayors, ex-Aldermen and Assistants of the cities of New York, Brooklyn and other cities.

Heads of Departments and Officers of the City Government.

Foreign Ministers and Consuls.

Judges of the United States, State and City Courts.

District Attorney. Members of the Bar.

Members of the Press.

Sheriff, Under-Sheriff and Deputies of the City of New York.

Register, County Clerk and Coroner of the City of New York, with their officers.

Police Magistrates, with staves.

Marshal of the United States for the Southern District of New York, with his Deputies and other Officers.

United States District Attorney, Collector of the Port of New York, with the Clerks and other Officers of his Department, Surveyor, Naval Officer, and other officers connected with their Department.

Postmaster of the City of New York, with his Secretary, Assistant and Clerks.

The Board of Education of the City of New York, Preceded by its President and Clerk.

President, Trustees, Faculty and Students of Columbia College.

President, Council, Faculty and Students of University of New York.

College of Physicians and Surgeons.

Young Men's Debating Society.

New York Academy of Medicine.

New York Medical Society and Physicians and Students.

Teachers and Pupils of Grammar School of

Columbia College and University.
Professors of the Free Academy, with Pupils of the same.
College of Pharmacy.
New York Historical Society.
United States Naval Lyceum.
National Academy of Design.
Engineers' Institute.
Chamber of Commerce.
General Society of Mechanics and Tradesmen.
American Institute.
Mechanics' Institute, Officers and Members.
The several Printers' Societies of the City of New York.
Board of Trade.
Masters, Wardens and Harbor Masters of the Port of New York.
Pilots of the Port of New York.
Members of the Industrial Congress.
Teachers' Association.
Teachers and Pupils of the several Public, Ward and Private Schools.
President, Superintendent, Officers and Pupils of the Deaf and Dumb, and Blind Institutions.
Veterans of 1812, in carriages.

Fourth Division.

Col. A. A. BREMNER, Aid to Grand Marshal.
S. S. WARD, Esq., Aid.

Band.

Civic Societies of the cities of Brooklyn, Jersey City, Newark, Williamsburgh, Paterson and Newburgh.
Civic Societies of adjoining Cities.

Fifth Division.

ADAM P. PENTZ, Esq., Aid to Grand Marshal.
HENRY B. COOK, Esq., Aid.

Band.

Firemen of Brooklyn, Jersey City, Williamsburgh, and other cities and villages.

Exempt Firemen.

Fire Department of the City of New York.

Sixth Division.

Capt. WM. H. UNDERHILL, Aid to Grand Marshal.
JOHN T. OGDEN, Esq., Aid.

Band.

Grand Lodge, State of New York, Free and Accepted Masons.*

Seventh Division.

ELIJAH F. PURDY, Esq., Aid to Grand Marshal.
ROBERT SMITH, Esq., Aid to Grand Marshal.

Band.

Young Men's Democratic General Committee. Young Men's Whig General Committee.

* This Division presented an imposing appearance, the different orders marching with appropriate banners, each member wearing the insignia of his order, with a rich mourning badge on the left arm. The whole fraternity was escorted by a large body of Knights Templars, mounted, and dressed in the splendid military costume, incident to their order, and the days of chivalry and the crusades. An interesting and most valuable relic was carried by the St. Johns' Lodge, No. 1. This was the Bible which was used by Chancellor ROBERT R. LIVINGSTON, in administering the first oath of office to Gen. GEORGE WASHINGTON, as President of the United States, in 1789. It is only used on the most solemn occasions, and was brought out to-day in honor to the illustrious HENRY CLAY, who was an honorary member of the lodge. A detachment of Washington Continentals acted as guard of honor, in their uniform, the same as that worn by the Father of his Country.

Democratic Whig General Committee.

Democratic Republican Gen. Committee.

Whig General Committee of the City of Williamsburgh.

Society of Tammany, or Columbian Order.

Clay Clubs of Newburgh.

Clay Festival Association.

Young Guard Henry Clay Association.

Central Clay Committee of 1844.

Various Clay Clubs of the City and County of New York.

Eighth Ward Scott Legion.

Eighth Division.

WM. T. CHILD, Esq., Aid to Grand Marshal.

JAMES ACKERMAN, Esq., Aid.

Band.

Order of United Americans.

Ninth Division.

Col. ROBERT B. BOYD, Aid to Grand Marshal.

J. J. KELLY, Esq., Aid.

Band.

Butchers' Association of the cities of New York, Brooklyn, Jersey City, Williamsburgh, and other cities and villages, mounted.

Cartmen's Association of the city of New York, mounted.

Tenth Division.

Col. J. C. BURNHAM, Aid to Grand Marshal.

Dr. H. F. QUACKENBOSS, Aid.

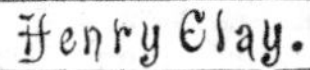

Band.

Gold and Silver Artisans.

Protestant Association.

Omnibus Proprietors' Mutual Association.

Eleventh Division.

SAMUEL OSGOOD, Esq., Aid to Grand Marshal.
ERASTUS GROVER, Esq., Aid.

Band.

Grand Division Sons of Temperance.

Cadets of Temperance.

Independent Order of Rechabites.

Roman Catholic Temperance Society.

Shamrock Benevolent Society.

Twelfth Division.

WILLIAM DINSMORE, Esq., Aid to Grand Marshal.
JOHN A. BUNTING, Esq., Aid.

Band.

Tailors' Societies.

Employees of the Express Establishments, with Express Wagons, decorated.

Thirteenth Division.

RUFUS E. CRANE, Esq., Aid to Grand Marshal.
GEORGE H. E. LYNCH, Esq., Aid.

Band.

Whitehall Association.

Eureka Association, and the various Benevolent Societies of the city of New York.

Fourteenth Division.

Garret H. Striker, Esq., Aid to Grand Marshal.
Jordan Mott, Esq., Aid.

Band.

Citizens of Fifth and other Wards.

Fifteenth Division.

Samuel Rogers, Esq., Aid to Grand Marshal.
Clarkson Crolius, Esq., Aid.

Band.

Mechanics' Societies.

ORDER OF ARRANGEMENTS.

The Societies, Associations and Trades, are requested to appear in the order prescribed, and to walk six abreast.

Bands will play Funeral Dirges in *common* time.

Such societies and associations as have not yet reported, will be assigned places in the order in which they shall report themselves to the Grand Marshal.

No banner bearing political devices or inscriptions will be admitted in the procession.

The First Division of New York State Militia, and the civic societies, will assemble at two o'clock, precisely, at the following places, preparatory to being brought into column:

The Division of Militia in Broadway, left resting on Chambers street.

Officiating Clergymen, Orator of the Day, the Clergy and Pall-Bearers, in the Governor's room.

Mayors of the several cities, and ex-Presidents, Foreign Ministers and Consuls, in the Mayor's office.

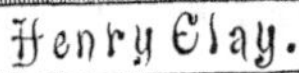

Common Councils of New York, Brooklyn, Jersey City, Newark, Williamsburgh, and the Trustees of the villages of Hoboken and Jamaica, together with their officers, in room No. 8, City Hall.

Governors, Lieutenant-Governors, Heads of Departments, Members of the Senate and Assembly, Senators and Members of Congress, in the Governor's room.

Society of Cincinnati, Revolutionary Soldiers, ex-Mayors, ex-Members of the Common Council, and Heads of Departments of the City Government, in the Library room.

Officers of the Army and Navy, in the Keeper's room.

Veterans of 1812, in carriages in Murray street.

Judges of the Courts, District Attorney, Members of the Bar, ex-Members of Congress, in the Law Library room, new City Hall.

Sheriff and his Deputies, in Sheriff's office.

County Clerk, Register and Coroner, with their officers and the Police Magistrates in the County Clerk's office.

United States District Attorney, United States Marshal and his Deputies, Collector and Surveyor of the Port, Naval Officer, Postmaster, and the Officers connected with their several Departments, in the United States Court.

Civic Societies of Brooklyn, Newark, Williamsburgh, Paterson and other places, in Park place.

President, Trustees, Council, Faculties and Students of Columbia College, and of the University, in the Supreme Court room, new City Hall.

Medical Societies and Students, College of Pharmacy, Historical Society, United States Naval Lyceum, National Academy of Design, Board of Trade, Masters, Wardens, Harbor Masters and Pilots of the Port, American Institute, Mechanics' Institute, in the Superior Court, new City Hall.

Officers and Pupils of Blind, and Deaf and Dumb Institutions, in office of Commissioner of Repairs and Supplies, new City Hall.

Other Associations, and gentlemen of the Third Division, rear of City Hall.

Fourth Division, Park place, front resting on Broadway.

Fifth Division, in Grand street, east of Broadway, front resting on Broadway.

Sixth Division, in Grand street, west of Broadway, front resting on Broadway.

Seventh Division, in Howard street, west of Broadway, front resting on Broadway.

Eighth Division, in Canal street, east of Broadway, front resting on Broadway.

Ninth Division, in Canal street, west of Broadway, front resting on Broadway.

Tenth Division, in Lispenard street, front resting on Broadway.

Eleventh Division, in Walker street, west of Broadway, front resting on Broadway.

Twelfth Division, in White street, west of Broadway, front resting on Broadway.

Thirteenth Division, in Franklin street, west of Broadway, front resting on Broadway.

Fourteenth Division, in Leonard street, east of Broadway, front resting on Broadway.

Fifteenth Division, in Leonard street, west of Broadway, front resting on Broadway.

The closing ceremonies, consisting of the Prayer, Oration and Benediction, will take place on the esplanade, in front of the City Hall.

The troops of the United States, stationed at the different posts in this harbor, are requested to fire minute-guns, from noon till sunset.

The Veteran Corps will fire minute-guns, from the Battery, during the procession.

The carriages for the use of the Pall-Bearers, and Society of the Cincinnati and Revolutionary soldiers, will be under the direction of ASHER TAYLOR, First Marshal of the city.

The owners and proprietors of all public and licensed carriages and vehicles, are directed to withdraw the same from the streets through which the procession is to pass, after the hour of one o'clock, P. M.

The Chief of Police is charged with the enforcement of the above order.

The owners of private carriages and vehicles are also respectfully requested to conform with the wishes of the Committee in this respect.

No obstruction of any kind will be permitted in the streets through which the procession is to pass.

WILLIAM H. CORNELL, WESLEY SMITH, WILLIAM J. BRISLEY, WILLIAM M. TWEED, JAMES M. BARD, S. L. H. WARD, JOHN BOYCE, RICHARD T. COMPTON, Pres't.	*Committee of the Board of Aldermen.*
ISAAC O. BARKER, THOMAS WOODWARD, JOHN J. TAIT, WILLIAM ANDERSON, WILLIAM H. WRIGHT, S. BENSON McGOWN, J. H. VALENTINE, JONATHAN TROTTER, Pres't.	*Committee of the Board of Assistant Aldermen.*

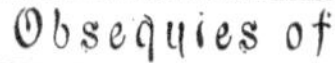

Ceremonies in the Park.

About 7 o'clock the head of the procession entered the Park. Upon the arrival of the funeral car in front of the City Hall, it received the honors of a marching salute from the military, as they filed around the esplanade, and occupied the entire space in front of the Hall. Each division as it passed through the Park, in review, was dismissed, they returning to their respective quarters.

The Common Council, with his Honor the Mayor, the Orator of the day, the officiating Clergy, the Grand Marshal and his Aids, Invited Guests, Pall-Bearers, Officers of the Army and Navy, Officers of the First Division New

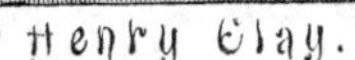

York State Militia, Heads of Departments, Veterans of 1812, and others, occupied the platform. The Aids to the Grand Marshal and the Guard of Honor, were drawn up in line in front, when the Grand Marshal, General WILLIAM HALL, introduced the

REV. JOHN M. KREBS, D.D.,

who offered up the following impressive

Prayer.

O GOD, our dwelling-place in all generations. By Thee kings reign and princes decree justice. Thou art our Lord. Thou art our refuge. In grace and tenderness hast Thou ruled us, and hast made the lines to fall to us in pleasant places. Thanks to Thy name, for our goodly heritage. Thanks for Thy mercies to our fathers—for their wisdom, integrity and valor, which achieved for us our blessings; and for all those whom Thou hast raised up to guide our counsels, to frame and to administer our laws, and to defend us in danger. While we, this day, deplore the decease of the eminent statesman whose prudent counsel, eloquent speech, and manifold services of patriotism were Thy gift to our country, we are both admonished not to put our trust in man, whose breath is in his nostrils, and are encouraged to look unto the hills from whence all our help cometh. When Thou with rebukes dost correct man for iniquity, Thou makest his beauty to consume like the moth. Surely every man is vanity. The princes perish; but Thou, O GOD, art our strong, as Thou art our only, confidence. Hear Thou, then, our prayer. To Thee, and to the word of Thy grace, we commend her, the widowed partner, and the family, whose honored head Thou hast taken away.

Comfort them with Thy mercy, which is in JESUS CHRIST Thy Son, our Redeemer. We give thanks to Thee, that amid the temptations of a public life so laborious and so protracted, Thou wert pleased to imbue the mind of our departed fellow-citizen with Thy saving truth, and to lead his faith to the Lamb of GOD, the sacrifice for our sins; and for the open avowal of that faith in Thine earthly courts.

We thank Thee for the supporting power of the Gospel hope which he enjoyed in his dying hour, and for the clear testimony which, living and dying, he bore to the attraction and the exclusive fitness and priceless value of the salvation of the Cross. May this blessedness be the portion of all who mourn his death. May his example and his testimony not be lost upon our rulers and our statesmen, nor upon any class of our countrymen. But may they be mindful, amid all the aims and pursuits of life, that they all need for themselves that personal interest in CHRIST, that purifying trust in Him, which alone shall associate them with those who have inherited salvation, and shall convey to them that wisdom and righteousness which fit men to bear rule and to enjoy freedom. May they all be mindful of their accountability to Heaven. Thus bless thy servant, the President of the United States—the National Congress, from whom Thou hast called away one of their most illustrious members—our governors, legislators, and judges—our counselors and advocates—the Mayor and the Common Council of this city, who have ordered these solemn obsequies. Death has come to teach them that there is One higher than the highest. May they disdain bribes and hate covetousness; may they consult and determine only for the public good; for their country; for GOD; for

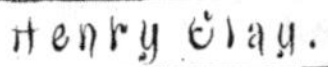

truth; may they be just, ruling in the fear of GOD. Give grace to our people that they may ever select such for office and authority; and so may we all lead a quiet and peaceful life in all godliness and honesty. And, to this end, we humbly beseech Thee, both forgive and allay the bitterness and injuries of party strife. Our shame, and our sin, we confess this day, over the grave, where obloquy and calumny are hushed; where political animosity is rebuked, and enmity is buried; where our citizens mingle their praises and regrets for the statesman and the patriot, whom we all have lost.

Extend Thy gracious sway and Thy protecting arm over this land. Be Thou its glory and its trust. And let the saving rule of Thine Anointed dispense peculiar blessings and salvation through all our borders, and throughout the world. And, now, most merciful LORD and Savior, grant unto us the free and the full pardon of our personal and of our national sins. Teach us to consider our latter end, and the measure of our days what it is. Renew our hearts by Thy Holy Spirit. And give unto us all grace, that we may live by the faith of the Son of GOD; and die the death of Thy saints, and dwell forever with the LORD. We ask it all, for the merits' sake of JESUS CHRIST, our Mediator and Advocate. Amen.

At the conclusion of the prayer,

DODWORTH'S CORNET BAND

Performed the celebrated

Requiem,

From MENDELSSOHN'S Oratorio of ST. PAUL. After which, the Grand Marshal introduced to the vast assemblage, the Orator of the day,

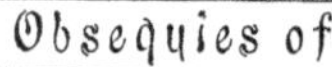

N. BOWDITCH BLUNT,

Who delivered, in a most impressive manner, the following

Oration.

HENRY CLAY is dead!

Such was the startling intelligence which, but a few days since, flashing on the wings of the lightning, was diffused throughout the entire republic. Commencing with a rumor, at whose faintest whisper Senators and Representatives abandoned the halls of legislation, it burst upon the country a dread reality. The statesman heard it with a thrill of awe; the politician with a subdued spirit; the hum of business was hushed in the crowded mart; the artisan and laborer ceased from their toil; the courts of justice were closed; the husbandman watered the furrows with his tears, and the sailor, looking to the half mast flag, whispered with white lips, our defender is dead. The tolling bell and booming minute-gun, proclaimed the departure of a mighty spirit. The sombre decorations of funereal show betokened the darkness and gloom of the land. All felt that sorrow and grief which follows the death of the cherished and the loved. The nation mourned the nation's loss.

There is a fitness in such manifestations. They give hope and encouragement to the future, for they teach us that however transient may be our mortal lingering, men's deeds live after them. The immortal spirit shall not die, and the genius, the eloquence, and the patriotism which inspired, aroused and encouraged his compatriots, still remain in the fruits of his efforts, constituting the eternal monument upon which is inscribed the deathless name of HENRY CLAY.

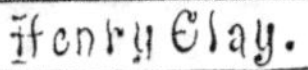

So long as liberty shall endure; so long as the history of American freedom shall exist; in every clime, and wherever the English language shall be spoken or read, the name of the great American Commoner will be joined with the orators, statesmen and patriots of past, present and future ages.

> "Ne'er to the chambers, where the mighty rest,
> Since their foundation, came a nobler guest;
> Nor e'er was to the bowers of bliss conveyed,
> A fairer spirit, or more welcome shade."

The cardinal feature of our form of government is that great and noble principle which recognizes equality as the basis of civil right. It forms the corner-stone of our political fabric. To the humble youth it proclaims, that wealth and honor are within the reach of all; that the child of the poorest native of the soil may in turn become the elective chief of the state; that fortune and fame depend not upon hereditary estate, nor ancestorial pride; that here, man, under Providence, is the architect of his own character and position; and that, upon himself, and the appropriate use of the talents wherewith God has endowed him, rest his estimate among his countrymen, and his responsibility hereafter. No more striking illustration of this peculiar character of our institutions can be found than he, who, from the humble position of the "Mill Boy of the Slashes," self-prompted and self-sustained, became foremost among a nation's sons;

> "Primus inter pares."

Well may his country cherish his fame, for he emphatically lived for his country. The glare of military achievements, the red trophies of conquest, the blood-stained triumphs of the warrior belonged not to him. His was the proud independence, the intellectual power, the eloquent fire, before which the haughtiest quailed; but his acts were those of peace; his offerings were on the shrine of liberty; his deeds are written in the prosperity, the progress and glory of his country. Nor were his efforts in behalf of human freedom, limited by his country's bounds.

> " Where Greece unsheathed her olden blade
> For glory in the haunted shade—
> Where Chimborazo stands sublime
> A landmark by the sea of Time,
> His name shall, as a blessing given
> For man, Oh! never to depart,
> Peal from the gladdened earth to heaven
> The warm, wild music of the heart."

HENRY CLAY is no more! He has passed the fatal stream, which can never be repassed by mortal. The vital spark is extinguished; the music of his voice is hushed. Cold and silent he sleeps the sleep that knows no earthly waking.

Reverently we acknowledge this dispensation of Divine Providence, and, as we bend with solemn awe, we feel within us that inspiration which teaches us there is an immortality beyond the grave. In this assurance we are comforted with the reflection that he died in Christian faith and with a Christian hope; and we involuntarily exclaim within ourselves " may our last end be like his."

Mr. CLAY, in his brief review of the character of Chancellor WYTHE, has furnished the key to his own career. Up to the time of his connection with this illustrious man, we know him only as the boy, an epitome of whose previous life was so graphically given by Mr. ROBERT HUGHES, at Campbell Court House, Virginia : "He and

I were born close to the slashes of old Hanover. He worked barefooted, and so did I. He went to mill, and so did I. He was good to his mamma, and so was I." His acquaintance with this venerable man opened a new field to his view. Before him spread the broad extent of legal study, which, in those times especially, served to appal the faint-hearted explorer, while it infused energy and vigor into the ardent and determined mind. Few were the opportunities afforded to the young men of that day. The republic was yet in its infancy; the shock of the Revolution had left behind its ravages, and the country was slowly recovering from the effects of the mighty throes which had given birth to a free and independent nation. Public libraries were comparatively unknown, and the student was left to depend mainly upon his own efforts, aided by the private libraries and instruction of his teacher. The common law of England, previously recognized as the law of the colonies, was undergoing a process of modification adapted to the changed relations of the countries, and the peculiar character of our government. International law was more especially the subject of close and searching investigation. The French revolution, with its results upon the peace of Europe; the clashing of hostile commercial interests; the claims of belligerent powers upon the one side, and the rights of neutrals on the other, were topics of discussion among the statesmen of both worlds.

It was under these circumstances, that the attention of Chancellor WYTHE was called to the humble boy, who was then commencing a career destined to become so glorious. He saw the germ of that intellect, which in its development, was afterward to sway the minds of juries, to charm and convince listening senates, to arouse public enthusiasm, to direct the course of legislation, and to control the energies of a mighty people. The Chancellor and the boy became friends. The youth has left the impression of his matured greatness upon the records of his country's history, and the character of the patron has been well portrayed by the touching testimonial of Mr. CLAY himself in a letter to a friend.

Shortly after Mr. CLAY's admission to the bar, in 1797, he removed to Kentucky, and at once assumed a high position at the bar of his adopted state. At this period of his life, he was remarkable for a fearless independence, undaunted courage, keen sarcasm, and brilliant rhetoric, which, united to a tall and graceful person, an eye that never quailed, and a voice whose tones now ringing like a trumpet, and again pleading with the softness of a woman, intimidated the turbulent, commanded the respect of his compeers, and captivated the rude spirits of his hearers. These attributes continued to his death.

The soil itself was congenial to his mind. The native forests were yet unsubdued. Here and there a clearing, a settlement, and a community indicated the inroads of civilization upon the fastnesses of the savage. The Indian still claimed his birth-right, and the tales of savage warfare, and the horrors of border life are chronicled in the traditions which designate the state as the "dark and bloody ground." Amid scenes like these, aloof from the luxuries of polished life, surrounded by primeval forests, where nature alone reigned supreme, the future statesman and legislator was trained and matured. They furnished nutriment to his fancy, vigor to his mind, and, above all, encouraged and strengthened that self-reliant spirit which in after years sustained him amid the turmoil of politics, the struggles of faction, the assaults of calumny, the encounters of political debate, and the forensic disputations of the bar.

Three-fourths of a century have passed since that memorable declaration which declared to the world our emancipation from colonial thraldom, and demanded our separation from our British brethren, "holding them, as we hold the rest of mankind, enemies in war; in peace, friends." The year succeeding to that which gave birth to the nation, hailed the birth of him who was destined to leave the impress of his spirit upon the age. In the language of a biographer, "born and cradled in the agonies of a revolution, HENRY CLAY seems to have been destined by Providence to sympathize with its great principles of freedom, and to be the leading champion of human rights for the age in which he has lived."

His career as a legislator commenced in the General Assembly of Kentucky, in 1803, from which he was speedily elevated to the Senate of the United States, in 1806, for the unexpired term of Hon. JOHN ADAIR. In 1809, he was again returned to the Senate; and in 1811, foregoing the higher dignity, he became a candidate for the House of Representatives, and at the Special Session, Nov. 4, 1811, was elected Speaker of the House, to which post he was subsequently re-elected six times; occupying that position in all about thirteen years. In 1814, he resigned, upon being appointed one of the Commissioners to negotiate peace with England. In 1825, he became Secretary of State, under Mr. Adams; and in 1831, was returned to the Senate, where, with a brief interval, consequent upon his voluntary retirement, in 1842, he continued until his death, being a period of nearly fifty years' public service from his first entrance into public life. It was in these various capacities of legislator, diplomatist, and Minister of State, that Mr. CLAY developed those views and principles of public policy which have given to him the designation of "The Father of the American System." By this I do not mean that single, isolated measure known as the Tariff; but that great expansive system of public policy which, based upon the laws of nature and the rights of nations, has commanded the respect of the world, while it has advanced the true prosperity of the country. Part of this system was the enforcement of our rights as a neutral power, and the protection of our seamen against the arrogant pretensions of the imperious self-styled "Mistress of the Seas."

It is not too much to say, that no person occupied a more prominent position in the origin and support of the war of 1812, than Mr. CLAY. "The war was declared because Great Britain arrogated to herself the pretension of regulating our foreign trade, under the delusive name of retaliatory Orders in Council—because she persisted in the practice of impressing American seamen; because she had instigated the Indians to commit hostilities against us, and because she had refused indemnity for her past injuries upon our commerce." The results of the struggle are known, and in the termination so honorable to ourselves, and so beneficial to American interests, Mr. CLAY was again, as one of the Commissioners at Ghent, mainly instrumental.

The recognition of South American Independence, and the fearless and determined stand assumed by Mr. Monroe, counseled and sustained by Mr. CLAY, against foreign intervention in the affairs of the South American States;

his instructions, as Secretary of State, to the ministers to the proposed Congress at Panama; his correspondence, growing out of the difficulties in relation to the Colonial trade and the navigation of the St. Lawrence, and the commercial treaties negotiated by him, constitute the international feature of his American policy. Internal improvements, the protection and encouragement of American industry, and the complete development of American resources, and their independence of foreign control, formed the domestic portion of his scheme, and though others have honestly differed as to the expediency of some of his proposed measures, no one will question the motives of patriotism which prompted their advocate.

More than all, and above all, he cherished the integrity of the Union. For this he labored; to this end he strove. Placing himself upon the Constitution, he stood before the country the advocate of concord and fraternal harmony—the stern, unyielding opponent of discord and disunion. Amid the clashing of sectional jealousies and discordant interests; the denunciations of heated zealots, and the threats of vindictive partisans, his eye quailed not; his voice was not hushed. His eagle glance surveyed the scene; and anon, amid the whirl of conflict and political strife, above the howlings of the storm, rung out his clarion tones of comfort for the faint-hearted, and encouragement to the despairing. Born to command the human passions, and skilled to rule the infirmities of our nature, he now threatened the defiant, now persuaded the self-willed. The tempest was stayed. At the sound of his voice, ringing out the notes of warning and alarm, millions sprang to the rescue—the war of passions ceased, discord fled, and the elements of peace and happiness again shone forth.

In 1821, when the storm of dissolution threatened the country upon the Missouri question, the almost superhuman efforts of Mr. CLAY alone averted the result. Again, in 1833, when nullification reared its hideous head, he interposed, and the spectre was exorcised. And when, at last, disunion showed its horrid front,

> "And o'er our fathers' yet green graves,
> The sons of those who side by side
> Struck down the lion banner's pride,
> Were arming for fraternal strife,
> For blow for blow, and life for life—"

again stood forth that Old Man Eloquent. He had seen most of his children fall around him, one upon the battle-field, others by the hand of disease and unexpected death. He had felt the anguish and sorrow of the sudden rupture of the holiest of ties; he had wept over the graves of his own loved offspring, but his country remained. There she stood a beacon of liberty to the enthralled of other shores. The ever-burning altars of freedom were on her hilltops, and the smoke of their incense was diffusing itself throughout the world. The sails of her commerce whitened every sea, and her flag proudly floated, a sure token of protection to all beneath its folds. The oppressed of Europe looked to her and her example as their refuge and hope. Tyrants and traitors alone hated and feared her. All this he saw and knew. Again he donned his armor, and battling in the foremost rank with the noble spirits who yet survive, and who, forgetful of party and party ties stood side by side in defence of our ancient bond of brotherhood, his last blows were in the cause of his country, constitutional liberty and union.

Glorious termination of a well-spent life! Children of

America! revere his memory—imitate his example—emulate his virtue!

> "Be just and fear not;
> Let all the ends thou aims't at be thy Country's,
> Thy God's, and Truth's."

Thus shall you acquire "the high, the exalted, the sublime emotions of a patriotism which, soaring toward heaven, rises above all mean, low or selfish things, and is absorbed by one soul-transporting thought of the good and the glory of one's country. That patriotism which, catching its inspiration from the immortal GOD, and leaving, at an immeasurable distance below, all lesser groveling personal interests and feelings, animates and prompts to deeds of self-sacrifice, of valor, of devotion, and of death itself. THAT IS PUBLIC VIRTUE; THAT IS THE NOBLEST, THE SUBLIMEST OF PUBLIC VIRTUES." That was the PUBLIC VIRTUE OF HENRY CLAY.

Women of America! ye around whom our affections cluster and upon whom they depend—cherish in your heart of hearts the memory of the departed patriot, and to the lisping infant chant the story of his greatness and his honest fame. Tell your children of his filial reverence and devotion; of his untiring energy, his lofty aims, his noble bearing, and his self-sacrificing spirit; and teach them—be ye, too, the guardians and defenders of that Union which *he* struggled to preserve.

Men of America! be steadfast in your country's cause. Falter not! Here, over the grave of the departed sage, by that courage which failed him not, by the memorials of his greatness, by the records of his patriotism, by his unfaltering devotion to the cause of freedom, by his undying fame, and by that divine faith and resignation which cheered, consoled and comforted his glorious death, swear ye that ye will transmit unimpaired, to your posterity, the inheritance ye possess—"Our glorious Union, now and forever, one and indivisible."

REV. BENJAMIN J. HAIGHT, D.D.,

concluded the beautiful obituary ceremonies with the following

Benediction.

Unto God, and to His glorious mercy and protection, I commit you. May the Lord preserve and keep you, and may He make His voice to shine upon you, and be gracious unto you. May the light of His countenance be upon you, and give you peace, now and evermore. Amen.

The funeral solemnities in honor of the universally beloved and honored American statesman, the illustrious and lamented Henry Clay, having been accomplished, your Committee have great reason to congratulate themselves upon the very general assistance cheerfully rendered by the inhabitants of this and the adjacent cities, in the discharge of the melancholy, though grateful, duties assigned them. Sensible of the high responsibilities resting on them, they know that they would be wanting in their duty, did they fail to acknowledge, with sentiments of gratitude, the promptness and alacrity, as well as the deep feelings of sympathy manifested by their fellow-citizens in carrying out the various duties of the ceremonial, in the discharge of which they seemed to feel themselves highly honored. Party spirit was completely forgotten; political differences entirely laid aside, and men of every class and station vied with each other in rendering appropriate honors to the "mighty dead." All parties claimed him—for *he was of his whole country.* The citizens of the Republic acted and felt as ONE PEOPLE—with a common interest in cherishing the memory of the great and good. His was one of the few instances in which a great man, passing through a long and active life, closely identified with the exciting political questions of the day, and placed in the front rank in the discussion of subjects of vital importance to the interests of the country—lived through and outlived all sectional prejudice; every party vituperation, and ambitious sordid hypocrisy. His honest, his intense, his devoted love of country, endeared him to the whole nation. "He was American through and through; American in his feelings, American in his aims, American in his policy and projects. The influence, the grandeur, the dominion of America were the dreams of his boyhood, and the intense effort of his riper years. For this he valued power, and for this he used it." Of him every citizen in the country could justly say—

> "His life was gentle; and the elements
> So mix'd in him, that Nature might stand up,
> And say to all the world,—*This was a man!*"

Your Committee would dwell, for a few moments, upon the *ensemble* of the pageant. From an early part of the day set apart for the purpose, the city was given up to preparation for the imposing solemnities about to take place. Precisely at the hour designated in the programme, the various military companies, public bodies, associations, societies and citizens, having arrived in detachments at their several places of rendezvous, were formed into column by the respective Aids to the Grand Marshal, who, upon the signal by the tolling bell, placed himself at the head of the procession, which then commenced its march. A common sentiment of veneration pervaded the entire line of the procession, and the sympathy between it and the throngs that embordered its entire route, was made manifest in many exhibitions of tenderness. Thousands of buildings in all parts of the city bore, upon their neatly decorated fronts, undeniable evidences of the love which was felt for HENRY CLAY. Devices of unique and classic conception, and recorded sentiments, setting forth the exalted character and virtues of the deceased—his eventful life and tranquil death—were suspended from eaves, balconies, stagings, and windows. Funereal draperies, streaming from house-top to the street; flags, heavily shrouded, at half mast, among the shipping in the harbor, and upon every flag staff in the city; the booming minute-gun, consecutively fired from the Battery, and answered again from the forts in the harbor, at the Navy Yard, from Brooklyn and Bergen Heights, from Governor's, Ellis', Bedlow's and Staten Islands, reverberating mournfully through the city, and echoing along the bay, until their deafening sounds were lost in the distance; the tolling bells, ringing their sad knell in notes that betoken the dissolution of man's earthly career—the same mournful sounds distinctly heard from the bells in Brooklyn, Jersey City, and Williamsburgh, chiming in doleful concert with those of this city; the solemn dirge; the muffled drum; the heavy tramp of the mournful procession, as it wended, in its slow and measured length, along the streets; all gave the strongest tokens of the deep sympathy pervading the hearts of the thousands that had come from their business and homes to render their last tribute of love and homage to the memory of a Nation's departed son. Though during the early part of the day, the sun shone forth with its highest splendor, darting its torrid rays with unusual vigor, yet toward the afternoon, the heavens, like the earth, put on their sable mantling; a cooling and shadowy cloud intervened between the burning rays of the sun and the earth, and threw a singularly gloomy aspect over the whole city—appropriate to the mournful solemnities of the day. All business was suspended, and at an early hour, every part of the city, save on the line of the procession, was deserted. Perfect order reigned everywhere; thousands of strangers from the adjacent cities thronged our streets as participators in the mournful obsequies. The entire route of the procession, on every side, was lined with inscriptions, busts, monuments, and other imposing reminiscences of respect to the great man's memory. Many of the devices and inscriptions exhibited a refined taste, with great appropriateness; and very frequently, as some thrilling tribute of affection was met, the civic portion of the procession uncovered and remained so until they passed it.

The procession was probably the longest ever seen in this city, and one general feeling marked every section of its immense numbers, illustrative of the beautiful sentiment of the occasion—*its sincerity*. It was no unmeaning mockery of woe; no mere seeming of regret, but the true and real mourning of an appreciating, a grateful and a bereaved people. To no man, living or dead, has America ever paid a higher tribute of respect than that which she rendered to the memory of HENRY CLAY. The subject is full of material for reflection—an encouragement for others to walk with uprightness, and in the paths of virtue and integrity, following him as an example, worthy of all imitation.

"Lives of great men all remind us,
We can make our lives sublime;
And departing, leave behind us,
Footprints in the sands of time,
Footprints, that perhaps another,
Sailing o'er life's troubled main,
Some forlorn and shipwrecked brother,
Seeing, may take heart again."

In conclusion, your Committee beg leave to express their sincere thanks to the Grand Marshal and his Aids; the military, political and civic bodies; the clergy, citizens of this and adjacent cities, and all others who united with them upon this melancholy occasion, for their valuable and essential services in carrying into effect the detailed arrangements of the day; and most especially for the cheerful, prompt and efficient manner with which they all responded, in every instance, to the wishes of the Committee in giving effect to this solemn and well merited pageant.

Your Committee also desire, before closing the labors of their report, to state, that as solemnities of an appropriate and imposing character were celebrated in the city of Brooklyn, by order of the corporate authorities, upon the evening of the day on which the obsequies were performed in this city, in a manner commensurate with their sincere and devoted attachment to the illustrious deceased; and upon this, as well as on all former occasions of this character, the Common Council and citizens of Brooklyn were efficient participants in the obsequies of our mutually

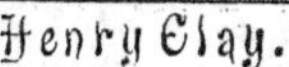

respected and lamented dead, your Committee deem the subject and its interests, in this connection, so closely allied as to demand some proper consideration at their hands, and the official proceedings of that body, adopted upon that occasion, together with the ceremonies, should occupy a space in this report; therefore, in accordance with these views, your Committee present the following

PROCEEDINGS IN BROOKLYN.

COMMON COUNCIL.—SPECIAL MEETING.

THURSDAY, JULY 1st, 1852.

A special meeting of the Common Council was held this evening, for the purpose of taking some action relative to the death of Henry Clay. On the assembling of the Board, the following communication from the Mayor was submitted :

Gentlemen :—The country has been called to lament the loss of one of its most illustrious citizens. A statesman, to whom the eyes of the nation have been turned for counsel in every hour of peril and disaster for nearly the last half century, has closed his brilliant and honorable career of public service, and has ceased to be of earth. Henry Clay, a Senator of the United States, from the State of Kentucky, died at the city of Washington on the 29th of June last. The feeling of public sorrow for this national bereavement is so universal and profound, that you will, no doubt, feel called upon to make some public and suitable expression of the sentiments of this community on the occasion. I shall be happy to concur with you in whatever measures may be deemed appropriate to do honor to the memory of the lamented and venerated dead, and justice to the emotions of a people proud of his fame, and stricken with a deep sense of a great public loss.

Respectfully yours,

CONKLIN BRUSH, *Mayor.*

Aldermen MARVIN, FOWLER and HARTEAU made some brief and appropriate remarks on the subject of the communication, when, on motion, Aldermen MARVIN, FOWLER, MORRIS, HARTEAU, SPINOLA and BAYLIS were appointed a a committee to draft resolutions expressive of the sense of the Board, who, after a short deliberation, reported the following:

Whereas, This Common Council having been officially informed of the decease at Washington, on the 29th of June last, of HENRY CLAY, and desiring, with feelings of profound sensibility, to unite with their fellow-citizens throughout the land in the general expression of sorrow for a great national bereavement, in the loss of one of the most distinguished citizens of the Republic; it is therefore

Resolved, That this Common Council, representing a community in which the name of HENRY CLAY has long been known and cherished, desires to place upon the records of the city an expression of its sense of the exalted character of the departed patriot and statesman. Commencing his career in the service of the United States as a senator in 1806; in 1852, at the close of nearly half a century of diversified and brilliant civic employments, death found him there at his post, and he fell with his "harness on"—"without fear and without reproach." Greatness, as applied to HENRY CLAY, was a word of large significance. He was a great lawyer; a great patriot; a great statesman, a great orator, and combining the radiance of all these distinguished titles to admiration and honor, he was, in the most general and highest sense, a truly noble and great man. His laurels were never wet with the tears of widows and orphans, and his trophies have never cost the nation its treasure or its blood. These free United States, whose prosperity has been advanced, and whose union has been cemented by his wisdom, will hereafter, with eyes purged from the mists of party prejudice, read the glorious annals which record his brilliant career with pride, in his comprehensive views of public policy; in his integrity; in his unfaltering courage, and in his unwavering fidelity in the long, difficult and dangerous path of public life which he trod, will hold up his example for the study and imitation of their ingenuous youth, and their rising statesmen; and will, through all the coming ages of the Republic, cherish his as

> "On of the few immortal names
> That were not born to die."

Resolved, That it be referred to a Special Committee of six, to make arrangements for the delivery, before this Common Council, and our fellow-citizens, of a discourse upon the life and services of HENRY CLAY, and to make such arrangements as they may think proper.

In pursuance of the foregoing resolution, the undersigned would respectfully announce to their fellow-citizens and others, that the Rev. SAMUEL H. COX, D. D., will deliver a discourse on the life and services of HENRY CLAY, in the Second Presbyterian Church, Clinton street, (under the pastoral charge of the Rev. I. S. SPENCER, D. D.,) on Tuesday, 20th inst., at 8 o'clock, P. M.

The Committee respectfully recommend his Honor the Mayor, to issue his proclamation, suggesting to the citizens to close their places of business on the afternoon of that day, and to attend the evening services in honor of the lamented dead.

ABM. B. BAYLIS,
CHAS. R. MARVIN,
C. C. FOWLER,
FREDERICK MORRIS,
HENRY HARTEAU,
F. B. SPINOLA,
Special Com. of Arrangements.

PROCLAMATION.

MAYOR'S OFFICE,
BROOKLYN, JULY 17, 1852.

The citizens are recommended to unite in the public services, on Tuesday evening, the 20th of July, at 8 o'clock, at the church of the Rev. Dr. SPENCER, in honor of the memory of HENRY CLAY, and to close their places of business during the afternoon of that day. A discourse, commemorative of Mr. CLAY's distinguished services and career, has been deemed more appropriate than a public pageant, to express the profound and universal sorrow of our citizens, on occasion of an irreparable national loss, in the decease of the great American statesman.

CONKLIN BRUSH, *Mayor*.

Pursuant to the foregoing unanimous action of the Common Council, a very large and respectable auditory assembled in the Second Presbyterian Church, generously offered for the purpose. His Honor, CONKLIN BRUSH, Mayor, presiding; the Common Council, with officers of the Army and Navy, and other distinguished citizens participating. The impressive ceremonies were commenced with the following impressive

Prayer,

which was offered up to the Throne of Grace by the Rev. GEORGE W. BETHUNE, D. D.

O LORD, Thou art GOD alone; before the mountains were brought forth, or ever Thou didst form the earth and the sea, Thou wert alone in Thy glory and perfections, and from Thy will all things have come. Thou callest man into being, and when Thou hast served Thy purposes with him upon earth, Thou sendest him again to the dust, and bringest his spirit before Thee into judgment. There is none that can stay Thy hand, none that can escape the purpose of Thy will. It becometh us, O Lord, to bow down before Thee at this time, in remembrance of Thy majesty and of our littleness. Thou alone art the Author, and the Preserver, and the Governor and the Judge. We come to Thee in this hour of solemn warning and affliction. We come bending our hearts, as we trust to receive the lessons which Thou teachest, and beseeching Thee to grant us the blessings which we need. We give Thee thanks, O God, that from Thy high, majestic throne, Thou hast taken notice of Thy people. Especially do we, dwellers in this land, give Thee thanks for Thy favor to our fathers in all their history; in their settlement of this commonwealth, in their struggles for freedom, in their laying the foundation of this government, and the preservation of it amidst all the vicissitudes which are inevitable from the imperfections of man. We thank Thee that Thou didst lay the basis of our institutions deep in the hearts of the people; that Thou hast permitted them to build upon that foundation a superstructure so massive and so lofty. Blessed be Thy name, O Lord; for unless Thou buildest the city, those that build it work in vain. We thank Thee that our fathers cared for their country; and devoted their interests, and affection, and time, to the institutions of their native land. In Thy hands are the hearts of all men. From Thee have come our statesmen, our rulers, our orators, and all those who have contributed to build up this land; all those who have been permitted to serve their country. Especially at this time would we bow down before Thee, and while we acknowledge this severe affliction which Thy hand hath made the country to feel, we would thank Thee that Thou didst raise him up and qualify his mind, and Thou didst enlarge his heart and give to him a talent and an inclination to do all these things for his country, which have tended to its prosperity. We thank Thee that Thou hast granted unto us now the memory of one who was faithful to that land which he served. We thank Thee that Thy people of all parties and opinions may meet together, and with sincerity mourn over the dust of him for whom these pageants of mourning have been raised to-day. We thank Thee, O

God, for him, and for those who have been associated with him in time when the crisis of our nation's interests required self-sacrificing men to secure the welfare of the whole nation, and to bind in stronger union the various parties of this mighty confederacy, in the arch upon which the political liberties of the world are built. And we thank Thee that Thou didst shed the consolations of the Gospel through his mind, and that he whose life was one of constant toil and agitation, was permitted quietly and sweetly to expire in the hope of a glorious immortality. Blessed be God that we may receive through that darkness which hangs over the tomb, the anticipation of the bliss which is beyond. Yea, that we may have faith, by knowing that he who sleeps in Jesus, God will bring with him. We thank Thee that we are permitted to ask of Thee to continue Thy favors to our beloved land; that thou wouldst raise up from time to time, men of good counsel, of honest hearts and determined courage, who shall fearlessly and untiringly pursue the right. Remember the prayers of those who founded this nation, in their zeal, for Thy name. Remember the prayers of Thy people, which go up to Thee from the pulpit, the fireside, and the closet, calling down Thy blessing upon this land, incomparably more favored than ever Israel was. We are sinners before Thee, and now feel the truth that sentence of death hath passed upon all men, we are subject to that sentence which came into the world by sin. Sanctify our hearts by Thy peace, that we may live humbly mindful of death. Amen.

AN ADDRESS

ON THE LIFE AND CHARACTER OF THE LATE

HON. HENRY CLAY,

DELIVERED BEFORE THE

MAYOR AND COMMON COUNCIL OF BROOKLYN, AND A LARGE ASSEMBLAGE OF CITIZENS,

BY

SAMUEL HANSON COX, D. D.

— videbatur omnino mori non debuisse —

Mr. Mayor, Members of the Common Council, and other Honored and Intelligent Persons present, Ladies and Gentlemen:

We have met on a rare and a solemn occasion! Our nation celebrates the funeral of Henry Clay. Our loss is national. Not many a Washington, or a Lafayette, or an Adams, or a Clay, had our country to lose. Such statesmen, such heroes, such patriots, such champions, such useful and distinguished and exemplary citizens, are not to be found frequent in any country. Ours has had her full and appropriate share of great men. Her firmament is rich with constellations, and each of these adorned with stars of the first magnitude. Hereafter, not Kentucky, but America, not the party, but the nation, claims Henry Clay, as her own. Alas! that she mourns him dead, because with the fleeting and inconstant minority alive, he ceases to be numbered.

Henry Clay.

In obedience to your call, my honored hearers, I stand before you, willing to meet the awe-inspiring occasion, with what I best may offer; not without the subduing consciousness of my incompetency to do it justice. I respond, honored civic Fathers of Brooklyn, and fellow-citizens, under the fond ideas that we are together performing one of the high duties of patriotism; that this social and moral service is done and due to the collective interests of our country, our great, our beloved, our whole country; that it is proper, useful, and sublimely national; that all these observances and commemorations are beneficial and cementing to our mighty and our magnificent UNION; that we are enacting, in these tributary honors, what the Great Fathers and Founders of the REPUBLIC, what WASHINGTON, and FRANKLIN, and HAMILTON, would approve; that every concert movement of this moral and patriotic sort, tends natively to consolidate the strength, and to assimilate the members, and to render homogeneous for good all the correlated portions and sections of our vast and our wonderful confederacy; that with it we profitably lose the littleness of sectionalism, in the expansive sympathies of our vast and united country, realizing, in the conscious imprint of our mingled hearts, the conservative, and the economic grandeur of our noble national motto, which our bird imperial, grasping the arrows and the bolts of war in one talon, and in the other, this the dexter, waving the olive branch of peace preferred; which motto, I say, our soaring eagle, with pinions spread among the stars of heaven, lifts to the gaze and the admiration of the universe—E PLURIBUS UNUM! Yes! the idea that in this we forget, for an auspicious season, all that is little and local and partial; know no east, no west, no north, no south, no distinction of ocean boundaries or mountain ranges, liquefied indeed with the grief of patriotism and confluent in the feelings of funereal sympathy, we celebrate the death of CLAY, our lofty senator; we solemnize his exit, as that of another of the great patriarchs of our common country, and do this in concert simultaneous with millions of our countrymen; this idea befits us, ennobles us, benefits the nation, makes us united and assimilated more, is proper in all relations, and even our divine Christianity sanctions and inspires this homage, in its wide spread and memorable and excellent magnificence.

We have privileges as citizens of this country, dignities, and consequent duties too, at once ennobling and stupendous, which are equally enjoyed by no other people under heaven. As Christians and worshippers of the true God, how precious to the enlightened mind, how good and how paramount, are our civic and political liberties! And how base and abominable, to possess them with no gratitude, with no appreciation, with no sensibility. And what is it better than squalid degradation, and criminal selfishness, to occupy and enjoy these high advantages, with no generous sentiment, either to the Sovereign of the Universe, who vouchsafes to confer them on us, or to those proximate instruments of his beneficence, through whom, and by whose vigilance and care and skill and faithfulness, under God, we derive and retain them all. With this view, my respected hearers, are we ready to denounce the man, of soul so dead, could we find him in our city or our country—yet would I not accuse any portion of our happy land of harboring the monster, who thinks that he owes no gratitude to our departed senator; who grudges these honors to his hearse; who feels no grief, no sense of bereavement, in common with the nation and the world, at the funeral of HENRY CLAY—we denounce him, as unfit to live in our country, as an ingrate, or a simpleton, or a traitor.

If such there live, go mark him well;
For him no minstrel raptures tell.
High though his titles, proud his name,
Boundless his wealth as wish may claim;
Despite those titles, power, and pelf,
The wretch concentred all in self,
Living, shall forfeit fair renown,
And, doubly dying, shall go down,
To the vile dust from whence he sprung,
Unwept, unhonored and unsung.

Our theme was an American of the Americans. He was an exemplar, and a noble specimen of genuine American greatness. Born to no princely fortune, the scion of no factitious family honors, he was, under God, as he was ever fond to confess, the architect of his own high fortunes, the maker of his own large patent of nobility, the honest earner of his own accomplished fame. He rose from obscurity, from poverty, from orphanage, and even from a very limited education, to rank among the first and the most estimable of human personages, beloved by his countrymen and celebrated through the world. He rose legitimately; not by ignominious boasting, or mercenary patronage, or the caprice of prodigies and events, or by flattering the populace, or by the flooded puissance of bribes, or by some *coup d'etat* of revolutionary exigence, or by cunning and the low arts of demagogism; but—hear it, O ye ingenuous and aspiring youth of our country, HENRY CLAY rose by industry, by assiduous application, by honesty, by consistency, by deserving the confidence of the people, by studying and pursuing the true interests of his country, by evincing what he was, so that enemies had to own it, by practical wisdom, by love of liberty, by illustrating the true nature of American statesmanship, by vivid alertness in the cause of humanity, by enlightened and devout attachment to the interests of the nation; by studying and mastering the full philosophy of constitutional law, and bodying the CONSTITUTION in his living conduct; by unfeigned attachment to our noble and inviolable national UNION; by self-sacrificing devotion to the vernacular cause, whenever he apprehended its true interest, or its latent foe, or its real danger; by being justly and on proper occasions superior to popular clamor, where he knew and could distinguish between the hosannahs of the mob and the fame of history; by loving party only for his country's sake, and utterly forgoing it, when it seemed to stand in his country's way; by illustrating, *dignus discipulus dignissimo patre*, the principles of the school of WASHINGTON; and by maintaining those principles, effulgent and true, throughout his whole career of public life. Added to this, indeed, we are to credit his rare endowments and capacities, his form and bearing, his natural and oaken eloquence, his grandeur of person and persuasion of address, his nurture among the people, his nativity and growth in this country, and the formative times and crises both of the chivalrous young State of his adoption, and the prodigious and wonder-working country of his birth and his affections—his Kentucky and his America. And last, not least, in this mighty host of consecutive influences, his general instinct and homage in favor of religion; his sense, luminous and manly, of dependence on the providence and care of the Supreme Being—his accountability to GOD, the truth of the Bible, the mission of the SAVIOR, the destinations of eternity.

This last was a mighty element of his character—even when he quenched its flame, counterworked its proper effects by yielding to temptation, and sinned consciously, as alas! such millions do, against its tenderness, its persuasion, and its warning voice. Still, HENRY CLAY was no infidel. In his deviations, it was not his way to disparage and condemn religion, in order to frame an excuse for himself. He knew that religion was no pensioner on human opinion, or praise, or conduct; men depending on it, not it on men; it depending alone on GOD, its author and avenger; and GOD depending on himself alone—rather, depending not at all, the Being of Beings, existing absolute, necessary, immutable, perfect, eternal, JEHOVAH.

For the last half century, identified so nearly with the first half of the nineteenth century, so pregnant with great events throughout all Christendom, the events of our political history as a nation, in peace and in war, in prosperity and in adversity, in tranquillity and in agitation, in security and in fear, in hope and in despondency—their history could not be written without writing also the biography of HENRY CLAY. He was complicated with them, perpetually, prominently, practically, usefully, honorably—and whether in office and in public, or as a citizen and a patriot in private. Without a correct knowledge of the deeds of JOHN QUINCY ADAMS, HENRY CLAY and DANIEL WEBSTER, that great national triumvirate, no man could write the history of that distinguished period. And no man could judge correctly of their public acts, especially —shall I say—of the acts of Mr. CLAY, without some expansive comprehension at once of the state of the country, its relation to other nations, and the peculiar principles of its political organization, so wonderfully and yet harmoniously constituted and compounded, as a nation of nations, or a State of States, THIRTY-ONE from THIRTEEN, and to be augmented by still greater accessions from our vast territories. Here, to understand a part, one must understand the whole; and act at once for the interests of the immense national body, and for those of each related and constituent member. Here impulse is often in conflict with wisdom; partial regards are seemingly irreconcilable with those provincial or universal; the strength of government tends to operate menacingly in collision with popular rights; and the balance of power, and the adjustment of interests, in so multifarious an administration, is no problem for boys to solve, or for men of one idea, or even for empyrics and parvenues of five! or for any thing short of illumined American statesmanship, in full conjunction with sound patriotism and large experience and resolute integrity. Beside, what we often forget in the plain, of the men whom WE, THE PEOPLE, place on the summit of the pyramid of office, as our servants and our targets, as well as our spectacles and our themes of calumny, we solemnly swear them, when they take office, to abide by the constitution, to be incorruptible and impartial, and to seek the common good of the people, even against their importunities, and in spite of their criticisms and complaints, for the moment. This is no easy task for sentient flesh and blood to perform—and when I think of this, justice tells me, to respect the rulers and the magistrates of my country; to construe kindly, and magnanimously, and with liberal allowance, all their public acts, and even their private conduct; to pray for them, and to remember that it is one thing to supersede them in office, and often quite another to replace them with their superiors.

Will the episode be allowed me, not wholly inappropriate, if I venture to remind you of ten great principles, which are properly fundamental to all others, in the government of our country—a decade of main principles, without honoring which, we may boldly aver, no man is fit for office in it, unless inconsistency and perjury are among the prime of his qualifications; principles, we believe, which no man better understood and exemplified than our exalted senator and statesman; and without approving which, no man is competent to judge his acts or qualified to understand them; and to oppose which, ought to be a brand on the face of any citizen, who in that way should practice implicit treason, deserving a sentence of popular relegation from the country, still too good to harbor such a parricide in the capacious and genial bosom of its own outraged maternity.

1. All governments on earth, as fabrics, human in form and movement, all political organizations and administrations, as history too copiously shows, are imperfect; and hence though improvements are to be expected, and wisely sought and attempted, in the progressions of society, yet perfection, as a practical reality, will not be enjoyed in the present world.

2. The character of government is therefore comparative, as better or worse, on a scale of many gradations; while that of our country, we well and wisely accredit, as relatively the least faulty, and therefore the best in the world.

3. The Union of our States in one grand nationality, is the great fundamental and the normal and the indispensable condition, at once of our strength, and our safety, and our perpetuity, and our prosperity, if not properly of

our being, as a people, and a nation, and a powerful republic among the nations of the earth.

4. In order to this, concessions and compromises, as well as faithful covenant-keeping, are absolutely necessary, among the causes *sine qua non* of our confederated and our national existence.

5. The supremacy of mind over matter, that is the subordination of the military to the civil power, the sword to the pen, the army and the navy to the law-making and the law-interpreting and the law-executing functions; so that the proper magistracy of the country shall be the central mind of its government; this is AMERICANISM, THIS OUR WISDOM.

6. The inviolableness of the CONSTITUTION, with the just interpretation and the due performance of all its provisions.

7. The moral omnipotence of law; which, as law, is not to be resisted anywhere; but must ever be despotic and supreme, while it remains law; or, the rights of the people are gone, protection is defunct, and the individual is neither safe, nor free, at home or abroad, in seclusion or in society.

8. The subordinate independence and distinct sovereignty of each state in the confederacy, with all its constitutional prerogatives and rights, in its own jurisdiction and sphere.

9. The rights of legislation, representation, petition, and free speech, to all; with that of the ballot-box, as the masterly resource of freemen.

10. Religious freedom, with Church and State mutually related and serviceable, but not united; and the rights of conscience universally and impartially protected.

Let a man digest these principles, before he presumes to censure our great statesmen, who, for generations and for

ages now, and in times of peril and experiment, when precedents were less to be followed than created, have figured with honor and consistency in the service of their country. Their posts have been difficult, their duties arduous, their perils formidable, their acts stupendous, and their great success a glorious innovation on the scroll of universal history. As for HENRY CLAY—great without our highest office, I feel profoundly how much, under God, the whole nation is his debtor; and now, to pay that debt, is forever impossible. History will write his eulogium. Posterity will do him justice.

His country's heart is his funeral urn—
And should sculptured stone be denied him,
There will his name be found, when in turn
We lay our heads beside him.

HENRY CLAY was born in Virginia, that state of so many classic nativities and renowned memories in our country's annals, on the twelfth of April, seventeen hundred and seventy-seven, in the commencement of the war, about nine months after the Declaration of Independence. He was the son of a worthy clergyman, whose early exit, left him in tender years to the care and kindness of a worthy mother—bless her memory! who laid the foundation of all that was good and great in his maturer life, by sowing in a rich soil the seeds of Christian wisdom; thence illustrating the excellent stanza of Watts,

Though seed lie buried long in dust
It shant deceive the hope;
The precious grain can ne'er be lost
For grace insures the crop.

He struggled with no common difficulties in his nurture and development—but I am not his biographer, in this rapid sketch of approximations. His success was such as wealth and outward prosperity could never have secured to him. Adversity, a rude nurse, but oft a useful one, trained him and developed him, as no palace could, for great thoughts and mighty deeds.

His mind was distinguished for originality and strength. His intelligence was sound and his knowledge digested and accurate. His magnanimity was proverbial, the better counterpart of his large majestic frame. His courage was not fool-hardy or inconsiderate; but there was enough of it, always of the right kind, to meet any emergency. His self-command was remarkable. He fixed it in his mind, that, to lose his balance would never assist his strength or aid his victory; and few men have lived with a COMPOS SUI more rational and philosophic, or more commonly "harnessed in order serviceable." In the forum, or among surrounding and enthusiastic multitudes, or in the House of Representatives, or the Speaker's chair, or the senate "grave with primate wisdom," he was always sure of his identity as HENRY CLAY; with character, and plan, and object, and principle, that made others sure of the same. His perseverance was wonderful and his power of achievement was its result. His natural eloquence was real; but like DEMOSTHENES and CICERO and BURKE and AMES, he tried to make five talents ten—and he succeeded. His eloquence is a vernacular model; and many an unborn youth will it yet inspire, and many a young politician shall it hereafter discipline, to feel that, in a legitimate way, they also can rise, can be something, and do something, for the country, to vindicate their title to the honors of American birthright and American citizenship. And who could be an exemplar or a counselor, for our youthful Americans, more safe, more true, more just, more noble than HENRY CLAY.

It were worthy of a master hand to portray our illustrious statesman, in some of those scenes of peril and perplexity, as of honor and conspicuity and noble service to his country, in which he at once figured well, and acted gallantly, and was greatly tried, and showed in the result eminently prosperous, and enviably victorious, in the memorable arena. A few of these I select and mention, though I scarce can venture more. I pass all the initial stages of his ardent juvenility and his chivalrous behavior; all the scenery of his introduction to public life and the councils of his country; all the ways in which he conciliated the love and the confidence of his countrymen, and won the admiration of mankind; all his development and rise in congress, and all his popularity in the nation at large; and mention only a few of the maturer and the later passages of his history, in which, with many others, I own that I have peculiarly admired him.

1. At the treaty of Ghent, as one of the five American Commissioners, by whose wise and masterly diplomacy PEACE was negotiated. His colleagues were JOHN QUINCY ADAMS, ALBERT GALLATIN, JAMES A. BAYARD and JONATHAN RUSSELL; and their British opponents were the Right Honorable Lord GAMBIER, and the Honorable HENRY GOULBURN and WILLIAM ADAMS. In that august convention, while the American power and tact were radiant and ascendant, inspiring a just deference in the British Commissioners which they did not anticipate; while each of the five that represented America, was excellent in some peculiar way, and all combined were quite superior to all the antagonist forces on the part of King George, that is, the Prince Regent, it is well known that the influence and power of HENRY CLAY were much credited and renowned in the ar-

duous process and the pacific result. True indeed, the state of things in Europe and some casual events conspired to favor pacification. The cabinets of the continent, in conjunction with that of insular Europe, were all astir with ominous preparation; alliances were forming, and armies preparing, and prognostications circulating about the state of things and their drear issues, just before the great battle of Waterloo, which achieved the downfall of NAPOLEON: and now it was quite inconvenient for England to be at war in any other direction. But—none the less were the talent and the bravery of our Commissioners to be esteemed and praised, as more than a match for their opponents in the whole engagement. It is sufficient for my purpose in this sketch to add, that among his peers the genius and the address of CLAY did signal service to our cause. They all figured in the eye of Europe and the world; they were all well selected and admirably combined; but among them HENRY CLAY, PRIMUS INTER PARES, if not FACILE PRINCEPS, exerted a commanding influence, is said to have impressed usefully the British negotiators, and was owned by his colleagues as having contributed greatly to the happy consummation.

2. After his return, his services to the country were still continued and still distinguished, eminently masterly and eminently beneficial; till, on the accession of Mr. ADAMS to the Presidency in 1825, Mr. CLAY accepted the office of Secretary of State—and however misunderstood and misrepresented in that entire transaction, it is now confessed and known, that no bargain, no corruption, no collusion, no duplicity, but only reasonable and honorable management, at the time, constrained him, in accepting a seat in the cabinet of Mr. ADAMS, as in ordering or aiding the

operation of the antecedents that led to it. He filled the office with no injury, but only with increasing tributes to his culminating fame, and the good of his country.

3. In 1844 his name was before the people in the presidential canvass. I name this, passing many allied topics that obtrude themselves on our recollection, only to say, not that after a close and perilous contest, his friends and voters were defeated, but that the manner in which he bore the disappointment, evinced magnificently the superiority of the great national patriarch, who had other resources and compensations than popular appreciation, and who, we know, "had rather be RIGHT than be PRESIDENT." Was he sullen or morose; did he retire in the spirit of vindictive misanthropy; was his patriotism worn out or its occupation gone? none of these! He was HENRY CLAY afterward; only emerging from the civic agony, more a philosopher, more the genuine son of the nation, more the American Nestor, than he was before! To such a noble of the republic, the presidential chair could confer no greatness; to such a patriot, a kingly throne would be a degradation.

4. In 1850, though now in his seventy-fourth year, the infirmities of age requiring his release from fatigue and care amid the rural solaces of his loved ASHLAND, his tranquil, hospitable home, yet it was a national crisis; and HENRY CLAY was at his post, with WEBSTER, and FILLMORE, and other men of might, at WASHINGTON, meeting that crisis, and elaborately effectuating the pacification of the country. Oh! it was a time of gloom and perplexity. Questions complicated were to be met and resolved, relations in many a labyrinth were to be harmonized, friends and foes to conciliate, north and south to be affianced in a

mutual and inviolable pact, concessions and compromises adjusted, and the whole completed, defended, enacted, till in eventful consummation the whole was done and established. And for this, shall we censure and denounce him, or praise and thank him only? Here indeed opinions vary —since men of impulse, party, short-sightedness, prejudice, of one idea—or at most of two or three, are all at variance with him; nor am I the one to re-echo their tirades of malediction, their vile and blasphemous opprobriums. The casuistry of the matter is in the abstract here—half a loaf is better than no bread, especially to a starving man; better this, with some deductions and privations entailed, than blood and murder and civil war inaugurated in all the nation; this, rather than a worse alternative, an infinitely worse one; this, when the worse was the only alternative— and all men of reflection and serenity knew it, felt it, appreciated it, and did in the circumstances the best they could!

Yes! says one, but why not set the slaves all free at once, and be done with it? sure enough—and why does not the querist do it himself? He is just exactly as able to do it, as was HENRY CLAY. Shame to the wicked simpletons. Mr. CLAY knew what he was about, was superior to the asinine clamor and objurgation which he both anticipated and compassionated or despised. He did the best he could in the circumstances and relations in which he acted, with such far-reaching wisdom, such comprehension, such vigor, such consistency, and such resulting good to all concerned, that now the whole nation are beginning to see and own it—and woe to the busy pragmatical lunatic, who attempts wildly to disturb that result or to do mischief in the premises in any other way!

5. See him again in his own death chamber, last winter,

in his interview with KOSSUTH. "As a dying man I denounce your doctrine and your plan of intervention," said he, to the startled Hungarian Governor. There it is, MULTUM IN PARVO! I denounce it too. What! are we to go a crusade to set things right, at the point of the bayonet, in all Europe, and in all the world? and this with the stupid self-contradictory paradox of—INTERVENTION FOR THE SAKE OF NON-INTERVENTION? This I hope will be administered, if at all, in very infinitesimal doses; though its grand principle would reverse the apophthegm of SIMILIA SIMILIBUS CURANTUR. Our doctrine, as taught us by WASHINGTON and all the fathers of the republic, is far better—FREE INTERCOURSE WITH ALL NATIONS; ENTANGLING ALLIANCES WITH NONE. Should we march to Hungary, or to Vienna, or St. Petersburgh, in the cause of the Great Magyar, we could soon do a wholesale business in that way. We might stop at France on our march, and teach their young nephew of his uncle some lessons of duty about keeping his oath of office to the adjourned republic. We could find also some employment for our reforming arms in England itself—and then in Italy, in Greece, in Turkey, and a thousand other places. No! Our wisdom is to keep clear the logic and the rhetoric of our republican example. This will teach lessons that must convince even tyrants themselves. It will go where electricity itself cannot follow it—into the consciences of all men. This we can always consistently and legitimately do, and none can blame, none refute us. The other plan—quixotic as well as impracticable, would exhaust our national resources, waste our blood and our treasure in foreign continents and oceans, insure signal and ignominious defeat, make us the laughing-stock of Europe and the pity of the world. Sometimes indeed our example may be specially direct, and even aggressive, in its action. We may serve them with some documentary American logic, like that of the immortal HULLSEMAN paper, in which our Great Secretary of State, with characteristic thunder in a clear sky, or visible lightning in the darkness of a transatlantic atmosphere, uttered the protest of freemen with consternation to the smitten heart of despotism.

Look again to his death-bed chamber and reconnoiter with me, that memorable scene—contemplate it, so picturesque, so characteristic, so instructive, such a lesson for our country, such a demonstration of wisdom, and courage, and sincerity, truly American! Were I a painter, or a gifted artist of the chisel, and endowed with fame-enacting genius, as a GUIDO, a RUBENS, a VANDYCK, a RAPHAEL, a PHIDIAS, or a PRAXITELES, that scene should always speak to posterity. The breathing marble, or the sculptured stone, or the grouping and more social canvas, should rehearse the lesson, with lucid and impressive and almost living, certainly enduring eloquence, to unborn generations of Americans. What a scene of grandeur, I repeat it, for some favored devotee of the fine arts—who is at the same time an intelligent lover of his country! It might be done, with power intelligible and electric. It has in it all the elements that should stimulate native talent and reward artistic enterprise, and make, for its own graphic achievement, a coronation, and an ovation in the country—elements of sublimity, of sapient instruction, of patriotic statesmanship, of Christian self-possession, of oraculous solemnity, of fortitude invincible snd of unchangeable policy, and of example national, stupendous, magnanimous, never to be forgotten; anticipating, for the reproductive art, that immortality of fame, which the excellence of the sentiment, so deservedly national, so justly American, must receive at last from the sober and the honorary registrations of history.

KOSSUTH indeed advocated the noble doctrine of the sodality of nations—and with him we both admire and believe it; nay, in a qualified sense, we go it with him—but, in his way, not at all! No, indeed! Our wisdom is still identified, on the contrary, with that of the FAREWELL ADDRESS of the FATHER OF HIS COUNTRY; which we brook no stranger to expound, or rectify, or pervert, for us. Our doctrine is at once with that protest of the dying senator; and as such, orthodox, tried, American.

We laud the sentiment; but, for the way,
The Great Magyar we doubt—and more obey
Our WASHINGTON, our WEBSTER, and our CLAY.

6. It remains, for a moment, to contemplate HENRY CLAY in the chamber of death; where, prisoned so long, he could meditate, and pray, and seek his GOD, with the solemn consciousness that soon he must appear, accountable before him! Yes! and this, we think, with reason, he did. GOD dealt with him in merciful loving-kindness. Gradual was the approach of death, the last enemy; and its illapse was gentle, gradual, seen only in result, "as sinks the summer's sun in cloudless sky." There, with his servant and his pastor, he received the communion; professed his faith and his hope in JESUS CHRIST alone; confessed, with humiliation, his sins; and on his bended knees, when he could, and on his bed when this was all his strength allowed, before the apprehended and holy majesty of Almighty GOD, only wise, and in the name of the gracious Redeemer and Savior of the lost, who *came into the world*

to save sinners, even the chief, who died for us on the cross, in whom we have redemption through his blood, the forgiveness of sins according to the riches of his grace, he often and devoutly prayed, for pardoning grace and full salvation; he prayed for his friends, for his country, for the Church of GOD, for the world of man, commending himself and all he chiefly loved and valued, to the grace and care of our FATHER and our GOD, our SOVEREIGN and our SAVIOR, forever.

And now, what shall we say? I answer with two concessions—He had faults and sins;—He had foes hardly to be placated or reconciled.

How could a man so eminent as CLAY
Not be a target for the hosts beneath?
Star in the darkness, with potential sway
He shone, a sun that changed it into a day;
While listening Senates, hearing, held their breath,
Defeated rivals, rigorous as death,
Found him the hindrance in ambition's way;
Envied his fame and grudged its bright display.
Such ever is of genius the career,
The meed of talents faithful in their sphere.
He who ascends the mountain crest shall find
Its loftiest peak most wrapt in cloud and snow;
As who surpasses or subdues mankind
Must look down on the hate of those below;
Though far above the sun of glory glow,
As far beneath the earth and ocean spread,
Round him are icy rocks, and fiercely blow,
Contending tempests on his naked head;
And thus reward the toils and cares that to those summits led.
Hence who aspires, distinguished, prosperous, high,
Meets thunder—from the earth, if not the sky.
Even patriot chiefs must find ungrateful war,
Or win too late their just—EXCELSIOR.
So while he lived as glory's first-born son
And freedom's sire, it raged on WASHINGTON.
With fame in just proportion envy grows,
And he who makes a character makes foes.
Some in such carnivals alone are seen;

On others' greatness feasts their envy keen;
Great only in the ravage of their spleen.
Yet greatness scorns or quite forgets their rage
While worthy purposes its thought engage.
The alternative, ignoble, craven, mean,
  Obscure as nothing, thwarting glory's plan;
  No! do your duty, show yourself a man,
Nor useless live, dying unblest, unseen—
  Your warrant this--I'M AN AMERICAN.
Thus, come what will, the patriot Christian dares
To think, speak, act, with wisdom's sacred cares;
Serve GOD, bless men, trust truth, do right, with praises and with prayers.

[Altered and enlarged from a known quotation.]

As to the former, his faults and sins, my argument is brief. If *angels rejoice over one sinner that repenteth,* who are you, O cruel caviler, to send your dissonance into their harmony, or utter your groans of malignity among their pæans and praises to the *grace that reigneth, through righteousness to eternal life, by Jesus Christ our Lord? Let him that is without sin among you cast at him the first stone.* He had sins? I know it—in part; GOD knows it altogether; knows the same of you and of me! What if GOD also knows that HENRY CLAY was a sincere penitent—as he solemnly professed to be? Then is he now in heaven, among the glorified millions of the ransomed of the Lamb. Better employed than caviling, and grudging the persuasion, which so much evidence sustains, that his great heart broke with the love of CHRIST and dissolved in penitence at his feet, by the grace of the Holy Ghost; better employed, I say, should we all be, in searching and seeking to secure our own preparation for glory, before that dread moment, when death, at the order of the Son of Man, sweeps us away from the vision of the living. Here I wish to forget all his faults and all his sins; being a sinner myself, humbly hoping for forgiveness and *acceptance in the* BELOVED.

In all the life and actions of HENRY CLAY, however far his deviations might at times have gone, there appears, on just and peculiar occasions, a noble and sincere remorse, that did homage to GOD and goodness, boldly, in the eye and ear of the observant world. All his great speeches, and often his brief and incidental ones, more or less evince his deep religious convictions, and contain honest tribute to the inspired and eternal truth of Christianity. I remember one, and can in the main, or in its drift, reproduce it; which affected many at the time, and myself with others, about twenty or more years ago, when the Asiatic cholera was giving signs of a visit to our country, after having coursed its way of desolation round the globe; seeming like the angel of wrath, hovering on our borders, displayed at meridian altitude in the midst of heaven, bending his bow and brandishing his shafts, and awaiting the signal from the throne of GOD, to take his fatal aim, and empty his capacious quiver, on places and on victims selected for doom. It was in the Senate of the United States that he uttered his solemn and appropriate eloquence; so apposite to the formidable crisis, when Europe was in funereal weeds; so corresponsive to the religious awe of our favored and guilty people, before high heaven, at a time so proper for solemnity and humiliation, that GOD might see before him a universe in tears, a nation at his feet, a whole people, with their conscious millions, deprecating his terrific and righteous judgments, and supplicating, *O Lord, in wrath remember mercy!* His words were good and true. "I am not," said he, "a Christian. I ought to be, I wish I was; I hope I shall be, ere long. At such an hour, we ought all to be prepared. This pestilence is the terror of nations and the scourge of GOD.

Who can stand before it? It is the cholera asphyxia, which with force electric sheds paralysis through the human frame, when the muscular and the nervous powers obey no more the will, and the mass of the smitten body collapses in inexorable death. It goes, sir, where it is sent. No prophylactic skill can parry its assault. Science knows not its way, and prognosis attempts in vain to forecast the place of its revel or the path of its commissioned progress. GOD alone can defend our country or limit its desolations."

There is one, a worthy colleague, formerly of the Senate, whom I have known and honored increasingly, now for more than forty years; who deserved the confidence of HENRY CLAY, and knew from converse and correspondence with him, more of his religious heart probably than any other person; and whose sound Christian faith and immaculate Christian example, were, in my own judgment, blest to his arrested and confiding regard; and whose pure and sound intelligence, as a judge in these sacred relations, there lives no one to question; such a one, whose opinion in his favor might well sway and accomplish ours, touching his Christian sincerity of faith; whose letters and counsel to him, were worthy of the confidential affection with which they were always received and answered; and whose influence was, I trust, used and owned of GOD, to render him a brother in the kingdom, and a friend to all eternity, in the loves and the hopes of the Redeemer. I allude to the President of the American Bible Society, and my own personal friend, HONORABLE THEODORE FRELINGHUYSEN, LL. D., late Chancellor of the University of the city of New York; now President of Rutgers' College, New Brunswick, New Jersey.

As to the foes of CLAY, I trust there are very few of posthumous continuance—very few remaining—few hyenas of the *genus homo*, conscious or confessed, now to desecrate the sleep of the grave! For one foe he had comparatively twenty friends—I should rather say, five hundred, throughout the nation; Whig and Democrat, Slaveholder and Abolitionist, Protestant and Romanist, Episcopalian and Baptist, Methodist and Presbyterian, Black and White, Bond and Free, Indian and Mulatto, Native and Adopted, Jew and Quaker, ay! and all Americans are now the friends of HENRY CLAY, as they are of his great archetype, WASHINGTON. As to the foes he had, alas! what great man has them not, especially if he acts in public life? if there he has an opinion of his own, and speaks it? if he takes a position, and maintains it? if he is not in the market to be bought or sold, but acts as truth and duty seem to him clearly to marshal his way? There is reason for the *woe* pronounced on that piece of imbecility, *of whom all men speak well!* Prejudice, ignorance, selfishness, partyism, narrow views, wrong-headedness, mental wildness, natural ferocity of character, superficial thinking, partial conceits, and social meanness; these abounding vices of society may account for it, that some, nay, many of the greatest and the best in human form, thus far vouchsafed from heaven to earth, have been the most hated by many of their cotemporaries—who, after death, mingle in the wail of the general bereavement, and build their sepulchres, as if their best friends' corpses were resting in them? The man most hated in his life, and most murdered in his death, by men on earth, was—our blessed Savior, the LORD from heaven—the LORD JESUS CHRIST.

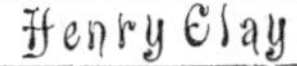

OBITUARY ADDRESSES

ON THE

OCCASION OF THE DEATH

OF THE

HON. HENRY CLAY,

DELIVERED IN THE

SENATE AND HOUSE OF REPRESENTATIVES OF THE UNITED STATES,

JUNE 30, 1852.

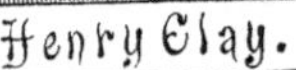

SENATE OF THE UNITED STATES.

After the reading of the Journal, Mr. UNDERWOOD rose and addressed the Senate, as follows:

Mr. PRESIDENT: I rise to announce the death of my colleague, Mr. CLAY. He died at his lodgings, in the National Hotel of this city, at seventeen minutes past eleven o'clock yesterday morning, in the seventy-sixth year of his age. He expired with perfect composure, and without a groan or struggle.

By his death our country has lost one of its most eminent citizens and statesmen; and, I think, its greatest genius. I shall not detain the Senate by narrating the transactions of his long and useful life. His distinguished services as a statesman are inseparably connected with the history of his country. As Representative and Speaker in the other house of Congress, as Senator in this body, as Secretary of State, and as Envoy abroad, he has, in all these positions, exhibited a wisdom and patriotism which have made a deep and lasting impression upon the grateful hearts of his countrymen. His thoughts and his actions have already been published to the world in written biography; in congressional debates and reports; in the journals of the two houses; and in the pages of American history. They have been commemorated by monuments erected on the wayside. They have been engraven on medals of gold. Their memory will survive the monuments of marble and the medals of gold; for these are effaced and decay by the friction of ages. But the thoughts and actions of my late colleague have become identified with the immortality of the human mind, and will pass down from generation to generation as a portion of our national inheritance, incapable of annihilation so long as genius has an admirer, or liberty a friend.

Mr. President, the character of HENRY CLAY was formed and developed by the influence of our free institutions. His physical, mental, and moral faculties were the gift of GOD. That they were greatly superior to the faculties allotted to most men cannot be questioned. They were not cultivated, improved, and directed by a liberal or collegiate education. His respectable parents were not wealthy, and had not the means of maintaining their children at college. Moreover, his father died when he was a boy. At an early period, Mr. CLAY was thrown upon his own resources, without patrimony. He grew up in a clerk's office in Richmond, Virginia. He there studied law. He emigrated from his native state and settled in Lexington, Kentucky, where he commenced the practice of his profession, before he was of full age.

The road to wealth, to honor, and fame, was open before him. Under our constitution and laws he might freely employ his great faculties unobstructed by legal impediments, and unaided by exclusive privileges. Very soon Mr. CLAY made a deep and favorable impression upon the people among whom he began his career. The excellence of his natural faculties was soon displayed. Necessity stimulated him in their cultivation. His assiduity, skill, and fidelity in professional engagements secured public confidence. He was elected member of the legislature of Kentucky, in which body he served several sessions prior to 1806. In that year he was elevated to a seat in the Senate of the United States.

At the bar and in the General Assembly of Kentucky, Mr. CLAY first manifested those high qualities as a public speaker which have secured to him so much popular applause and admiration. His physical and mental organization eminently qualified him to become a great and impressive orator. His person was tall, slender and commanding. His temperament ardent, fearless, and full of hope. His countenance clear, expressive and variable—indicating the emotion which predominated at the moment with exact similitude. His voice, cultivated and modulated in harmony with the sentiment he desired to express, fell upon the ear like the melody of enrapturing music. His eye beaming with intelligence and flashing with coruscations of genius. His gestures and attitudes graceful and natural. These personal advantages won the prepossessions of an audience, even before his intellectual powers began to move his hearers; and when his strong common sense, his profound reasoning, his clear conceptions of his subject in all its bearings, and his striking and beautiful illustrations, united with such personal qualities, were brought to the discussion of any question, his audience was enraptured, convinced and led by the orator as if enchanted by the lyre of Orpheus.

No man was ever blessed by his Creator with faculties of a higher order of excellence than those given to Mr. CLAY. In the quickness of his perceptions, and the rapidity with which his conclusions were formed, he had few equals and no superior. He was eminently endowed with a nice discriminating taste for order, symmetry and beauty. He detected in a moment every thing out of place or deficient in his room, upon his farm, in his own or the dress of others. He was a skillful judge of the form and qualities of his domestic animals, which he delighted to raise on his farm. I could give you instances of the quickness and minuteness of his keen faculty of observation which never overlooked any thing. A want of neatness and order was offensive to him. He was particular and neat in his handwriting, and his apparel. A slovenly blot or negligence of any sort met his condemnation; while he was so organized that he attended to, and arranged little things to please and gratify his natural love for neatness, order and beauty, his great intellectual faculties grasped all the subjects of jurisprudence and politics with a facility amounting almost to intuition. As a lawyer, he stood at the head of his profession. As a statesman, his stand at the head of the Republican Whig party for nearly half a century, establishes his title to pre-eminence among his illustrious associates.

Mr. Clay was deeply versed in all the springs of human action. He had read and studied biography and history. Shortly after I left college, I had occasion to call on him in Frankfort, where he was attending court, and well I remember to have found him with Plutarch's Lives in his hands. No one better than he knew how to avail himself of human motives, and all the circumstances which surrounded a subject, or could present them with more force and skill to accomplish the object of an argument.

Mr. Clay, throughout his public career, was influenced by the loftiest patriotism. Confident in the truth of his convictions and the purity of his purposes, he was ardent, sometimes impetuous, in the pursuit of objects which he believed essential to the general welfare. Those who

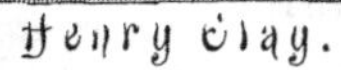

stood in his way were thrown aside without fear or ceremony. He never affected a courtier's deference to men or opinions which he thought hostile to the best interests of his country; and hence he may have wounded the vanity of those who thought themselves of consequence. It is certain, whatever the cause, that at one period of his life Mr. CLAY might have been referred to as proof that there is more truth than fiction in those profound lines of the poet—

> "He who ascends to mountain-tops shall find
> The loftiest peaks most wrapt in clouds and snow;
> He who surpasses or subdues mankind,
> Must look down on the hate of those below.
> Though high above the sun of glory glow,
> And far beneath the earth and ocean spread;
> Round him are icy rocks, and loudly blow
> Contending tempests on his naked head,
> And thus reward the toils which to those summits led."

Calumny and detraction emptied their vials upon him. But how glorious the change! He outlived malice and envy. He lived long enough to prove to the world that his ambition was no more than a holy aspiration to make his country the greatest, most powerful, and best governed on the earth. If he desired its highest office, it was because the greater power and influence resulting from such elevation would enable him to do more than he otherwise could for the progress and advancement—first of his own countrymen, then of his whole race. His sympathies embraced all. The African slave, the Creole of Spanish America, the children of renovated classic Greece—all families of men, without respect to color or clime, found in his expanded bosom and comprehensive intellect a friend of their elevation and amelioration. Such ambition as that, is GOD's implantation in the human heart for raising the down-trodden nations of the earth, and fitting them for regenerated existence in politics, in morals and religion.

Bold and determined as Mr. CLAY was in all his actions he was, nevertheless, conciliating. He did not obstinately adhere to things impracticable. If he could not accomplish the best, he contented himself with the nighest approach to it. He has been the great compromiser of those political agitations and opposing opinions which have, in the belief of thousands, at different times, endangered the perpetuity of our Federal Government and Union.

Mr. CLAY was no less remarkable for his admirable social qualities than for his intellectual abilities. As a companion, he was the delight of his friends; and no man ever had better or truer. They have loved him from the beginning, and loved him to the last. His hospitable mansion at Ashland was always open to their reception. No guest ever thence departed without feeling happier for his visit. But, alas! that hospitable mansion has already been converted into a house of mourning; already has intelligence of his death passed with electric velocity to that aged, and now widowed lady, who, for more than fifty years, bore to him all the endearing relations of wife, and whose feeble condition prevented her from joining him in this city, and soothing the anguish of life's last scene by those endearing attentions which no one can give so well as woman and a wife. May GOD infuse into her heart and mind the Christian spirit of submission under her bereavement. It cannot be long before she may expect a reunion in Heaven. A nation condoles with her and her children on account of their irreparable loss.

Mr. Clay, from the nature of his disease, declined very gradually. He bore his protracted sufferings with great equanimity and patience. On one occasion, he said to me, that when death was inevitable, and must soon come, and when the sufferer was ready to die, he did not perceive the wisdom of praying to be "delivered from sudden death." He thought, under such circumstances, the sooner suffering was relieved by death the better. He desired the termination of his own sufferings, while he acknowledged the duty of patiently waiting and abiding the pleasure of God. Mr. Clay frequently spoke to me of his hope of eternal life, founded upon the merits of Jesus Christ as a Savior; who, as he remarked, came into the world to bring "life and immortality to light." He was a member of the Episcopalian Church. In one of our conversations he told me, that as his hour of dissolution approached, he found that his affections were concentrating more and more upon his domestic circle—his wife and children. In my daily visits he was in the habit of asking me to detail to him the transactions of the Senate. This I did, and he manifested much interest in passing occurrences. His inquiries were less frequent as his end approached. For the week preceding his death he seemed to be altogether abstracted from the concerns of the world. When he became so low that he could not converse without being fatigued, he frequently requested those around him to converse. He would then quietly listen. He retained his mental faculties in great perfection. His memory remained perfect. He frequently mentioned events and conversations of recent occurrence, showing that he had a perfect recollection of what was said and done. He said to me that he was grateful to God for continuing to him the blessing of reason, which enabled him to contemplate and reflect on his situation. He manifested during his confinement the same characteristics which marked his conduct through the vigor of his life. He was exceedingly averse to give his friends "*trouble*," as he called it. Some time before he knew it we commenced waiting through the night in an adjoining room. He said to me, after passing a painful day, "Perhaps some one had better remain all night in the parlor." From this time he knew some friend was constantly at hand ready to attend to him.

Mr. President, the majestic form of Mr. CLAY will no more grace these halls. No more shall we hear that voice which has so often thrilled and charmed the assembled representatives of the American people. No more shall we see that waving hand and eye of light, as when he was engaged unfolding his policy in regard to the varied interests of our growing and mighty republican empire. His voice is silent, on earth, forever. The darkness of death has obscured the lustre of his eye. But the memory of his services—not only to his beloved Kentucky, not only to the United States, but for the cause of human freedom and progress throughout the world—will live through future ages, as a bright example, stimulating and encouraging his own countrymen and the people of all nations in their patriotic devotions to country and humanity.

With Christians, there is yet a nobler and a higher thought in regard to Mr. CLAY. They will think of him in connection with eternity. They will contemplate his immortal spirit occupying its true relative magnitude among the moral stars of glory in the presence of GOD.

They will think of him as having fulfilled the duties allotted to him on earth, having been regenerated by Divine grace, and having passed through the valley of the shadow of death, and reached an everlasting and happy home in that "house not made with hands, eternal in the heavens."

On Sunday morning last, I was watching alone at Mr. CLAY's bedside. For the last hour he had been unusually quiet, and I thought he was sleeping. In that, however, he told me I was mistaken. Opening his eyes and looking at me, he said, "Mr. UNDERWOOD, there may be some question where my remains shall be buried. Some persons may designate Frankfort. I wish to repose at the cemetery in Lexington, where many of my friends and connections are buried." My reply was, "I will endeavor to have your wish executed."

I now ask the Senate to have his corpse transmitted to Lexington, Kentucky, for sepulture. Let him sleep with the dead of that city, in and near which his home has been for more than half a century. For the people of Lexington, the living and the dead, he manifested, by the statement made to me, a pure and holy sympathy, and a desire to cleave unto them, as strong as that which bound RUTH to NAOMI. It was his anxious wish to return to them before he died, and to realize what the daughter of MOAB so strongly felt and beautifully expressed: "Thy people shall be my people, and thy GOD my GOD. Where thou diest will I die, and there will I be buried."

It is fit that the tomb of HENRY CLAY should be in the city of Lexington. In our Revolution, liberty's first libation-blood was poured out in a town of that name in Massachusetts. On hearing it, the pioneers of Kentucky consecrated the name, and applied it to the place where Mr. CLAY desired to be buried. The associations connected with the name, harmonize with his character; and the monument erected to his memory at the spot selected by him will be visited by the votaries of genius and liberty with that reverence which is inspired at the tomb of WASHINGTON. Upon that monument let his epitaph be engraved.

Mr. President, I have availed myself of Dr. JOHNSON'S paraphrase of the epitaph on THOMAS HANMER, with a few alterations and additions, to express, in borrowed verse, my admiration for the life and character of Mr. CLAY; and with this heart-tribute to the memory of my illustrious colleague, I conclude my remarks:

Born when Freedom her stripes and stars unfurl'd,
When Revolution shook the startled world—
Heroes and sages taught his brilliant mind
To know and love the rights of all mankind.
"In life's first bloom his public toils began,
At once commenced the Senator and man;
In business dext'rous, weighty in debate,
Near fifty years he labor'd for the State,
In every speech persuasive wisdom flow'd,
In every act refulgent virtue glow'd;
Suspended faction ceased from rage and strife,
To hear his eloquence and praise his life.
Resistless merit fixed the Members' choice,
Who hail'd him Speaker with united voice."
His talents ripening with advancing years—
His wisdom growing with his public cares—
A chosen envoy, war's dark horrors cease,
And tides of carnage turn to streams of peace.
Conflicting principles, internal strife,
Tariff and slavery, disunion rife,
All are *compromised* by his great hand,
And beams of joy illuminate the land.
Patriot, Christian, Husband, Father, Friend,
Thy work of life achieved a glorious end!

I offer the following resolutions:

Resolved, That a committee of six be appointed by the President of the Senate, to take order for superintending the funeral of HENRY CLAY, late a member of this body, which will take place to-morrow at twelve o'clock, M., and that the Senate will attend the same.

Resolved, That the members of the Senate, from a sincere desire of showing every mark of respect to the memory of the deceased, will go into mourning for one month, by the usual mode of wearing crape on the left arm.

Resolved, As a further mark of respect entertained by the Senate for the memory of HENRY CLAY, and his long and distinguished services to his country, that his remains, in pursuance of the known wishes of his family, be removed to the place of sepulture selected by himself at Lexington, in Kentucky, in charge of the Sergeant-at-Arms, and attended by a committee of six senators, to be appointed by the President of the Senate, who shall have full power to carry this resolution into effect.

Mr. CASS.

Mr. PRESIDENT: Again has an impressive warning come to teach us, that in the midst of life we are in death. The ordinary labors of this hall are suspended, and its contentions hushed, before the power of him, who says to the storm of human passion, as he said of old to the waves of Galilee, PEACE, BE STILL. The lessons of His providence, severe as they may be, often become merciful dispensations, like that which is now spreading sorrow through the land, and which is reminding us that we have higher duties to fulfill, and graver responsibilities to encounter, than those that meet us here, when we lay our hands upon His holy word, and invoke His holy name, promising to be faithful to that Constitution, which He gave us in His mercy, and will withdraw only in the hour of our blindness and disobedience, and of His own wrath.

Another great man has fallen in our land, ripe indeed in years and in honors, but never dearer to the American people than when called from the theatre of his services and renown to that final bar where the lofty and the lowly must all meet at last.

I do not rise, upon this mournful occasion, to indulge in the language of panegyric. My regard for the memory of the dead, and for the obligations of the living, would equally rebuke such a course. The severity of truth is, at once, our proper duty and our best consolation. Born during the revolutionary struggle, our deceased associate was one of the few remaining public men who connect the present generation with the actors in the trying scenes of that eventful period, and whose names and deeds will soon be known only in the history of their country. He was another illustration, and a noble one, too, of the glorious equality of our institutions, which freely offer all their rewards to all who justly seek them; for he was the architect of his own fortune, having made his way in life by self-exertion; and he was an early adventurer in the great forest of the West, then a world of primitive vegetation, but now the abode of intelligence and religion, of prosperity and civilization. But he possessed that intellectual superiority which overcomes surrounding obstacles, and which local seclusion cannot long withhold from general knowledge and appreciation.

It is almost half a century since he passed through Chillicothe, then the seat of government of Ohio, where I was a member of the legislature, on his way to take his place in this very body, which is now listening to this reminiscence, and to a feeble tribute of regard from one who then saw him for the first time, but who can never forget the impression he produced by the charms of his conversation, the frankness of his manner, and the high qualities with which he was endowed. Since then he has belonged to his country, and has taken a part, and a prominent part, both in peace and war, in all the great questions affecting her interest and her honor; and though it has been my fortune often to differ from him, yet I believe he was as pure a patriot as ever participated in the councils of a nation, anxious for the public good, and seeking to promote it, during all the vicissitudes of a long and eventful life. That he exercised a powerful influence, within the sphere of his action, through the whole country, indeed, we all feel and know; and we know, too, the eminent endowments to which he owed this high distinction. Frank and fearless in the expression of his opinion, and in the performance of his duties, with rare powers of eloquence, which never failed to rivet the attention of his auditory, and which always commanded admiration, even when they did not carry conviction—prompt in decision, and firm in action, and with a vigorous intellect, trained in the contests of a stirring life, and strengthened by enlarged experience and observation, joined withal to an ardent love of country, and to great purity of purpose,—these were the elements of his power and success; and we dwell upon them with mournful gratification now, when we shall soon follow him to the cold and silent tomb, where we shall commit "earth to earth, ashes to ashes, dust to dust," but with the blessed conviction of the truth of that Divine revelation which teaches us that there is life and hope beyond the narrow house, where we shall leave him alone to the mercy of his God and ours.

He has passed beyond the reach of human praise or censure; but the judgment of his contemporaries has preceded and pronounced the judgment of history, and his name and fame will shed lustre upon his country, and will be proudly cherished in the hearts of his countrymen for long ages to come. Yes, they will be cherished and freshly remembered, when these marble columns, that surround us, so often the witnesses of his triumph—but in a few brief hours, when his mortal frame, despoiled of the immortal spirit, shall rest under this dome for the last time, to become the witnesses of his defeat in that final contest, where the mightiest fall before the great destroyer—when these marble columns shall themselves have fallen, like all the works of man, leaving their broken fragments to tell the story of former magnificence, amid the very ruins which announce decay and desolation.

I was often with him during his last illness, when the world and the things of the world were fast fading away, before him. He knew that the silver cord was almost loosened, and that the golden bowl was breaking at the fountain; but he was resigned to the will of Providence, feeling that He who gave has the right to take away, in His own good time and manner. After his duty to his Creator, and his anxiety for his family, his first care was for his country, and his first wish for the preservation and perpetuation of the Constitution and the Union—dear to him in the hour of death, as they had ever been in the vigor of life. Of that Constitution and Union, whose defence in the last and greatest crisis of their peril, had called forth all his energies, and stimulated those memorable and powerful exertions, which he who witnessed can never forget, and which no doubt hastened the final catastrophe a nation now deplores, with a sincerity and unanimity, not less honorable to themselves than to the memory of the object of their affections. And when we shall enter that narrow valley, through which he has passed before us, and which leads to the judgment-seat of GOD, may we be able to say, through faith in his Son our Savior, and in the beautiful language of the hymn of the dying Christian—dying, but ever living and triumphant—

> "The world recedes; it disappears!
> Heav'n opens on my eyes! my ears
> With sounds seraphic ring;
> Lend, lend your wings! I mount—I fly!
> Oh, Grave! where is thy victory?
> Oh, Death! where is thy sting?"

"Let me die the death of the righteous, and let my last hour be like his."

Mr. HUNTER:

Mr. PRESIDENT: We have heard, with deep sensibility, what has just fallen from the Senators who have preceded me. We have heard, sir, the voice of Kentucky—and, upon this occasion, she had a right to speak—in mingled accents of pride and sorrow; for it has rarely fallen to the lot of any state to lament the loss of such a son. But Virginia, too, is entitled to her place in this procession; for she cannot be supposed to be unmindful of the tie which bound her to the dead. When the earth opens to receive the mortal part which she gave to man, it is then that affection is eager to bury in its bosom every recollection but those of love and kindness. And, sir, when the last sensible tie is about to be severed, it is then that we look with anxious interest to the deeds of the life, and to the emanations of the heart and the mind, for those more enduring monuments which are the creations of an immortal nature.

In this instance, we can be at no loss for these. This land, sir, is full of the monuments of his genius. His memory is as imperishable as American history itself, for he was one of those who made it. Sir, he belonged to that marked class who are the men of their century; for it was his rare good fortune not only to have been endowed with the capacity to do great things, but to have enjoyed the opportunities of achieving them. I know, sir, it has been said and deplored, that he wanted some of the advantages of an early education; but it, perhaps, has not been remembered that, in many respects, he enjoyed such opportunities for mental training as can rarely fall to the lot of man. He had not a chance to learn as much from books, but he had such opportunities of learning from men as few have ever enjoyed. Sir, it is to be remembered that he was reared at a time when there was a state of society, in the commonwealth which gave him birth, such as has never been seen there before nor since. It was his early privilege to see how justice was administered by a PENDLETON and a WYTHE, with the last of whom he was in the daily habit of familiar intercourse. He had constant opportunities to observe how forensic questions were managed by a MARSHALL and a WICKHAM. He was old enough, too,

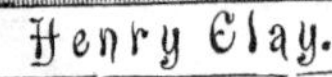

to have heard and to have appreciated the eloquence of a PATRICK HENRY, and of GEORGE KEITH TAYLOR. In short, sir, he lived in a society in which the examples of a JEFFERSON, and a MADISON, and MONROE were living influences, and on which the setting sun of a WASHINGTON cast the mild effulgence of its departing rays.

He was trained, too, as has been well said by the Senator from Michigan, [Mr. CASS,] at a period when the recent revolutionary struggle had given a more elevated tone to patriotism, and imparted a higher cast to public feeling and to public character. Such lessons were worth, perhaps, more to him than the whole encyclopedia of scholastic learning. Not only were the circumstances of his early training favorable to the development of his genius, but the theatre upon which he was thrown, was eminently propitious for its exercise. The circumstances of the early settlement of Kentucky, the generous, daring and reckless character of the people—all fitted it to be the theatre for the display of those commanding qualities of heart and mind, which he so eminently possessed. There can be little doubt but that those people and their chosen leader exercised a mutual influence upon each other; and no one can be surprised that with his brave spirit and commanding eloquence, and fascinating address, he should have led not only there but elsewhere.

I did not know him, Mr. President, as you did, in the freshness of his prime, or in the full maturity of his manhood. I did not hear him, sir, as you have heard him, when his voice roused the spirit of his countrymen for war—when he cheered the drooping, when he rallied the doubting through all the vicissitudes of a long and doubtful contest. I have never seen him, sir, when, from the height of the chair, he ruled the House of Representatives by the energy of his will, or when, upon the level of the floor, he exercised a control almost as absolute by the mastery of his intellect. When I first knew him his sun had a little passed its zenith. The effacing hand of time had just begun to touch the lineaments of his manhood. But yet, sir, I saw enough of him to be able to realize what he might have been in the prime of his strength, and in the full vigor of his maturity. I saw him, sir, as you did, when he led the "opposition" during the administration of Mr. VAN BUREN. I had daily opportunities of witnessing the exhibition of his powers during the extra session under Mr. TYLER's administration. And I saw, as we all saw, in a recent contest, the exhibition of power on his part, which was most marvellous in one of his years.

Mr. President, he may not have had as much of analytic skill as some others, in dissecting a subject. It may be, perhaps, that he did not seek to look quite so far ahead as some who have been most distinguished for political forecast. But it may be truly said of Mr. CLAY, that he was no exaggerator. He looked at events through neither end of the telescope, but surveyed them with the natural and the naked eye. He had the capacity of seeing things as the people saw them, and of feeling things as the people felt them. He had, sir, beyond any other man, whom I have ever seen, the true mesmeric touch of the orator—the rare art of transferring his impulses to others. Thoughts, feelings, emotions, came from the ready mould of his genius, radiant and glowing, and communicated their own warmth to every heart which received them. His, too, was the power of wielding the higher and intenser forms of passion with a majesty and an ease, which none but the great masters of the human heart can ever employ. It was his rare good fortune to have been one of those who form, as it were, a sensible link, a living tradition which connects one age with another, and through which one generation speaks its thoughts and feelings, and appeals to another. And, unfortunate is it for a country, when it ceases to possess such men, for it is to them that we chiefly owe the capacity to maintain the unity of the great Epos of human history, and preserve the consistency of political action.

Sir, it may be said that the grave is still new-made which covers the mortal remains of one of those great men who have been taken from our midst, and the earth is soon to open to receive another. I know not whether it can be said to be a matter of lamentation, so far as the dead are concerned, that the thread of this life has been clipped when once it had been fully spun. They escape the infirmities of age, and they leave an imperishable name behind them. The loss, sir, is not theirs, but ours; and a loss the more to be lamented that we see none to fill the places thus made vacant on the stage of public affairs. But it may be well for us, who have much more cause to mourn and to lament such deaths, to pause amidst the business of life for the purpose of contemplating the spectacle before us, and of drawing the moral from the passing event. It is when death seizes for its victims those who are, by "a head and shoulders, taller than all the rest," that we feel most deeply the uncertainty of human affairs, and that "the glories of our mortal state are shadows, not substantial things." It is, sir, in such instances as the present that we can best study by the light of example the true objects of life, and the wisest ends of human pursuit.

Mr. Hale.

Mr. President: I hope I shall not be considered obtrusive, if on this occasion, for a brief moment, I mingle my humble voice with those that, with an ability that I shall neither attempt nor hope to equal, have sought to do justice to the worth and memory of the deceased, and at the same time appropriately to minister to the sympathies and sorrows of a stricken people. Sir, it is the teaching of inspiration that "no man liveth and no man *dieth* unto himself."

There is a lesson taught no less in the death than in the life of every man—eminently so in the case of one who has filled a large space and occupied a distinguished position in the thoughts and regard of his fellow-men. Particularly instructive at this time is the event which we now deplore, although the circumstances attending his decease are such as are calculated to assuage rather than aggravate the grief which it must necessarily cause. His time had fully come. The threescore and ten, marking the ordinary period of human life, had for some years been passed, and, full of years and of honors, he has gone to his rest. And now, when the nation is marshaling itself for the contest which is to decide "who shall be greatest," as if to chasten our ambition, to restrain and subdue the violence of passion, to moderate our desires and elevate our hopes, we have the spectacle of one who, by the force of his intellect and the energy of his own purpose, had achieved a reputation which the highest official honors of the Republic might have illustrated, but could not have enhanced, laid low in death—as if, at the very outset of this political contest, on which the nation is now entering, to teach the

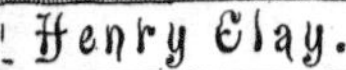

ambitious and aspiring the vanity of human pursuit and end of earthly honor. But, sir, I do not intend to dwell on that moral which is taught by the silent lips and closed eye of the illustrious dead, with a force such as no man ever spoke with; but I shall leave the event with its silent and mute eloquence, to impress its own appropriate teachings on the heart.

In the long and eventful life of Mr. Clay, in the various positions which he occupied, in the many posts of public duty which he filled, in the many exhibitions which his history affords of untiring energy; of unsurpassed eloquence, and of devoted patriotism, it would be strange indeed if different minds, as they dwell upon the subject, were all to select the same incidents of his life as pre-eminently calculated to challenge admiration and respect.

Sir, my admiration—aye, my affection for Mr. Clay—was won and secured many years since, even in my schoolboy days—when his voice of counsel, encouragement and sympathy was heard in the other hall of this capitol, in behalf of the struggling colonies of the southern portion of this continent, who, in the pursuit of their inalienable rights, in imitation of our own forefathers, had unfurled the banner of liberty, and, regardless of consequences, had gallantly rushed into that contest where "life is [illegible] t or freedom won." And again, sir, when Greece, i[illegible] the memories of the past, awoke from the slu[illegible] oppression and centuries of shame, and [illegible]

"To call her virtues back, and conquer time [illegible]

there, over the plains of that classic land, above the din of battle and the clash of arms, mingling with the shouts of the victors and the groans of the vanquished, were heard the thrilling and stirring notes of that same eloquence, excited by a sympathy which knew no bounds, wide as the world, pleading the cause of Grecian liberty before the American Congress, as if to pay back to Greece the debt which every patriot and orator felt was her due. Sir, in the long and honorable career of the deceased, there are many events and circumstances upon which his friends and posterity will dwell with satisfaction and pride, but none which will preserve his memory with more unfading lustre to future ages, than the course he pursued in the Spanish-American and Greek revolutions.

Mr. CLEMENS.

Mr. PRESIDENT: I should not have thought it necessary to add any thing to what has already been said, but for a request preferred by some of the friends of the deceased. I should have been content to mourn him in silence, and left it to other tongues to pronounce his eulogy. What I have now to say shall be brief—very brief.

Mr. President, it is now less than three short years ago since I first entered this body. At that period it numbered among its members many of the most illustrious statesmen this Republic has ever produced, or the world has ever known. Of the living, it is not my purpose to speak; but, in that brief period, death has been busy here; and as if to mark the feebleness of human things, his arrows have been aimed at the highest, the mightiest of us all. First, died CALHOUN. And well, sir, do I remember the deep feeling evinced on that occasion by him whose death has been announced here to-day, when he said: "I was his senior in years—in nothing else. In the course of nature I ought to have preceded him. It has been decreed otherwise; but I know that I shall linger here only a short time, and shall soon follow him." It was genius mourning over his younger brother, and too surely predicting his own approaching end.

He, too, is now gone from among us, and left none like him behind. That voice, whose every tone was music, is hushed and still. That clear, bright eye is dim and lustreless, and that breast, where grew and flourished every quality which could adorn and dignify our nature, is cold as the clod that soon must cover it. A few hours have wrought a mighty change—a change for which a lingering illness had, indeed, in some degree, prepared us; but which, nevertheless, will still fall upon the nation with crushing force. Many a sorrowing heart is now asking, as I did yesterday, when I heard the first sound of the funeral bell—

> "And is he gone?—the pure of the purest,
> The hand that upheld our bright banner the surest,
> Is he gone from our struggles away?
> But yesterday lending a people new life,
> Cold, mute, in the coffin to-day."

Mr. President, this is an occasion when eulogy must fail to perform its office. The long life which is now ended is a history of glorious deeds too mighty for the tongue of praise. It is in the hearts of his countrymen that his best epitaph must be written. It is in the admiration of a world that his renown must be recorded. In that deep love of country which distinguished every period of his life, he may not have been unrivaled. In loftiness of intellect he was not without his peers. The skill with which he touched every chord of the human heart may have been equaled. The iron will, the unbending firmness, the fearless courage, which marked his character, may have been shared by others. But where shall we go to find all these qualities united, concentrated, blended into one brilliant whole, and shedding a lustre upon one single head, which does not dazzle the beholder only because it attracts his love and demands his worship?

I scarcely know, sir, how far it may be allowable, upon an occasion like this, to refer to party struggles which have left wounds not yet entirely healed. I will venture, however, to suggest, that it should be a source of consolation to his friends that he lived long enough to see the full accomplishment of the last great work of his life, and to witness the total disappearance of that sectional tempest which threatened to whelm the Republic in ruins. Both the great parties of the country have agreed to stand upon the platform which he erected, and both of them have solemnly pledged themselves to maintain unimpaired the work of his hands. I doubt not the knowledge of this cheered him in his dying moments, and helped to steal away the pangs of dissolution.

Mr. President, if I knew any thing more that I could say, I would gladly utter it. To me he was something more than kind, and I am called upon to mingle a private with the public grief. I wish that I could do something to add to his fame. But he built for himself a monument of immortality, and left to his friends no task but that of soothing their own sorrow for his loss. We pay to him the tribute of our tears. More we have no power to bestow. Patriotism, honor, genius, courage, have all come to strew their garlands about his tomb; and well they may, for he was the peer of them all.

Mr. Cooper.

Mr. President: It is not always by words that the living pay to the dead the sincerest and most eloquent tribute. The tears of a nation, flowing spontaneously over the grave of a public benefactor, is a more eloquent testimonial of his worth, and of the affection and veneration of his countrymen, than the most highly-wrought eulogium of the most gifted tongue. The heart is not necessarily the fountain of words, but it is always the source of tears, whether of joy, gratitude or grief. But sincere, truthful and eloquent, as they are, they leave no permanent record of the virtues and greatness of him on whose tomb they are shed. As the dews of heaven falling at night are absorbed by the earth or dried up by the morning sun, so the tears of a people, shed for their benefactor, disappear without leaving a trace to tell to future generations of the services, sacrifices, and virtues of him to whose memory they were a grateful tribute. But as homage paid to virtue is an incentive to it, it is right that the memory of the good, the great, and noble of the earth should be preserved and honored.

The ambition, Mr. President, of the truly great, is more the hope of living in the memory and estimation of future ages than of possessing power in their own. It is this hope that stimulates them to perseverance; that enables them to encounter disappointment, ingratitude and neglect, and to press on through toils, privations and perils to the end. It was not the hope of discovering a world, over which he should himself exercise dominion, that sustained Columbus in all his trials. It was not for this he braved danger, disappointment, poverty and reproach. It was not for this he subdued his native pride, wandered from kingdom to kingdom, kneeling at the feet of princes, a suppliant for means to prosecute his sublime enterprise. It was not for this, after having at last secured the patronage of ISABELLA, that he put off in his crazy and ill-appointed fleet into unknown seas, to struggle with storms and tempests, and the rage of a mutinous crew. It was another and nobler kind of ambition that stimulated him to contend with terror, superstition and despair, and to press forward on his perilous course, when the needle in his compass, losing its polarity, seemed to unite with the fury of the elements and the insubordination of his crew in turning him back from his perilous but glorious undertaking. It was the hope which was realized at last, when his ungrateful country was compelled to inscribe, as an epitaph on his tomb—

"Columbus has given a new world to the kingdoms of Castile and Leon,"

that enabled him, at first, to brave so many disappointments, and at last, to conquer the multitude of perils that beset his pathway on the deep. This, sir, is the ambition of the truly great—not to achieve present fame, but future immortality. This being the case, it is befitting here to-day, to add to the life of HENRY CLAY the record of his death, signalized as it is by a nation's gratitude and grief. It is right that posterity should learn from us, the contemporaries of the illustrious deceased, that his virtues and services were appreciated by his country, and acknowledged by the tears of his countrymen poured out upon his grave.

The career of HENRY CLAY was a wonderful one. And what an illustration of the excellence of our institutions would a retrospect of his life afford! Born in an humble station, without any of the adventitious aids of fortune by which the obstructions on the road to fame are smoothed, he rose, not only to the most exalted eminence of position, but likewise to the highest place in the affections of his countrymen. Taking into view the disadvantages of his early position, disadvantages against which he had always to contend, his career is without a parallel in the history of great men. To have seen him a youth, without friends or fortune, and with but a scanty education, who would have ventured to predict for him a course so brilliant and beneficent, and a fame so well deserved and enduring? Like the pine, which sometimes springs up amidst the rocks on the mountain side, with scarce a crevice in which to fix its roots, or soil to nourish them, but which, nevertheless, overtops all the trees of the surrounding forest, HENRY CLAY, by his own inherent, self-sustaining energy and genius, rose to an altitude of fame almost unequaled in the age in which he lived. As an orator, legislator and statesman, he had no superior. All his faculties were remarkable, and in remarkable combination. Possessed of a brilliant genius and fertile imagination, his judgment was sound, discriminating and eminently practical. Of an ardent and impetuous temperament, he was nevertheless persevering and firm of purpose. Frank, bold and intrepid, he was cautious in providing against the contingencies and obstacles which might possibly rise up in the road to success. Generous, liberal, and entertaining broad and expanded views of national policy, in his legislative course he never transcended the limits of a wise economy.

But, Mr. President, of all his faculties, that of making friends and attaching them to him was the most remarkable and extraordinary. In this respect, he seemed to possess a sort of fascination, by which all who came into his presence were attracted toward, and bound to him by ties which neither time nor circumstances had power to dissolve or weaken. In the admiration of his friends was the recognition of the divinity of intellect; in their attachment to him a confession of his generous personal qualities and social virtues.

Of the public services of Mr. CLAY, the present occasion affords no room for a sketch more extended than that which his respected colleague [Mr. UNDERWOOD] has presented. It is, however, sufficient to say, that for more than forty years he has been a prominent actor in the drama of American affairs. During the late war with England, his voice was more potent than any other in awakening the spirit of the country, infusing confidence into the people, and rendering available the resources for carrying on the contest. In our domestic controversies, threatening the peace of the country and the integrity of the Union, he has always been first to note danger as well as to suggest the means of averting it. When the waters of the great political deep were upheaved by the tempest of discord, and the ark of the Union, freighted with the hopes and destinies of freedom, tossing about on the raging billows, and drifting every moment nearer to the vortex which threatened to swallow it up, it was his clarion voice, rising above the storm, that admonished the crew of impending peril, and counseled the way to safety.

But, Mr. President, devotedly as he loved his country, his aspirations were not limited to its welfare alone. Wherever freedom had a votary, that votary had a friend in HENRY CLAY; and in the struggle of the Spanish colonie or independence he uttered words of encouragement

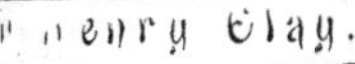

which have become the mottoes on the banners of freedom in every land. But neither the services which he has rendered his own country, nor his wishes for the welfare of others, nor his genius, nor the affection of friends, could turn aside the destroyer. No price could purchase exemption from the common lot of humanity. HENRY CLAY, the wise, the great, the gifted, had to die; and his history is summed up in the biography which the Russian poet has prepared for all, kings and serfs:

> * * * * "born, living, dying,
> Quitting the still shore for the troubled wave,
> Struggling with storm-clouds, over shipwrecks flying,
> And casting anchor in the silent grave."

But though time would not spare him, there is still this of consolation: he died peacefully and happy, ripe in renown, full of years and of honors, and rich in the affections of his country. He had, too, the unspeakable satisfaction of closing his eyes whilst the country he had loved so much and served so well, was still in the enjoyment of peace, happiness, union and prosperity—still advancing in all the elements of wealth, greatness and power.

I know, Mr. President, how unequal I have been to the apparently self-imposed task of presenting, in an appropriate manner, the merits of the illustrious deceased. But if I had remained silent on an occasion like this, when the hearts of my constituents are swelling with grief, I would have been disowned by them. It is for this reason—that of giving utterance to their feelings as well as of my own—that I have trespassed on the time of the Senate. I would that I could have spoken fitter words; but, such as they are, they were uttered by the tongue in response to the promptings of the heart.

Mr. Seward.

Mr. President: Fifty years ago, Henry Clay, of Virginia, already adopted by Kentucky, then as youthful as himself, entered the service of his country, a representative in the unpretending legislature of that rising state; and having thenceforward, with ardor and constancy, pursued the gradual paths of an aspiring change through halls of Congress, Foreign courts and Executive councils, he has now, with the cheerfulness of a patriot, and the serenity of a Christian, fitly closed his long and arduous career, here in the Senate, in the full presence of the Republic, looking down upon the scene with anxiety and alarm, not merely a Senator like one of us who yet remain in the Senate house, but filling that character which, though it had no authority of law, and was assigned without suffrage, Augustus Cæsar nevertheless declared was above the title of Emperor, *Primus inter Illustres*—the Prince of the Senate.

Generals are tried, Mr. President, by examining the campaigns they have lost or won, and statesmen by reviewing the transactions in which they have been engaged. Hamilton would have been unknown to us, had there been no Constitution to be created; as Brutus would have died in obscurity, had there been no Cæsar to be slain.

Colonization, Revolution, and Organization—three great acts in the drama of our national progress—had already passed when the western patriot appeared on the public stage. He entered in that next division of the majestic scenes which was marked by an inevitable reaction of political forces, a wild strife of factions and ruinous embarrassments in our foreign relations. This transition stage is always more perilous than any other in the career of nations, and especially in the career of republics. It proved fatal to the Commonwealth in England. Scarcely any of the Spanish-American states have yet emerged from it; and more than once it has been sadly signalized by the ruin of the republican cause in France.

The continuous administration of WASHINGTON and JOHN ADAMS had closed under a cloud which had thrown a broad, dark shadow over the future; the nation was deeply indebted at home and abroad, and its credit was prostrate. The revolutionary factions had given place to two inveterate parties, divided by a gulf which had been worn by the conflict in which the Constitution was adopted, and made broader and deeper by a war of prejudices concerning the merits of the belligerents in the great European struggle that then convulsed the civilized world. Our extraordinary political system was little more than an ingenious theory, not yet practically established. The union of the states was as yet only one of compact; for the political, social and commercial necessities to which it was so marvellously adapted, and which, clustering thickly upon it, now render it indissoluble, had not then been broadly disclosed, nor had the habits of acquiescence and the sentiments of loyalty, always slow of growth, fully ripened. The bark that had gone to sea, thus unfurnished and untried, seemed quite certain to founder by reason of its own inherent frailty, even if it should escape unharmed in the great conflict of nations which acknowledged no claims of justice and tolerated no pretensions of neutrality. Moreover, the territory possessed by the nation was inadequate to commercial exigencies and indispensable social expansion; and yet no provision had been made for enlargement, nor for extending the political system over distant regions, inhabited or otherwise, which must inevitably be acquired. Nor could any such acquisition be made, without disturbing the carefully-adjusted balance of powers among the members of the confederacy.

These difficulties, Mr. President, although they grew less with time and by slow degrees, continued throughout the whole life of the statesman whose obsequies we are celebrating. Be it known, then, and I am sure that history will confirm the instruction, that Conservatism was the interest of the nation, and the responsibility of its rulers, during the period in which he flourished. He was ardent, bold, generous, and even ambitious; and yet, with a profound conviction of the true exigencies of the country, like ALEXANDER HAMILTON, he disciplined himself and trained a restless nation, that knew only self-control, to the rigorous practice of that often humiliating conservatism which its welfare and security in that particular crisis so imperiously demanded.

It could not happen, sir, to any citizen to have acted alone, nor even to have acted always the most conspicuous part in a trying period so long protracted. HENRY CLAY, therefore, shared the responsibilities of government, with not only his proper contemporaries, but also survivors of the Revolution, as well as also many who will succeed himself. Delicacy forbids the naming of those who retain their places here, but we may, without impropriety, recall among his compeers a Senator of vast resources and inflexible resolve, who has recently withdrawn from this chamber, but I trust not altogether from public life, (Mr. BENTON;) and another, who, surpassing all his contemporaries within his country, and even throughout the world, in proper eloquence of the forum, now in autumnal years, for a second time dignifies and adorns the highest seat in the Executive Council, (Mr. WEBSTER.) Passing by these eminent and noble men, the shades of CALHOUN, JOHN QUINCY ADAMS, JACKSON, MONROE and JEFFERSON rise up before us—statesmen whose living and local fame has ripened already into historical and world wide renown.

Among geniuses so lofty as these, HENRY CLAY bore a part in regulating the constitutional freedom of political debate; establishing that long-contested and most important line which divides the sovereignty of the several states from that of the states confederated; asserting the right of neutrality, and vindicating it by a war against Great Britain, when that just but extreme measure became necessary; adjusting the terms on which that perilous yet honorable contest was brought to a peaceful close; perfecting the army and the navy, and the national fortifications; settling the fiscal and financial policy of the government in more than one crisis of apparently threatened revolution; asserting and calling into exercise the powers of the government for making and improving internal communications between the states; arousing and encouraging the Spanish-American colonies on this continent to throw off the foreign yoke, and to organize governments on principles congenial to our own, and thus creating external bulwarks for our own national defence; establishing equal and impartial peace and amity with all existing maritime powers; and extending the constitutional organization of government over all the vast regions secured in his lifetime by purchase or by conquest, whereby the pillars of the republic have been removed from the banks of the St. Mary, to the borders of the Rio Grande, and from the margin of the Mississippi to the Pacific coast. We may not yet discuss here the wisdom of the several measures which have thus passed in review before us, nor of the positions which the deceased statesman assumed in regard to them, but we may, without offence, dwell upon the comprehensive results of them all.

The Union exists in absolute integrity, and the republican system is in complete and triumphant development. Without having relinquished any part of their individuality, the states have more than doubled already, and are increasing in numbers and political strength and expansion more rapidly than ever before. Without having absorbed any state, or having even encroached on any state, the confederation has opened itself so as to embrace all the new members who have come, and now with capacity for further and indefinite enlargements has become fixed, enduring and perpetual. Although it was doubted only half a century ago whether our political system could be maintained at all, and whether, if maintained, it could guarantee the peace and happiness of society, it stands now confessed by the world the form of government not only most adapted to empire, but also most congenial with the constitution of human nature.

When we consider that the nation has been conducted to this haven, not only through stormy seas, but altogether, also, without a course and without a star; and when we consider, moreover, the sum of happiness that has already been enjoyed by the American people, and still more the influence which the great achievement is exerting for the advancement and melioration of the condition of mankind, we see at once that it might have satisfied the highest ambition to have been, no matter how humbly, concerned in so great transaction.

Certainly, sir, no one will assert that HENRY CLAY, in that transaction, performed an obscure, or even a common part. On the contrary, from the day on which he entered the public service, until that on which he passed the gates of death, he was never a follower but always a leader; and he marshaled either the party which sustained or that which resisted every great measure, equally in the Senate and among the people. He led where duty seemed to him to indicate, reckless whether he encountered one president or twenty presidents; whether he was opposed by factions or even by the whole people. Hence it has happened, that although that people are not yet agreed among themselves on the wisdom of all, or perhaps of even any of his great measures, yet they are nevertheless unanimous in acknowledging that he was at once the greatest, the most faithful and the most reliable of their statesmen. Here the effort at discriminating praise of HENRY CLAY, in regard to his public policy, must stop in this place, even on this sad occasion which awakens the ardent liberality of his generous survivors.

But his personal qualities may be discussed without apprehension. What were the elements of the success of that extraordinary man? You, sir, knew him longer and better than I, and I would prefer to hear you speak of them. He was indeed eloquent—all the world knows that. He held the keys to the hearts of his countrymen, and he turned the wards within them with a skill attained by no other master.

But eloquence was nevertheless only an instrument, and one of many that he used. His conversation, his gesture, his very look was persuasive, seductive, irresistible. And his appliance of all these was courteous, patient and indefatigable. Defeat only inspired him with new resolution. He divided opposition by his assiduity of address, while he rallied and strengthened his own bands of supporters by the confidence of success which, feeling himself, he easily inspired among his followers. His affections were high, and pure, and generous, and the chiefest among them was that which the great Italian poet designated as the charity of native land. And in him that charity was an enduring and overpowering enthusiasm, and it influenced all his sentiments and conduct, rendering him more impartial between conflicting interests and sections than any other statesman who has lived since the Revolution. Thus, with very great versatility of talent and the most catholic equality of favor, he identified every question, whether of domestic administration or foreign policy, with his own great name, and so became a perpetual Tribune of the people. He needed only to pronounce in favor of a measure or against it, here, and immediately popular enthusiasm, excited as by a magic wand, was felt, overcoming all opposition in the senate chamber.

In this way he wrought a change in our political system, that I think was not foreseen by its founders. He converted this branch of the legislature from a negative position, or one of equilibrium between the executive and the house of representatives, into the active ruling power of the republic. Only time can disclose whether this great innovation shall be beneficent or even permanent. Certainly, sir, the great lights of the senate have set. The obscuration is not less palpable to the country than to us, who are left to grope our uncertain way here, as in a labyrinth, oppressed with self-distrust. The times, too, present new embarrassments. We are rising to another and a more sublime stage of natural progress—that of expanding wealth and rapid territorial aggrandizement. Our institutions throw a broad shadow across the St. Lawrence, and stretching beyond the valley of Mexico, reaches even to the plains of Central America; while the Sandwich Islands and the shores of China recognize its renovating influence. Wherever that influence is felt, a desire for protection under those institutions is awakened. Expansion seems to be regulated, not by any difficulties of resistance, but by the moderation which results from our own internal constitution. No one knows how rapidly that restraint may give way. Who can tell how far or how fast it ought to yield. Commerce has brought the ancient continents near to us, and created necessities for new positions—perhaps connections or colonies there—and with the trade and friendship of the elder nations their conflicts and collisions are brought to our doors and to our hearts. Our sympathy kindles, our indifference extinguishes, the fire of freedom in foreign lands. Before we shall be fully conscious that a change is going on in Europe, we may find ourselves once more divided by that eternal line of separation that leaves on the one side those of our citizens who obey the impulses of sympathy, while on the other are found those who submit only to the counsels of prudence. Even prudence will soon be required to decide whether distant regions, east and west, shall come under our own protection, or be left to aggrandize a rapidly spreading and hostile domain of despotism.

Sir, who among us is equal to these mighty questions? I fear there is no one. Nevertheless, the example of Henry Clay remains for our instruction. His genius has passed to the realms of light, but his virtues still live here for our emulation. With them there will remain also the protection and favor of the Most High, if, by the practice of justice, and the maintenance of freedom we shall deserve it. Let, then, the bier pass on. With sorrow, but not without hope, we will follow the revered form that it bears to its final resting-place; and then, when that grave opens at our feet to receive such an inestimable treasure, we will invoke the GOD of our fathers to send us new guides, like him that is now withdrawn, and give us wisdom to obey their instruction.

Mr. JONES, of Iowa.

Mr. PRESIDENT: Of the vast number, who mourn the departure of the great man whose voice has so often been heard in this hall, I have peculiar cause to regret that dispensation which has removed him from among us. He was the guardian and director of my collegiate days; four of his sons were my college-mates and my warm friends. My intercourse with the father was that of a youth and a friendly adviser. I shall never cease to feel grateful to him—to his now heart-stricken and bereaved widow and children, for their many kindnesses to me during four or five years of my life. I had the pleasure of renewing my acquaintance with him, first, as a delegate in congress, while he was a member of this body from 1835 to 1839, and again in 1848, as member of this branch of congress; and during the whole of which period, some eight years, none but the most kindly feeling existed between us.

As an humble and unimportant senator, it was my fortune to co-operate with him throughout the whole of the exciting session of 1849–'50—the labor and excitement of which is said to have precipitated his decease. That co-operation did not end with the accordant vote on this floor, but, in consequence of the unyielding opposition to the series of measures known as the "Compromise," extended to many private meetings held by his friends, at all of which Mr. CLAY was present. And whether in public or private life, he everywhere continued to inspire me with the most exalted estimate of his patriotism and statesmanship. Never shall I forget the many ardent appeals he made to senators, in and out of the senate, in favor of the settlement of our then unhappy sectional differences.

Immediately after the close of that memorable session of congress, during which the nation beheld his great and almost superhuman efforts upon this floor to sustain the wise counsels of the "Father of his Country," I accompanied him home to Ashland, at his invitation, to revisit the place where my happiest days had been spent, with the friends who there continued to reside. During that, to me, most agreeable and instructive journey, in many conversations he evinced the utmost solicitude for the welfare and honor of the Republic, all tending to show that he believed the happiness of the people and the cause of liberty throughout the world depended upon the continuance of our glorious Union, and the avoidance of those sectional dissensions which could but alienate the affections of one portion of the people from another. With the sincerity and fervor of a true patriot, he warned his companions, in that journey, to withhold all aid from men who labored, and from every cause which tended to sow the seeds of disunion in the land; and to oppose such, he declared himself willing to forego all the ties and associations of mere party.

At a subsequent period, sir, this friend of my youth, at my earnest and repeated entreaties, consented to take a sea voyage from New York to Havana. He remained at the latter place a fortnight, and then returned by New Orleans to Ashland. That excursion by sea, he assured me, contributed much to relieve him from the sufferings occasioned by the disease which has just terminated his eventful and glorious life. Would to Heaven that he could have been persuaded to abandon his duties as a senator, and to have remained during the past winter and spring upon that Island of Cuba! The country would not, now, perhaps, have been called to mourn his loss.

In some matters of policy connected with the administration of our general government, I have disagreed with him, yet the purity and sincerity of his motives I never doubted; and as a true lover of his country, as an honorable and honest man, I trust his example will be reverenced and followed by the men of this, and of succeeding generations.

Mr. Brooke.

Mr. President: As an ardent, personal admirer and political friend of the distinguished dead, I claim the privilege of adding my humble tribute of respect to his memory, and of joining in the general expression of sorrow that has gone forth from this chamber. Death, at all times, is an instructive monitor, as well as a mournful messenger; but when his fatal shaft hath stricken down the great in intellect and renown, how doubly impressive the lesson that it brings home to the heart, that the grave is the common lot of all—the great leveler of all earthly distinctions! But at the same time we are taught that in one sense the good and great can never die; for the memory of their virtues and their bright example will live through all coming time in an immortality that blooms beyond the grave. The consolation of this thought may calm our sorrow; and, in the language of one of our own poets, it may be asked:

> "Why weep ye, then, for him, who having run
> The bound of man's appointed years, at last,
> Life's blessings all enjoyed, life's labors done,
> Serenely to his final rest has passed;
> While the soft memory of his virtues yet
> Lingers, like twilight hues when the bright sun has set?"

It will be doing no injustice, sir, to the living or the dead to say, that no better specimen of the true American character can be found in our history than that of Mr. Clay. With no adventitious advantages of birth or fortune, he won his way by the efforts of his own genius to the highest distinction and honor. Ardently attached to the principles of civil and religious liberty, patriotism was with him both a passion and a sentiment—a passion that gave energy to his ambition, and a sentiment that pervaded all his thoughts and actions, concentrating them upon his country as the idol of his heart. The bold and manly frankness in the expression of his opinions which always characterized him, has often been the subject of remark; and in all his victories it may be truly said he never "stooped to conquer." In his long and brilliant political career, personal considerations never, for a single instant, caused him to swerve from the strict line of duty, and none have ever doubted his deep sincerity in that memorable expression to Mr. Preston, "Sir, I had rather be right than be President."

This is not the time nor occasion, sir, to enter into a detail of the public services of Mr. CLAY, interwoven as they are with the history of the country for half a century; but I cannot refrain from adverting to the last crowning act of his glorious life—his great effort in the Thirty-first Congress for the preservation of the peace and integrity of this great Republic, as it was this effort that shattered his bodily strength, and hastened the consummation of his death. The union of the states, as being essential to our prosperity and happiness, was the paramount proposition in his political creed, and the slightest symptom of danger to its perpetuity filled him with alarm, and called forth all the energies of his body and mind. In his earlier life he had met this danger and overcome it. In the conflict of contending factions it again appeared; and coming forth from the repose of private life, to which age and infirmity had carried him, with unabated strength of intellect, he again entered upon the arena of political strife, and again success crowned his efforts, and peace and harmony were restored to a distracted people. But, unequal to the mighty struggle, his bodily strength sank beneath it, and he retired from the field of his glory to yield up his life as a holy sacrifice to his beloved country. It has well been said that peace has its victories as well as war; and how bright upon the page of history, will be the record of this great victory of intellect, of reason, and of moral suasion, over the spirit of discord and sectional animosities!

We this day, Mr. President, commit his memory to the regard and affection of his admiring countrymen. It is a consolation to them and to us to know that he died in full possession of his glorious intellect, and, what is better, in the enjoyment of that "peace which the world can neither give nor take away." He sank to rest as the full-orbed king of day, unshorn of a single beam, or rather like the planet of morning, his brightness was but eclipsed by the opening to him of a more full and perfect day.

> "No waning of fire, no paling of ray,
> But rising, still rising, as passing away.
> Farewell, gallant eagle, thou'rt buried in light—
> God speed thee to heaven, lost star of our night."

The resolutions submitted by Mr. Underwood, were then unanimously agreed to.

Ordered, That the Secretary communicate these resolutions to the House of Representatives.

On motion of Mr. Underwood,

Resolved, That, as an additional mark of respect to the memory of the deceased, the Senate do now adjourn.

HOUSE OF REPRESENTATIVES.

A message was received from the Senate, by ASBURY DICKINS, Esq., its secretary, communicating information of the death of HENRY CLAY, late senator from the state of Kentucky, and the proceedings of the Senate thereon.

The resolutions of the Senate having been read,

Mr. BRECKENRIDGE the rose and said :

Mr. SPEAKER : I rise to perform the melancholy duty of announcing to this body the death of HENRY CLAY, late a senator in congress from the commonwealth of Kentucky.

Mr. CLAY expired at his lodgings in this city yesterday morning, at seventeen minutes past eleven o'clock, in the seventy-sixth year of his age. His noble intellect was unclouded to the last. After protracted sufferings, he passed away without pain; and so gently did the spirit leave his frame, that the moment of departure was not observed by the friends who watched at his bedside. His last hours were cheered by the presence of an affectionate son; and he died surrounded by friends who, during his long illness, had done all that affection could suggest to sooth his sufferings.

Although this sad event has been expected for many weeks, the shock it produced, and the innumerable tributes of respect to his memory exhibited on every side, and in every form, prove the depth of the public sorrow, and the greatness of the public loss.

Imperishably associated, as his name has been, for fifty years, with every great event affecting the fortunes of our country, it is difficult to realize that he is indeed gone forever. It is difficult to feel that we shall see no more his noble form within these walls—that we shall hear no more his patriot tones, now rousing his countrymen to vindicate their rights against a foreign foe; now imploring them to preserve concord among themselves. We shall see him no more. The memory and the fruits of his services alone remain to us. Amidst the general gloom, the capitol itself looks desolate, as if the genius of the place had departed. Already the intelligence has reached almost every quarter of the Republic, and a great people mourn with us, to-day, the death of their most illustrious citizen. Sympathizing, as we do, deeply, with his family and friends, yet private affliction is absorbed in the general sorrow. The spectacle of a whole community lamenting the loss of a great man, is far more touching than any manifestation of private grief. In speaking of a loss which is national, I will not attempt to describe the universal burst of grief with which Kentucky will receive these tidings. The attempt would be vain to depict the gloom that will cover her people, when they know that the pillar of fire is removed which has guided their footsteps for the life of a generation.

It is known to the country, that from the memorable session of 1849–'50, Mr. Clay's health gradually declined. Although several years of his senatorial term remained he did not propose to continue in the public service longer than the present session. He came to Washington chiefly to defend, if it should become necessary, the measures of adjustment, to the adoption of which he so largely contributed; but the condition of his health did not allow him, at any time, to participate in the discussions of the senate. Through the winter, he was confined almost wholly to his room, with slight changes in his condition, but gradually losing the remnant of his strength. Through the long and dreary winter, he conversed much and cheerfully with his friends, and expressed a deep interest in public affairs. Although he did not expect a restoration to health, he cherished the hope that the mild season of spring would bring to him strength enough to return to Ashland, and die in the bosom of his family. But, alas! spring, that brings life to all nature, brought no life nor hope to him. After the month of March, his vital powers rapidly wasted, and for weeks he lay patiently awaiting the stroke of death. But the approach of the destroyer had no terrors for him. No clouds overhung his future. He met the end with composure, and his pathway to the grave was brightened by the immortal hopes which spring from the Christian faith.

Not long before his death, having just returned from Kentucky, I bore to him a token of affection from his excellent wife. Never can I forget his appearance, his manner, or his words. After speaking of his family, his friends and his country, he changed the conversation to his own future, and looking on me with his fine eye undimmed, and his voice full of its original compass and melody, he said, "I am not afraid to die, sir. I have hope, faith, and some confidence. I do not think any man can be entirely certain in regard to his future state, but I have an abiding trust in the merits and mediation of our Savior." It will assuage the grief of his family to know that he looked hopefully beyond the tomb, and a Christian people will rejoice to hear that such a man, in his last hours, reposed with simplicity and confidence upon the promises of the Gospel.

It is the custom, on occasions like this, to speak of the parentage and childhood of the deceased, and to follow him, step by step, through life. I will not attempt to relate even all the great events of Mr. CLAY's life, because they are familiar to the whole country, and it would be needless to enumerate a long list of public services which form a part of American history.

Beginning life as a friendless boy, with few advantages, save those conferred by nature, while yet a minor, he left Virginia, the state of his birth, and commenced the practice of law at Lexington, in Kentucky. At a bar remarkable for its numbers and talent, Mr. CLAY soon rose to the first rank. At a very early age he was elected from the county of Fayette to the General Assembly of Kentucky, and was the speaker of that body. Coming into the senate of the United States, for the first time, in 1806, he entered upon a parliamentary career, the most brilliant and successful in our annals. From that time he remained habitually in the public eye. As a senator, as a member of this house and its speaker, as a representative of his country abroad, and as a high officer in the executive department of the government, he was intimately connected, for fifty years, with every great measure of American policy. Of the mere party measures of this period, I do not propose to speak. Many of them have passed away, and are remembered only as the occasions for the great intellectual efforts which marked their discussion. Concerning others, opinions are still divided. They will go into history, with the reasons on either side rendered by the greatest intellects of the time.

As a leader in a deliberative body, Mr. CLAY had no equal in America. In him, intellect, person, eloquence, and courage, united to form a character fit to command. He fired with his own enthusiasm, and controlled by his amazing will, individuals and masses. No reverse could crush his spirit, nor defeat reduce him to despair. Equally erect and dauntless in prosperity and adversity, when successful, he moved to the accomplishment of his purposes with severe resolution; when defeated, he rallied his broken bands around him, and from his eagle eye shot along their ranks the contagion of his own courage. Destined for a leader, he everywhere asserted his destiny. In his long and eventful life he came in contact with men of all ranks and professions, but he never felt that he was in the presence of a man superior to himself. In the assemblies of the people, at the bar, in the senate—everywhere within the circle of his personal presence he assumed and maintained a position of pre-eminence.

But the supremacy of Mr. CLAY, as a party leader, was not his only, nor his highest title to renown. That title is to be found in the purely patriotic spirit which, on great occasions, always signalized his conduct. We have had no statesman who, in periods of real and imminent public peril, has exhibited a more genuine and enlarged patriotsm than HENRY CLAY. Whenever a question presented itself actually threatening the existence of the Union, Mr. CLAY, rising above the passions of the hour, always exerted his powers to solve it peacefully and honorably. Although more liable than most men, from his impetuous and ardent nature, to feel strongly the passions common to us all, it was his rare faculty to be able to subdue them in a great crisis, and to hold, toward all sections of the confederacy, the language of concord and brotherhood.

Sir, it will be a proud pleasure to every true American heart to remember the great occasions when Mr. CLAY has displayed a sublime patriotism—when the ill-temper engendered by the times, and the miserable jealousies of the day, seemed to have been driven from his bosom by the expulsive power of nobler feelings—when every throb of his heart was given to his country; every effort of his intellect dedicated to her service. Who does not remember the three periods when the American system of government was exposed to its severest trials; and who does not know that when history shall relate the struggle which preceded, and the dangers which were averted by the Missouri compromise, the Tariff compromise of 1832, and the adjustment of 1850, the same pages will record the genius, the eloquence, and the patriotism of HENRY CLAY?

Nor was it in Mr. CLAY's nature to lag behind until measures of adjustment were matured, and then come forward to swell a majority. On the contrary, like a bold and real statesman, he was ever among the first to meet the peril, and hazard his fame upon the remedy. It is fresh in the memory of us all that, when lately the fury of sectional discord threatened to sever the confederacy, Mr. CLAY, though withdrawn from public life, and oppressed by the burden of years, came back to the senate—the theatre of his glory—and devoted the remnant of his strength to the sacred duty of preserving the union of the states.

With characteristic courage he took the lead in proposing a scheme of settlement. But while he was willing to assume the responsibility of proposing a plan, he did not, with petty ambition, insist upon its adoption to the exclusion of other modes; but, taking his own as a starting point for discussion and practical action, he nobly labored with his compatriots to change and improve it in such form as to make it an acceptable adjustment. Throughout the long and arduous struggle the love of country expelled from his bosom the spirit of selfishness, and Mr. CLAY proved, for the third time, that though he was ambitious and loved glory, he had no ambition to mount to fame on the confusions of his country. And this conviction is lodged in the hearts of the people; the party measures and the party passions of former times have not, for several years, interposed between Mr. CLAY and the masses of his countrymen. After 1850, he seemed to feel that his mission was accomplished; and, during the same period, the regards and affections of the American people have been attracted to him in a remarkable degree. For many months, the warmest feelings, the deepest anxieties of all parties, centered upon the dying statesman; the glory of his great actions shed a mellow lustre on his declining years; and to fill the measure of his fame, his countrymen, weaving for him the laurel wreath, with common hands, did bind it about his venerable brows, and send him crowned, to history.

The life of Mr. CLAY, sir, is a striking example of the abiding fame which surely awaits the direct and candid statesman. The entire absence of equivocation or disguise, in all his acts, was his master-key to the popular heart; for while the people will forgive the errors of a bold and open nature, he sins past forgiveness, who deliberately deceives them. Hence Mr. CLAY, though often defeated in his measures of policy, always secured the respect of his opponents, without losing the confidence of his friends. He never paltered in a double sense. The country was never in doubt as to his opinions or his purposes. In all the contests of his time, his position on great public questions was as clear as the sun in a cloudless sky. Sir, standing by the grave of this great man, and considering these things, how contemptible does appear the mere legerdemain of politics! What a reproach is his life on that false policy which would trifle with a great and upright people! If I were to write his epitaph, I would inscribe, as the highest eulogy, on the stone which shall mark his resting-place, "Here lies a man, who was in the public service for fifty years, and never attempted to deceive his countrymen."

While the youth of America should imitate his noble qualities, they may take courage from his career, and note the high proof it affords that, under our equal institutions, the avenues to honor are open to all. Mr. CLAY rose by the force of his own genius, unaided by power, patronage or wealth. At an age when our young men are usually advanced to the higher schools of learning, provided only with the rudiments of an English education, he turned his steps to the west, and amidst the rude collisions of a border-life, matured a character whose highest exhibitions were destined to mark eras in his country's history. Beginning on the frontiers of American civilization, the orphan boy, supported only by the consciousness of his own powers, and by the confidence of the people, surmounted all the barriers of adverse fortune, and won a glorious name in the annals of his country. Let the generous youth, fired with honorable ambition, remember that the American system of government offers on every hand bounties to merit. If, like CLAY, orphanage, obscurity, poverty, shall oppress him; yet, if, like CLAY, he feels the Promethean spark within, let him remember that his country, like a generous mother, extends her arms to welcome and to cherish every one of her children whose genius and worth may promote her prosperity or increase her renown.

Mr. Speaker, the signs of woe around us, and the general voice, announce that another great man has fallen. Our consolation is that he was not taken in the vigor of his manhood, but sank into the grave at the close of a long and illustrious career. The great statesmen who have filled the largest space in the public eye, one by one are passing away. Of the three great leaders of the senate one alone remains, and he must follow soon. We shall witness no more their intellectual struggles in the American forum; but the monuments of their genius will be cherished as the common property of the people, and their names will continue to confer dignity and renown upon their country.

Not less illustrious than the greatest of these will be the name of CLAY—a name pronounced with pride by Americans in every quarter of the globe; a name to be remembered while history shall record the struggles of modern Greece for freedom, or the spirit of liberty burn in the South American bosom; a living and immortal name—a name that would descend to posterity without the aid of letters, borne by tradition from generation to generation. Every memorial of such a man will possess

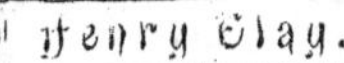

a meaning and a value to his countrymen. His tomb will be a hallowed spot. Great memories will cluster there, and his countrymen, as they visit it, may well exclaim—

"Such graves as his are pilgrim shrines,
Shrines to no creed or code confined;
The Delphian vales, the Palestines,
The Meccas of the mind."

Mr. Speaker, I offer the following resolutions:

Resolved, That the House of Representatives of the United States, has received, with the deepest sensibility, intelligence of the death of HENRY CLAY.

Resolved, That the officers and members of the House of Representatives will wear the usual badge of mourning for thirty days, as a testimony of the profound respect this House entertains for the memory of the deceased.

Resolved, That the officers and members of the House of Representatives, in a body, will attend the funeral of HENRY CLAY, on the day appointed for that purpose by the Senate of the United States.

Resolved, That the proceedings of this House, in relation to the death of HENRY CLAY, be communicated to the family of the deceased, by the clerk.

Resolved, That as a further mark of respect for the memory of the deceased, this House do now adjourn.

Mr. EWING rose, and said:

A noble heart has ceased to beat forever. A long life of brilliant and self-devoted public service is finished at last. We now stand at its conclusion, looking back through the changeful history of that life to its beginning, contemporaneous with the very birth of the Republic, and its varied events mingle, in our hearts and our memories, with the triumphs and calamities, the weakness and the power, the adversity and prosperity of a country we love so much. As we contemplate this sad event, in this place, the shadows of the past gather over us; the memories of events long gone crowd upon us, and the shades of departed patriots seem to hover about us, and wait to receive into their midst the spirit of one who was worthy to be a colaborer with them in a common cause, and to share in the rewards of their virtues. Henceforth he must be to us as one of them.

They say he was ambitious. If so, it was a grievous fault, and grievously has he answered it. He has found in it naught but disappointment. It has but served to aggravate the mortification of his defeats, and furnish an additional lustre to the triumph of his foes. Those who come after us may, aye, they will, inquire why his statue stands not among the statues of those whom men thought ablest and worthiest to govern.

But his ambition was a high and holy feeling, unselfish, magnanimous. Its aspirations were for his country's good, and its triumph was his country's prosperity. Whether in honor or reproach, in triumph or defeat, that heart of his never throbbed with one pulsation, save for her honor and her welfare. Turn to him in that last, best deed, and crowning glory of a life so full of public service and of honor, when his career of personal ambition was finished forever. Rejected again and again by his countrymen; just abandoned by a party which would scarce have had an existence without his genius, his courage, and his labors, that great heart, ever firm and defiant to the assaults of his enemies, but defenceless against the ingratitude of friends; doubtless wrung with the bitterest mortification of his life—then it was, and under such circumstances as these the gathering storm rose upon his country. All eyes turned to him; all voices called for those services which, in the hour of prosperity and security, they had so carelessly rejected. With no misanthropic chagrin; with no morose, selfish resentment, he forgot all but his country, and that country endangered. He returns to the scene of his labors and his fame which he had thought to have left forever. A scene—that American senate chamber—clothed in no gorgeous drapery, shrouded in no superstitious awe, or ancient reverence for hereditary power, but to a reflecting American mind more full of interest, or dignity, and of grandeur, than any spot on this broad earth, not made holy by religion's consecrating seal. See him as he enters there, tremblingly, but hopefully, upon the last, most momentous, perhaps most doubtful conflict of his life. Sir, many a gay tournament has been more dazzling to the eye of fancy, more gorgeous and imposing in the display of jewelry and cloth of gold, in the sound of heralds' trumpets, in the grand array of princely beauty and of royal pride. Many a battle field has trembled beneath a more ostentatious parade of human power, and its conquerors have been crowned with laurels, honored with triumphs, and apotheosized amid the demigods of history; but to the thoughtful, hopeful, philanthropic student of the annals of his race, never was there a conflict in which such dangers were threatened, such hopes imperiled, or the hero of which deserved a warmer gratitude, a nobler triumph, or a prouder monument.

Sir, from that long, anxious and exhausting conflict, he

never rose again. In that last battle for his country's honor and his country's safety, he received the mortal wound which laid him low, and we now mourn the death of a martyred patriot.

But never, in all the grand drama which the story of his life arrays, never has he presented a sublimer or a more touching spectacle than in those last days of his decline and death. Broken with the storms of state, wounded and scathed in many a fiery conflict, that aged, worn and decayed body, in such mournful contrast with the never-dying strength of his giant spirit, he seemed a proud and sacred, though a crumbling monument of past glory. Standing among us, like some ancient colossal ruin amid the degenerate and more diminutive structures of modern times, its vast proportions magnified by the contrast, he reminded us of those days when there were giants in the land, and we remembered that even then there was none whose prowess could withstand his arm. To watch him in that slow decline, yielding with dignity, and, as it were, inch by inch, to that last enemy, as a hero yields to a conquering foe the glorious light of his intellect blazing still in all its wonted brilliancy, and setting at defiance the clouds that vainly attempted to obscure it, he was more full of interest than in the day of his glory and his power. There are some men whose brightest intellectual emanations rise so little superior to the instincts of the animal, that we are led fearfully to doubt that cherished truth of the soul's immortality, which, even in despair, men press to their doubting hearts. But it is in the death of such a man as he, that we are reassured by the contemplation of a kindred, though superior spirit, of a soul which, immortal, like his fame, knows no old age, no decay, no death.

The wondrous light of his unmatched intellect may have dazzled a world; the eloquence of that inspired tongue may have enchanted millions, but there are few who have sounded the depths of that noble heart. To see him in sickness and in health, in joy and in sadness, in the silent watches of the night and in the busy day-time—this it was to know and love him. To see the impetuous torrent of that resistless will; the hurricane of those passions hushed in peace, breathe calmly and gently as a summer zephyr; to feel the gentle pressure of that hand in the grasp of friendship, which, in the rage of fiery conflict, would hurl scorn and defiance at his foe; to see that eagle eye, which oft would burn with patriotic ardor, or flash with the lightning of his anger, beam with the kindliest expressions of tenderness and affection—then it was, and then alone, we could learn to know and feel that that heart was warmed by the same sacred fire from above which enkindled the light of his resplendent intellect. In the death of such a man even patriotism itself might pause, and for a moment stand aloof, while friendship shed a tear of sorrow upon his bier.

> "His life was gentle; and the elements
> So mix'd in him, that Nature might stand up,
> And say to all the world,—*This was a man!*"

But who can estimate his country's loss? What tongue portray the desolation which, in this hour, throughout this broad land, hangs like a gloomy pall over his grief-stricken countrymen? How poorly can words like mine translate the eloquence of a whole people's grief for a patriot's death. For a nation's loss let a nation mourn. For that stupendous calamity to our country and mankind, be the heavens hung with black; let the wailing elements chant his dirge, and the universal heart of man throb with one common pang of grief and anguish.

Mr. CASKIE said:

Mr. SPEAKER: Unwell as I am, I must try to lay a single laurel leaf in that open coffin which is already garlanded by the eloquent tributes to the illustrious departed, which have been heard in this now solemn hall; for I come, sir, from the district of his birth. I represent on this floor that old Hanover, so proud of her HENRYS—her PATRICK HENRY and her HENRY CLAY. I speak for a people among whom he has always had as earnest and devoted friends as were ever the grace and glory of a patriot and statesman.

I shall attempt no sketch of his life. That you have had from other and abler hands than mine. Till yesterday that life was, of his own free gift, the property of his country; to-day it belongs to her history. It is known to all, and will not be forgotten. Constant, stern opponent of his political school as has been my state, I say, for her, that nowhere in this broad land are his great qualities more admired, or is his death more mourned, than in Virginia. Well may this be so; for she is his mother, and he was her son.

Mr. Speaker, when I remember the party strifes in which he was so much mingled, and through which we all, more or less, have passed, and then survey this scene, and think how far, as the lightning has borne the news that he is gone, half masted flags are drooping and church bells are tolling, and hearts are sorrowing, I can but feel that it is good for man to die. For when Death enters, O! how the unkindnesses, and jealousies, and rivalries of life do vanish, and how, like incense from an altar, do peace, and friendship, and all the sweet charities of our nature, rise around the corpse which was once a man! And of a truth, Mr. Speaker, never was more of veritable noble *manhood* cased in mortal mould than was found in him to whose memory this brief and humble, yet true and heart-felt tribute is paid. But his eloquent voice is hushed, his high heart is stilled. "Like a shock of corn fully ripe, he has been gathered to his fathers." With more than threescore years and ten upon him, and honors clustered thick about him; in the full possession of unclouded intellect, and all the consolations of Christianity, he has met the fate which is evitable by none. Lamented by all his countrymen, his name is bright on Fame's immortal roll. He has finished his course, and he has his crown. What more fruit can life bear? What can it give that HENRY CLAY has not gained?

Then, Mr. Speaker, around his tomb should be heard, not only the dirge that wails his loss, but the jubilant anthem which sounds that on the world's battle field another victory has been won—another *incontestable greatness* achieved.

Mr. CHANDLER, of Pennsylvania, said:

Mr. SPEAKER: It would seem as if the solemn invocation of the honorable gentleman from Kentucky, (Mr. EWING) was receiving an early answer, and that the heavens are hung in black, and the wailing elements are singing the funeral dirge of HENRY CLAY. Amid this elemental gloom, and the distress which pervades the nation at the death of HENRY CLAY, private grief should not obtrude itself upon notice, nor personal anguish seek for utterance. Silence is the best exponent of individual sorrow, and the heart that knoweth its own bitterness, shrinks from an exposition of its affliction.

Could I have consulted my own feelings on the event which occupies the attention of the house at the present moment, I should even have forborne attendance here, and in the solitude and silence of my chamber have mused upon the terrible lesson which has been administered to the people and the nation. But I represent a constituency who justly pride themselves upon the unwavering attachment they have ever felt and manifested to HENRY CLAY —a constant, pervading, hereditary love. The son has taken up the father's affection, and amid all the professions of political attachments to others, whom the accidents of party have made prominent, and the success of party has made powerful, true to his own instincts, and true to the sanctified legacy of his father, he has placed the name of HENRY CLAY forward and pre-eminent as the exponent of what is greatest in statesmanship and purest in patriotism. And even, sir, when party fealty caused other attachments to be avowed for party uses, the preference was limited to the occupancy of office, and superiority admitted for CLAY in all that is reckoned above party estimation.

Nor ought I to forbear to add that, as the senior member of the delegation which represents my commonwealth, I am requested to utter the sentiments of the people of Pennsylvania at large, who yield to no portion of this great Union in their appreciation of the talents, their reverence for the lofty patriotism, their admiration of the statesmanship, and hereafter their love of the memory of HENRY CLAY.

I cannot, therefore, be silent on this occasion without injustice to the affections of my constituency, even though I painfully feel how inadequate to the reverence and love my people have toward that statesman must be all that I have to utter on this mournful occasion.

I know not, Mr. Chairman, where now the nation is to find the men she needs in peril; either other calls than those of politics are holding in abeyance the talents which the nation may need, or else a generation is to pass undistinguished by the greatness of our statesmen. Of the noble minds that have swayed the senate, one yet survives in the maturity of powerful intellect, carefully disciplined and nobly exercised. May He, who has thus far blessed our nation, spare to her and the world, that of which the world must always envy our country the possession! But my business is with the dead.

The biography of HENRY CLAY, from his childhood upward, is too familiar to every American for me to trespass on the time of this house by a reference directly thereto; and the honorable gentlemen who have preceded me have, with affectionate hand and appropriate delicacy, swept away the dust which nearly fourscore years have scattered over a part of the record, and have made our pride greater in his life, and our grief more poignant at his death, by showing some of those passages which attract respect to our republican institutions, of which Mr. CLAY'S whole life was the able support and the most successful illustration.

It would, then, be a work of supererogation for me to renew that effort, though inquiry into the life and conduct of Henry Clay would present new themes for private eulogy, new grounds for public gratitude.

How rare is it, Mr. Speaker, that the great man, living, can with confidence rely on extensive personal friendship, or dying, think to awaken a sentiment of regret beyond that which includes the public loss or the disappointment of individual hopes. Yet, sir, the message which yesterday went forth from this city that Henry Clay was dead, brought sorrow, personal, private, special sorrow, to the hearts of thousands; each of whom felt that from his own love for, his long attachment to, his disinterested hopes in, Henry Clay, he had a particular sorrow to cherish and express, which weighed upon his heart separate from the sense of national loss.

No man, Mr. Speaker, in our nation, had the art so to identify himself with public measures of the most momentous character, and to maintain, at the same time, almost universal affection, like that great statesman. His business, from his boyhood was with national concerns, and he dealt with them as with familiar things. And yet his sympathies were with individual interests, enterprises, affections, joys, and sorrows; and while every patriot bowed in humble deference to his lofty attainments and heart-felt gratitude for his national services, almost every man in this great Republic knew that the great statesman was, in feeling and experience, identified with his own position. Hence the universal love of the people; hence their enthusiasm, in all times, for his fame. Hence, sir, their present grief.

Many other public men of our country have distinguished themselves and brought honor to the nation by superiority in some peculiar branch of public service, but it seems to have been the gift of Mr. CLAY to have acquired peculiar eminence in every path of duty he was called to tread. In the earnestness of debate, which great public interests and distinguished opposing talents excited in this house, he had no superior in energy, force or effect. Yet, as the presiding officer, by blandness of language, and firmness of purpose, he soothed and made orderly; and thus, by official dignity, he commanded the respect which energy had secured to him on the floor.

Wherever official or social duties demanded an exercise of his power, there was a pre-eminence which seemed prescriptively his own. In the lofty debate of the senate, and the stirring harangues to popular assemblages, he was the orator of the nation and of the people; and the sincerity of purpose and the unity of design evinced in all he said or did, fixed in the public mind a confidence strong and expansive as the affections he had won.

Year after year, sir, has HENRY CLAY been achieving the work of the mission with which he was intrusted; and it was only when the warmest wishes of his warmest friends were disappointed, that he entered on the fruition of a patriot's highest hopes, and stood in the full enjoyment of that admiration and confidence which nothing but the antagonism of party relations could have divided.

How rich that enjoyment must have been it is only for us to imagine. How eminently deserved it was, we and the world can attest.

The love and the devotion of his political friends were cheering and grateful to his heart, and were acknowledged in all his life—were recognized even to his death.

The contest in the senate chamber or the forum were rewarded with success achieved, and the great victor could enjoy the ovation which partial friendship or the gratitude of the benefit prepared. But the triumph of his life was no party achievement. It was not in the applause which admiring friends and defeated antagonists offered to his measureless success, that he found the reward of his labors, and comprehended the extent of his mission.

It was only when friends and antagonists paused in their contests, appalled at the public difficulties and national dangers which had been accumulating, unseen and unregarded; it was only when the nation itself felt the danger, and acknowledged the inefficacy of party action as a remedy, that HENRY CLAY calculated the full extent of his powers, and enjoyed the reward of their saving exercise. Then, sir, you saw, and I saw, party designations dropped, and party allegiance disavowed, and anxious patriots, of all localities and name, turn toward the country's benefactor as the man for the terrible exigencies of the hour; and the sick chamber of HENRY CLAY became the Delphos whence were given out the oracles that presented the means and the measures of our Union's safety. There, sir, and not in the high places of the country, were the labors and sacrifices of half a century to be rewarded and closed. With his right yet in that senate which he had entered the youngest, and lingered still the eldest member, he felt that his work was done, and the object of his life accomplished. Every cloud that had dimmed the noonday lustre had been dissipated; and the retiring orb, which sunk from the sight of the nation in fullness and beauty, will yet pour up the horizon a posthumous glory that shall tell of the splendor and greatness of the luminary that has passed away.

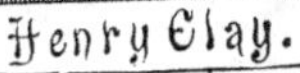

Mr. Bayly, of Virginia.

Mr. Speaker: Although I have been all my life a political opponent of Mr. Clay, yet from my boyhood I have been upon terms of personal friendship with him. More than twenty years ago, I was introduced to him by my father, who was his personal friend. From that time to this, there has existed between us as great personal intimacy as the disparity in our years and our political difference would justify. After I became a member of this house, and upon his return to the senate, subsequent to his resignation in 1842, the warm regard, upon his part, for the daughter of a devoted friend of forty years' standing, made him a constant visitor at my house, and frequently a guest at my table. These circumstances make it proper, that upon this occasion, I should pay this last tribute to his memory. I not only knew him well, as a statesman, but I knew him better in most unreserved social intercourse. The most happy circumstance, as I esteem it, of my political life, has been, that I have thus known each of our great congressional triumvirate.

I, sir, never knew a man of higher qualities than Mr. Clay. His very faults originated in high qualities. With as great self-possession, with greater self-reliance than any man I ever knew, he possessed moral and physical courage to as high a degree as any man who ever lived. Confident in his own judgment, never doubting as to his own course, fearing no obstacle that might lie in his way, it was almost impossible that he should not have been imperious in his character. Never doubting himself as to what, in his opinion, duty and patriotism required at his hands, it was natural that he should sometimes have been impatient with those more doubting and timid than himself. His were qualities to have made a great general, as they were qualities that did make him a great statesman, and these qualities were so obvious that, during the darkest period of our late war with Great Britain, Mr. MADISON had determined, at one time, to make him general-in-chief of the American army.

Sir, it is but a short time since the American Congress buried the first one that went to the grave of that great triumvirate. We are now called upon to bury another. The third, thank GOD! still lives, and long may he live to enlighten his countrymen by his wisdom, and set them the example of exalted patriotism. Sir, in the lives and characters of these great men, there is much resembling those of the great triumvirate of the British Parliament. It differs principally in this: BURKE preceded FOX and PITT to the tomb. WEBSTER survives CLAY and CALHOUN. When FOX and PITT died, they left no peer behind them. WEBSTER still lives, now that CALHOUN and CLAY are dead, the unrivaled statesman of his country. Like FOX and PITT, CLAY and CALHOUN lived in troubled times. Like FOX and PITT, they were each of them the leader of rival parties. Like FOX and PITT they were idolized by their respective friends. Like FOX and PITT, they died about the same time, and in the public service; and, as has been said of FOX and PITT, CLAY and CALHOUN died with "their harness upon them." Like FOX and PITT—

"With more than mortal powers endow'd,
How high they soar'd above the crowd;
Theirs was no common party race,
Jostling by dark intrigue for place—
Like fabled gods their mighty war
Shook realms and natio s in its jar.

Beneath each banner proud to stand,
Look'd up the noblest of the land.

* * * * *

Here let their discord with them die.
Speak not for those a separate doom;
Whom fate made brothers in the tomb;
But search the land of living men,
Where wilt thou find their like again?"

Mr. VENABLE, said:

Mr. SPEAKER: I trust that I shall be pardoned for adding a few words upon this sad occasion. The life of the illustrious statesman, which has just terminated, is so interwoven with our history, and the lustre of his great name so profusely shed over its pages, that simple admiration of his high qualities might well be my excuse. But it is a sacred privilege to draw near; to contemplate the end of the great and the good. It is profitable as well as purifying to look upon and realize the office of death in removing all that can excite jealousy or produce distrust, and to gaze upon the virtues which, like jewels, have survived his powers of destruction. The light which radiates from the life of a great and patriotic statesman is often dimmed by the mists which party conflicts throw around it. But the blast which strikes him down purifies the atmosphere which surrounded him in life, and it shines forth in bright examples and well-earned renown. It is then that we witness the sincere acknowledgment of gratitude by a people who, having enjoyed the benefits arising from the services of an eminent statesman, embalm his name in their memory and hearts. We should cherish such recollections as well from patriotism as self-respect. Ours, sir, is now the duty, in the midst of sadness, in this high place, in the face of our Republic, and before the world, to pay this tribute, by acknowledging the merits of our colleague, whose name has ornamented the journals of congress for nearly half a century. Few, very few, have ever combined the high intellectual powers and distinguished gifts of this illustrious senator. Cast in the finest mould by nature, he more than fulfilled the anticipations which were indulged by those who looked to a distinguished career as the certain result of that zealous pursuit of fame and usefulness upon which he entered in early life. Of the incidents of that life it is unnecessary for me to speak—they are as familiar as household words, and must be equally familiar to those who come after us. But it is useful to refresh memory by recurrence to some of the events which marked his career. We know, sir, that there is much that is in common in the histories of distinguished men. The elements which constitute greatness are the same in all times; hence those who have been the admiration of their generations present in their lives much which, although really great, ceases to be remarkable, because illustrated by such numerous examples—

> "But there are deeds which should not pass away,
> And names that must not wither."

Of such deeds the life of HENRY CLAY affords many and bright examples. His own name, and those with whom he associated, shall live with a freshness which time cannot impair, and shine with a brightness which passing years cannot dim. His advent into public life was as remarkable for the circumstances as it was brilliant in its effect. It was at a time in which genius and learning, statesmanship and eloquence, made the American congress the most august body in the world. He was the contemporary of a race of statesmen, some of whom—then administering the government, and others retiring and retired from office—presented an array of ability unsurpassed in our history. The elder ADAMS, JEFFERSON, MADISON, GALLATIN, CLINTON, and MONROE, stood before the Republic in the maturity of their fame; while CALHOUN, JOHN QUINCY ADAMS, LOWNDES, RANDOLPH, CRAWFORD, GASTON and CHEVES, with a host of others, rose a bright galaxy upon our horizon. He who won his spurs in such a field earned his knighthood. Distinction amid such competition was true renown—

> "The fame which a man wins for himself is best—
> That he may call his own."

It was such a fame that he made for himself in that most eventful era in our history. To me, sir, the recollections of that day, and the events which distinguish it, is filled with an overpowering interest. I never can forget my enthusiastic admiration of the boldness, the eloquence, and the patriotism of HENRY CLAY during the war of 1812. In the bright array of talent which adorned the congress of the United States; in the conflict growing out of the political events of that time; in the struggles of party, and amid the gloom and disasters which depressed the spirits of most men, and well-nigh paralyzed the energies of the administration, his cheerful face, high bearing, commanding eloquence and iron will, gave strength and consistency to those elements which finally gave, not only success, but glory, to the country. When dark clouds hovered over us, and there was little to save from despair, the country looked with hope to CLAY and CALHOUN, to

LOWNDES, and CRAWFORD, and CHEVES, and looked not in vain. The unbending will, the unshaken nerve, and the burning eloquence of HENRY CLAY did as much to command confidence and sustain hope as even the news of our first victory after a succession of defeats. Those great names are now canonized in history; he, too, has passed to join them on its pages. Associated in his long political life with the illustrious CALHOUN, he survived him but two years. Many of us heard his eloquent tribute to his memory in the senate chamber on the annunciation of his death. And we this day unite in a similar manifestation of reverential regard to him whose voice shall never more charm the ear, whose burning thoughts, borne on that medium, shall no more move the hearts of listening assemblies.

In the midst of the highest specimens of our race, he was always an equal; *he was a man among men.* Bold, skillful and determined, he gave character to the party which acknowledged him as a leader; impressed his opinions upon their minds, and an attachment to himself upon their hearts. No man, sir, can do this without being eminently great. Whoever attains this position must first overcome the aspirations of antagonist ambition; quiet the clamors of rivalry; hold in check the murmurs of jealousy, and overcome the instincts of vanity and self-love in the masses thus subdued to his control. But few men ever attain it. Very rare are the examples of those whose plastic touch forms the minds and directs the purposes of a great political party. This infallible indication of superiority belonged to Mr. CLAY. He has exercised that control during a long life; and now, through our broad land, the tidings of his death, borne with electric speed, have opened the fountains of sorrow. Every city, town, village and hamlet will be clothed with mourning; along our extended coast, the commercial and military marine, with flags drooping at half mast, own the bereavement; state-houses draped in black proclaim the extinguishment of one of the great lights of senates; and minute-guns sound his requiem!

Sir, during the last five years I have seen the venerable JOHN QUINCY ADAMS, JOHN C. CALHOUN and HENRY CLAY pass from among us, the legislators of our country. The race of giants who "were on the earth in those days" is well-nigh gone. Despite their skill, their genius, their might, they have sunk under the stroke of time. They were our admiration and our glory; a few linger with us, the monuments of former greatness, the beacon-lights of a past age. The death of HENRY CLAY cannot fail to suggest melancholy associations to each member of this house. These walls have re-echoed the silvery tones of his bewitching voice; listening assemblies have hung upon his lips. The chair which you fill has been graced by his presence, while his commanding person and unequaled parliamentary attainments inspired all with deference and respect. Chosen by acclamation because of his high qualifications, he sustained himself before the house and the country. In his supremacy with his party, and the uninterrupted confidence which he enjoyed to the day of his death, he seems to have almost discredited the truth of those lines of the poet LABERIUS—

"Non possunt primi esse omnes omni in tempore,
Summum ad gradum cum claritatis veneris,
Consistes ægre, et citius, quam ascendas, cades."

If not at all times first, he stood equal with the foremost, and a brilliant rapid rise knew no decline in the confidence of those whose just appreciation of his merits had confirmed his title to renown.

The citizens of other countries will deplore his death; the struggling patriots who, on our own continent, were cheered by his sympathies, and who must have perceived his influence in the recognition of their independence by this government, have taught their children to venerate his name. He won the civic crown, and the demonstrations of this hour own the worth of civil services.

It was with great satisfaction that I heard my friend from Kentucky, [Mr. BRECKENRIDGE] the immediate representative of Mr. CLAY, detail a conversation which disclosed the feelings of that eminent man in relation to his Christian hope. These, Mr. Speaker, are rich memorials, precious reminiscences. A Christian statesman is the glory of his age, and his memory will be glorious in after-times; it reflects a light coming from a source which clouds cannot dim nor shadows obscure. It was my privilege, also, a short time since, to converse with this distinguished statesman on the subject of his hopes in a future state. Feeling a deep interest, I asked him frankly what were his hopes in the world to which he was evidently hastening. "I am pleased," said he, "my friend, that you have introduced the subject. Conscious that I must die very soon, I love to meditate upon the most important of all interests. I love to converse and to hear conversations about them. The vanity of the world and its insufficiency to satisfy the soul of man has long been a settled conviction of my mind. Man's inability to secure, by his own merits, the approbation of GOD, I feel to be true. I trust in the atonement of the Savior of men as the ground of my acceptance and my hope of salvation. My faith is feeble, but I hope in His mercy and trust in His promises." To such declarations I listened with the deepest interest, as I did on another occasion, when he said: "I am willing to abide the will of Heaven, and ready to die when that will shall determine it."

He is gone, sir, professing the humble hope of a Christian. That hope, alone, sir, can sustain you, or any of us. There is one lonely and crushed heart that has bowed before this afflictive event. Far away, at Ashland, a widowed wife, prevented, by feeble health, from attending his bedside and soothing his painful hours, she has thought even the electric speed of the intelligence daily transmitted of his condition too slow for her aching, anxious bosom. She will find consolation in his Christian submission, and will draw all of comfort that such a case admits from the assurance that nothing was neglected by the kindness of friends which could supply her place. May the guardianship of the widow's God be her protection, and His consolations her support!

"All cannot be at all times first,
To reach the top-most step of glory; to stand there
More hard. Even swifter than we mount we fall."

Mr. Haven, said:

Mr. Speaker: Representing a constituency distinguished for the constancy of its devotion to the political principles of Mr. Clay, and for its unwavering attachment to his fortunes and his person—sympathizing deeply with those whose more intimate personal relations with him have made them feel most profoundly this general bereavement

—I desire to say a few words of him, since he has fallen amongst us, and been taken to his rest.

After the finished eulogies which have been so eloquently pronounced by the honorable gentlemen who have preceded me, I will avoid a course of remark which might otherwise be deemed a repetition, and refer to the bearing of some of the acts of the deceased upon the interests and destinies of my own state. The influence of his public life, and of his *purely American character*, the benefits of his wise forecast, and the results of his efforts for wholesome and rational progress, are nowhere more strongly exhibited than in the state of New York.

Our appreciation of his anxiety for the general diffusion of knowledge and education, is manifested in our twelve thousand public libraries, our equal number of common schools, and a large number of higher institutions of learning, all of which draw portions of their support from the share of the proceeds of the public lands, which his wise policy gave to our state. Our whole people are thus constantly reminded of their great obligations to the statesman, whose death now afflicts the nation with sorrow. Our extensive public works, attest our conviction of the utility and importance of the system of internal improvements he so ably advocated; and their value and productiveness, afford a most striking evidence of the soundness and wisdom of his policy. Nor has his influence been less sensibly felt in our agriculture, commerce, and manufactures. Every department of human industry acknowledges his fostering care, and the people of New York are in no small measure, indebted to his statesmanship for the wealth, comfort, contentment and happiness so widely and generally diffused throughout the state.

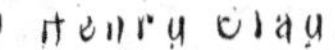

Well may New York cherish his memory and acknowledge, with gratitude, the benefits that his life has conferred. That memory will be cherished throughout the Republic.

When internal discord and sectional strife have threatened the integrity of the Union, his just weight of character, his large experience, his powers of conciliation and acknowledged patriotism, have enabled him to pacify the angry passions of his countrymen, and to raise the bow of promise and of hope upon the clouds which have darkened the political horizon.

He has passed from amongst us, ripe in wisdom and pure in character—full of years and full of honors—he has breathed his last amidst the blessings of a united and grateful nation. He was, in my judgment, particularly fortunate in the time of his death.

He lived to see his country, guided by his wisdom, come once again unhurt, out of trying sectional difficulties and domestic strife; and he has closed his eyes in death upon that country, whilst it is in the enjoyment of profound peace, busy with industry, and blessed with unequaled prosperity.

It can fall to the lot of but few to die amidst so warm a gratitude flowing from the hearts of their countrymen; and none can leave a brighter example, or a more enduring fame.

Mr. Brooks, of New York, said:

Mr. Speaker: I rise to add my humble tribute to the memory of a great and good man, now to be gathered to his fathers. I speak for, and from, a community in whose heart is enshrined the name of him whom we mourn; who, however much Virginia, the land of his birth, or Kentucky, the land of his adoption, may love him, is, if possible, loved where I live, yet more. If idolatry had been Christian, or allowable even, he would have been our idol. But as it is, for a quarter of a century now, his bust, his portrait, or some medal, has been one of our household gods, gracing not alone the saloons and the halls of wealth, but the humblest room or work-shop of almost every mechanic or laborer. Proud monuments of his policy as a statesman, as my colleague has justly said, are all about us; and we owe to him, in a good degree, our growth, our greatness, our prosperity and happiness as a people.

The great field of HENRY CLAY, Mr. Speaker, has been here, on the floor of this house, and in the other wing of the capitol. He has held other posts of higher nominal distinction, but they are all eclipsed by the brilliancy of his career as a congressman. What of glory he has acquired, or what most endear him to his countrymen, have been won, here, amid these pillars, under these domes of the capitol.

"Si quæris monumentum, circumspice."

The mind of Mr. CLAY has been the governing mind of the country, more or less, ever since he has been on the stage of public action. In a minority or majority—more, perhaps, even in a minority than in a majority, he seems to have had some commission, divine, as it were, to persuade, to convince, to govern other men. His patriotism, his grand conceptions, have created measures which the secret fascination of his manners, in-doors, or his irresistible eloquence without, have enabled him, almost always, to frame into laws. Adverse administrations have yielded to him, or been borne down by him, or he has taken them captive as a leader, and carried the country and congress with him. This power he has wielded now for nearly half a century, with nothing but reason and eloquence to back him. And yet, when he came here, years ago, he came from a then frontier state of this Union, heralded by no loud trumpet of fame, nay, quite unknown! unfortified even by any position, social or pecuniary;—to quote his own words, "My only heritage has been infancy, indigence, and ignorance."

In these days, Mr. Speaker, when mere civil qualifications for high public places—when long civil training and practical statesmanship are held subordinate—a most discouraging prospect would be rising up before our young men, were it not for some such names as LOWNDES, CRAWFORD, CLINTON, GASTON, CALHOUN, CLAY, and the like, scattered along the pages of our history, as stars or constellations along a cloudless sky. They shine forth and show us, that if the chief magistracy cannot be won by such qualifications, a memory among men can be—a hold upon posterity, as firm, as lustrous—nay, more imperishable. In the Capitolium of Rome there are long rows of marble slabs, on which are recorded the names of the Roman consuls; but the eye wanders over this wilderness of letters but to light up and kindle upon some CATO or CICERO. To win such fame, thus unsullied, as Mr. CLAY has won, is worth any man's ambition. And how was it won? By courting the shifting gales of popularity? No, never! By truckling to the schemes, the arts, and seductions of the demagogue? Never, never! His hardest battles, as a public man—his greatest, most illustrious achievements—have been against, at first, an adverse public opinion. To gain an imperishable name, he has often braved the perishable popularity of the moment. That sort of courage which, in a public man, I deem the highest of all courage, that sort of courage most necessary, under our form of government, to guide as well as to save a state, Mr. CLAY was possessed of more than any public man I ever knew. Physical courage, valuable, indispensable though it be, we share but with the brute; but moral courage, to dare to do right amid all temptations to do wrong, is, as it seems to me, the very highest species, the noblest heroism, under institutions like ours. "I had rather be right than be President," was Mr. CLAY'S sublime reply when pressed to refrain from some measure that would mar his popularity. These lofty words were the clue of his whole character—the secret of his hold upon the heads as well as hearts of the American people; nay, the key of his immortality.

Another of the keys, Mr. Speaker, of his universal reputation, was his intense nationality. When taunted, but recently, almost within our hearing, as it were, on the floor of the Senate by a southern senator, as being a southern man unfaithful to the south—his indignant but patriotic exclamation was, "I know no *south*, no north, no east, no west. The country, the *whole* country, loved, reverenced, adored such a man. The soil of Virginia may be his birth-place, the sod of Kentucky will cover his grave—what was mortal they claim—but the spirit, the soul, the genius of the mighty man, the immortal part, these belong to his country and to his GOD.

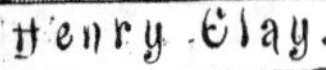

Mr. FAULKNER, of Virginia, said:

Representing, in part, the state which gave birth to that distinguished man whose death has just been announced upon this floor, and having for many years held toward him the most cordial relations of friendship, personal and political, I feel that I should fail to discharge an appropriate duty, if I permitted this occasion to pass by without some expression of the feeling which such an event is so well calculated to elicit. Sir, this intelligence does not fall upon our ears unexpectedly. For months the public mind has been prepared for the great national loss which we now deplore; and yet, as familiar as the daily and hourly reports have made us with his hopeless condition and gradual decline, and although

> " Like a shadow thrown
> Softly and sweetly from a passing cloud,
> Death fell upon him,"

it is impossible that a light of such surpassing splendor should be, as it is now, forever extinguished from our view, without producing a shock, deeply and painfully felt, to the utmost limits of this great Republic. Sir, we all feel that a mighty intellect has passed from among us; but, happily for this country, happily for mankind, not until it had accomplished, to some extent, the exalted mission for which it had been sent upon this earth; not until it had reached the full maturity of its usefulness and power; not until it had shed a bright and radiant lustre over our national renown; not until time had enabled it to bequeath the rich treasures of its thought and experience for the guidance and instruction of the present and of succeeding generations.

Sir, it is difficult,—it is impossible—within the limit allowed for remarks upon occasions of this kind, to do justice to a great historical character like HENRY CLAY. He was one of that class of men whom SCALIGER designates as *homines centenarii*—men that appear upon the earth but once in a century. His fame is the growth of years, and it would require time to unfold the elements which have combined to impart to it so much of stability and grandeur. Volumes have already been written, and volumes will continue to be written, to record those eminent and distinguished public services which have placed him in the front rank of American statesmen and patriots. The highest talents, stimulated by a fervid and patriotic enthusiasm, has already and will continue to exhaust its powers to portray those striking and generous incidents of his life—those shining and captivating qualities of his heart, which have made him one of the most beloved, as he was one of the most admired, of men; and yet the subject itself will remain as fresh and exhaustless as if hundreds of the best intellects of the land had not quaffed the inspiration of their genius from the ever-gushing and overflowing fountains of his fame. It could not be that a reputation so grand and collossal as that which attaches to the name of HENRY CLAY, could rest, for its base, upon any single virtue, however striking; nor upon any single act, no matter how marked or distinguished. Such a reputation as he has left behind him, could only be the result of a long life of illustrious public service. And such in truth it was. For nearly half a century he has been a prominent actor in all the stirring and eventful scenes of American history, fashioning and moulding many of the most important measures of public policy by his bold and sagacious mind, and arresting others by his unconquerable energy and resistless force of eloquence. And however much the members of this body may differ in opinion as to the wisdom of many of his views of national domestic policy, there is not one upon this floor—no, sir, not one in this nation—who will deny to him frankness and directness as a public man; a genius for statesmanship of the highest order; extraordinary capacities for public usefulness, and an ardent and elevated patriotism, without stain and without reproach.

In referring to a career of public service so varied and extended as that of Mr. Clay, and to a character so rich in every great and manly virtue, it is only possible to glance at a few of the most prominent of those points of his personal history, which have given to him so distinguished a place in the affections of his countrymen.

In the whole character of Mr. Clay, in all that attached or belonged to it, you find nothing that is not essentially American. Born in the darkest period of our revolutionary struggle; reared from infancy to manhood among those great minds which gave the first impulse to that mighty movement, he early imbibed and sedulously cherished those great principles of civil and political liberty which he so brilliantly illustrated in his subsequent life, and which has made his name a watch-word of hope and consolation to the oppressed of all the earth. In his intellectual training, he was the pure creation of our own republican soil. Few, if any, allusions are to be seen in his speeches or writings, to ancient or modern literature, or to the thoughts and ideas of other men. His country, its institutions, its policy, its interests, its destiny, form the exclusive topics of those eloquent harangues which, while they are destitute of the elaborate finish, have all the ardor and intensity of thought, the earnestness of purpose, the cogency of reasoning, the vehemence of style, and the burning patriotism, which mark the productions of the great Athenian orator.

One of the most distinguishing characteristics of Mr. CLAY, as a public man, was his loyalty to truth and to the honest convictions of his own mind. He deceived no man: he would not permit his own heart to be deceived by any of those seductive influences which too often warp the judgment of men in public station. He never paused to consider how far any step which he was about to take would lead to his own personal advancement; he never calculated what he might lose or what he might gain by his advocacy of, or his opposition to, any particular measure. His single inquiry was, Is it right? Is it in accordance with the Constitution of the land? Will it redound to the permanent welfare of the country? When satisfied upon these points, his determination was fixed; his purpose was immovable. "I would rather be right than President," was the expression of his genuine feelings, and the principle by which he was controlled in his public career—a saying worthy of immortality, and proper to be inscribed upon the heart of every young man in this Republic. And yet, sir, with all of that personal and moral intrepidity which so eminently marked the character of Mr. CLAY; with his well-known inflexibility of purpose and unyielding resolution, such was the genuine sincerity of his patriotism, and such his thorough comprehension of those principles of compromise, upon which the whole structure of our government was founded, that no one was more prompt to relax the rigor of his policy the moment he perceived that it was calculated to disturb the harmony of the states, or to endanger, in any degree, the stability of the government. With him the love of this Union was a passion—an absorbing sentiment—which gave color to every act of his public life. It triumphed over party; it triumphed over policy; it subdued the natural fierceness and haughtiness of his temper, and brought him into the most kindly and cordial relations with those who, upon all other questions, were deeply and bitterly opposed to him. It has been asserted, sir, upon high medical authority, and doubtless with truth, that his life was, in all probability, shortened ten years by the arduous and extraordinary labors which he assumed at the memorable session of 1850. If so, he has added the crowning glory of the MARTYR to the spotless fame of the PATRIOT; and we may well hope that a great national pacification, purchased at such a sacrifice, will long continue to cement the bonds of this now happy and prosperous Union.

Mr. CLAY possessed, in an eminent degree, the qualities of a great popular leader; and history, I will assume to say, affords no example in any republic, ancient or modern, of any individual that so fearlessly carried out the convictions of his own judgment, and so sparingly flattered the prejudices of popular feeling, who, for so long a period, exercised the same controlling influence over the public mind. Earnest in whatever measure he sustained, fearless in attack—dexterous in defence—abounding in intellectual resource—eloquent in debate—of inflexible purpose, and with a "courage never to submit or yield," no man ever lived with higher qualifications to rally a desponding party, or to lead an embattled host to victory. That he never attained the highest post of honorable ambition in this country, is not to be ascribed to any want of capacity as a popular leader, nor to the absence of those qualities which attract the fidelity and devotion of "troops" of admiring friends. It was the fortune of NAPOLEON, at a critical period of his destiny, to be brought into collision with the star of WELLINGTON; and it was the fortune of HENRY CLAY to have encountered, in his political orbit, another great and original mind, gifted with equal power for commanding success, and blessed with more fortunate elements, concurring at the time, of securing popular favor. The struggle was such as might have been anticipated from the collision of two such fierce and powerful rivals. For near a quarter of a century this great Republic has been convulsed to its centre by the divisions which have sprung from their respective opinions, policy and personal destinies; and even now, when they have both been removed to a higher and a better sphere of existence, and when every unkind feeling has been quenched in the triumphs of the grave, this country still feels, and for years will continue to feel, the influence of those agitations to which their powerful and impressive characters gave impulse.

But I must pause. If I were to attempt to present all the aspects in which the character of this illustrious man will challenge the applause of history, I should fatigue the House, and violate the just limit allowed for such remarks.

I cannot, however, conclude, sir, without making some more special allusion to Mr. CLAY, as a native of that state which I have the honor in part to represent upon this floor. We are all proud, and very properly proud, of the distinguished men to whom our respective states have given birth. It is a just and laudable emulation, and one, in a confederated government like ours, proper to be encouraged. And while men, like Mr. CLAY, very rapidly rise above the confined limits of a state reputation, and acquire a national fame, in which all claim, and all have an equal interest, still there is a propriety and fitness in preserving the relation between the individual and his state. Virginia has given birth to a large number of men who have, by their distinguished talent and services, impressed their names upon the hearts and memories of their countrymen; but certainly, since the colonial era, she has given birth to no man, who, in the massive and gigantic proportions of his character, and in the splendor of his native endowments, can be compared to HENRY CLAY. At an early age, he emigrated from his native state, and found a home in Kentucky. In a speech which he delivered in the Senate of the United States, in February, 1842,—and which I well remember—upon the occasion of his resigning his seat in that body, he expressed the wish that, when that event should occur, which has now clothed this city in mourning, and filled the nation with grief, his "earthly remains should be laid under the green sod of Kentucky, with those of her gallant and patriotic sons."

Sir, however gratifying it might be to us that his remains should be transferred to his native soil, to there mingle with the ashes of WASHINGTON, JEFFERSON, MADISON, LEE and HENRY, we cannot complain of the very natural preference which he has himself expressed. If Virginia did give him birth—Kentucky has nourished him in his manhood—has freely lavished upon him her highest honors—has shielded him from harm when the clouds of calumny and detraction gathered heavily and loweringly about him; and she has watched over his fame with the tenderness and zeal of a mother. Sir, it is not to be wondered that he should have expressed the wish he did, to be laid by the side of her gallant and patriotic sons. Happy Kentucky! Happy in having an adopted son so worthy of her highest honors. Happy, in the unshaken fidelity and loyalty with which, for near half a century, those honors have been so steadfastly and gracefully accorded to him.

Sir, whilst Virginia, in the exercise of her own proper judgment, has differed from Mr. CLAY in some of his views of national policy, she has never, at any period of his public career, failed to regard him with pride, as one of her most distinguished sons; to honor the purity and the manliness of his character, and to award to him the high credit of an honest and sincere devotion to his country's welfare. And now, sir, that death has arrested forever the pulsations of that mighty heart, and sealed in eternal silence those eloquent lips upon whose accents thousands have so often hung in rapture, I shall stand justified in saying, that a wail of lamentation will be heard from her people—her whole people—reverberating through her mountains and valleys, as deep, as genuine, and as sincere as that, which I know, will swell the noble hearts and the heaving bosoms of the people of his own cherished, and beloved Kentucky.

Sir, as I walked to the capitol this morning, every object which attracted my eye, admonished me that a nation's benefactor had departed from amongst us. He is gone! HENRY CLAY, the idol of his friends, the ornament of the senate chamber, the pride of his country; he whose presence gathered crowds of his admiring fellow-men around him, as if he had been one descended from above, has passed forever from our view.

> "His soul, enlarged from its vile bonds, has gone
> To that REFULGENT world, where it shall swim
> In liquid light, and float on seas of bliss."

But the memory of his virtues and of his services will be gratefully embalmed in the hearts of his countrymen, and generations yet unborn will be taught to lisp, with reverence and enthusiasm, the name of HENRY CLAY.

Mr. PARKER, of Indiana, said:

Mr. SPEAKER: This is a solemn—a consecrated hour. And I would not detain the members of the House from indulging in the silence of their own feelings, so grateful to hearts chastened as ours.

But I cannot restrain an expression from a bosom pained with its fullness.

When my young thoughts first took cognizance of the fact that I have a country—my eye was attracted by the magnificent proportions of HENRY CLAY.

The idea absorbed me then, that he was, above all other men, the embodiment of my country's genius.

I have watched him; I have studied him; I have admired him—and, GOD forgive me! for he was but a man, "of like passions with us"—I fear I have *idolized* him, until this hour.

But he has gone from among men; and it is for US now to awake and apply ourselves, with renewed fervor and increased fidelity, to the welfare of the country HE loved so well and served so truly and so long—the glorious country yet saved to us!

Yes, HENRY CLAY has fallen, at last!—as the ripe oak falls in the stillness of the forest. But the verdant and gorgeous richness of his glories will only fade and wither from the earth, when his country's history shall have been forgotten.

"One generation passeth away and another generation cometh." Thus it has been from the beginning, and thus it will be, until time shall be no longer.

Yesterday morning, at eleven o'clock, the spirit of HENRY CLAY—so long the pride and glory of his own country, and the admiration of all the world—was yet with us, though struggling to be free. Ere "high noon" came, it had passed over "the dark river," through the gate, into the celestial city, inhabited by all the "just men made perfect." May not our rapt vision contemplate him there, this day, in sweet communion with the dear friends that have gone before him?—with MADISON, and JEFFERSON, and WASHINGTON, and HENRY, and FRANKLIN—with the eloquent TULLY, with the "divine PLATO," with AARON the Levite, who could "speak well"—with all the great and good, since and before the flood!

His princely tread has graced these aisles for the last time. These halls will wake no more to the magic music of his voice.

Did that tall spirit, in its etherial form, enter the courts of the upper sanctuary, bearing itself comparable with the spirits there, as was his walk among men?

Did the mellifluous tones of his greeting there enrapture the hosts of Heaven, comparably with his strains "to stir men's blood" on earth?

Then, may we not fancy, when it was announced to the inhabitants of that better country, HE COMES! HE COMES!

there was a rustling of angel-wings—a thrilling joy—*up there*, only to be witnessed once in an earthly age?

Adieu!—a last adieu to thee, HENRY CLAY!

The hearts of all thy countrymen are melted, on this day, because of the thought that thou art gone.

Could we have held the hand of the "insatiate archer," thou hadst not died; but thou wouldst have tarried with us, in the full grandeur of thy greatness, until we had no longer need of a country.

But we thank our Heavenly Father that thou wast given to us; and that thou didst survive so long.

We would cherish thy memory while we live, as our country's JEWEL—than which none is richer. And we will teach our children the lesson of matchless patriotism thou hast taught us; with the fond hope that our LIBERTY and our UNION may only expire with

"The Last of Earth."

Mr. GENTRY, of Tennessee, said:

MR. SPEAKER: I do not rise to pronounce an eulogy on the life and character and public services of the illustrious orator and statesman, whose death this nation deplores. Suitably to perform that task, a higher eloquence than I possess might essay in vain. The gushing tears of the nation, the deep grief which oppresses the hearts of more than twenty millions of people, constitute a more eloquent eulogium upon the life and character and patriotic services of HENRY CLAY, than the power of language can express. In no part of our country is that character more admired, or those public services more appreciated, than in the state which I have the honor, in part, to represent. I claim for the people of that state a full participation in the general woe which the sad announcement of to-day will everywhere inspire.

Mr. BOWIE, of Maryland, said:

Mr. SPEAKER: I rise not to utter the measured phrases of premeditated woe, but to speak as my constituency would, if they stood around the grave now opening to receive the mortal remains, not of a statesman only, but of a beloved friend.

If there is a state in this Union, other than Kentucky, which sends up a wail of more bitter and sincere sorrow than another, that state is Maryland.

In her midst, the departed statesman was a frequent and a welcome guest. At many a board, and many a fire-side, his noble form was the light of the eyes, the idol of the heart. Throughout her borders, in cottage, hamlet, and city, his name is a household word, his thoughts are familiar sentences.

Though not permitted to be the first at his cradle, Maryland would be the last at his tomb.

Through all the phases of political fortune, amid all the storms which darkened his career, Maryland cherished him in her inmost heart, as the most gifted, patriotic, and eloquent of men. To this hour, prayers ascend from many domestic altars, evening and morning, for his temporal comfort and eternal welfare. In the language of inspiration, Maryland would exclaim, "There is a prince and a great man, fallen this day, in Israel." Daughters of America! weep for him "who hath clothed you in scarlet and fine linen."

The husbandman at his plough, the artisan at the anvil, and the seaman on the mast, will pause and drop a tear when he hears CLAY is no more.

The advocate of freedom in both hemispheres, he will be lamented alike on the shores of the Hellespont and the banks of the Mississippi and Orinoco. The freed men of Liberia, learning and practicing the art of self-government, and civilizing Africa, have lost in him a patron and protector, a father and a friend. America mourns the eclipse of a luminary, which enlightened and illuminated the continent; the United States, a counsellor of deepest wisdom and purest purpose; mankind, the advocate of human rights and constitutional liberty.

Mr. WALSH, of Maryland, said:

MR. SPEAKER: The illustrious man, whose death we this day mourn, was so long my political leader—so long almost the object of my personal idolatry—that I cannot allow that he shall go down to the grave, without a word at least of affectionate remembrance—without a tribute to a memory which will exact tribute as long as a heart shall be found to beat within the bosom of civilized man, and human agency shall be adequate, in any *form*, to give them an expression; and even, sir, if I had no heart-felt sigh to pour out here—if I had no tear for that coffin's lid, I should do injustice to those whose representative in part I am, if I did not, in this *presence*, and at this time, raise the voice to swell the accents of the profoundest public sorrow.

The state of Maryland has always vied with Kentucky in love and adoration of his name. Her people have gathered around him with all the fervor of a first affection, and with more than its *duration*. Troops of friends have ever clustered about his pathway with a personal devotion which each man of them regarded as the highest individual honor—friends, sir, to whose fire-sides the tidings of his death will go with all the withering influences which are felt when household ties are severed.

I wish, sir, I could offer now a proper memorial for such a subject and such an affection. But as I strive to utter it, I feel the disheartening influence of the well-known truth, that in view of death all minds sink into triteness. It would seem, indeed, sir, that the great leveler of our race would vindicate his *title* to be so considered, by making all men think alike in regard to his visitation—"the thousand thoughts that begin and end in one"—the *desolation* here—the eternal hope *hereafter*—are influences felt alike by the lowest intellect and the loftiest genius.

Mr. Speaker, a statesman for more than fifty years in the councils of his country, whose peculiar charge it was to see that the Republic suffered no detriment—a patriot for all times, all circumstances, and all emergencies—has passed away from the trials and triumphs of the world, and gone to his reward. Sad as are the emotions which such an event would ordinarily excite, their intensity is heightened by the matters so fresh within the memories of us all:

> "Oh! think how to his latest day,
> When death, just hovering, claim'd his prey,
> With Palinurus' unalter'd mood,
> Firm at his dangerous post he stood,
> Each call for needful rest repell'd,
> With dying hand the rudder held;
> Then while on freedom's thousand plains
> One unpolluted church remains,
> Whose peaceful bells ne'er sent around

The bloody tocsin's maddening sound,
But still, upon the hallow'd day,
Convoke the swains to praise and pray,
While faith and civil peace are dear,
Greet his cold marble with a tear,
He who preserved them—Clay lies here."

In a character, Mr. Speaker, so illustrious and beautiful, it is difficult to select any point for particular notice, from those which go to make up its noble proportions; but we may now, around his honored grave, call to grateful recollection that invincible spirit which no personal sorrow could sully, and no disaster could overcome. Be assured, sir, that he has, in this regard, left a legacy to the young men of the Republic, almost as sacred and as dear as that liberty of which his life was a blessed illustration.

We can all remember, sir, when adverse political results disheartened his friends, and made them feel even as men without hope, that his own clarion voice was still heard in the purpose and the pursuit of right, as bold and as eloquent as when it first proclaimed the freedom of the seas, and its talismanic tones struck off the badges of bondage from the lands of the Incas, and the plains of Marathon.

Mr. Speaker, in the exultation of the statesman he did not forget the duties of the man. He was an affectionate adviser on all points wherein inexperienced youth might require counsel. He was a disinterested sympathizer in personal sorrows that called for consolation. He was ever upright and honorable in all the duties incident to his relations in life.

To an existence so lovely, Heaven in its mercy granted a fitting and appropriate close. It was the prayer, Mr. Speaker, of a distinguished citizen, who died some years since in the metropolis, even while his spirit was fluttering for its final flight, that he might depart gracefully. It may not be presumptuous to say, that what was in that instance the aspiration of a chivalric *gentleman*, was in this the realization of the dying *Christian*, in which was blended all that human dignity could require, with all that Divine grace had conferred ; in which the firmness of the man was only transcended by the fervor of the penitent.

A short period before his death he remarked to one by his bedside, "that he was fearful he was becoming selfish, as his thoughts were entirely withdrawn from the world, and centered upon eternity." This, sir, was but the purification of his noble spirit from all the dross of earth – a happy illustration of what the religious muse has so sweetly sung :

"No sin to stain—no lure to stay
The soul, as home she springs ;
Thy sunshine on her joyful way,
Thy freedom in her wings."

Mr. Speaker, the solemnities of this hour may soon be forgotten. We may come back from the new-made grave only still to show that we consider "eternity the bubble, life and time the enduring substance." We may not pause long enough by the brink to ask which of us, revelers of to-day, shall next be at rest. But, be assured, sir, that upon the records of mortality will never be inscribed a name more illustrious than that of the statesman, patriot, and friend whom the nation mourns.

The question was then put on the adoption of the resolutions proposed by Mr. BRECKINRIDGE, and they were unanimously adopted.

www.ingramcontent.com/pod-product-compliance
Lightning Source LLC
LaVergne TN
LVHW010132110826
845151LV00002B/337

* 9 7 8 1 4 2 5 5 3 9 7 2 6 *